Alexander McKenzie

**Some Things Abroad**

Vol. 1

Alexander McKenzie

**Some Things Abroad**
*Vol. 1*

ISBN/EAN: 9783337419905

Printed in Europe, USA, Canada, Australia, Japan

Cover: Foto ©Andreas Hilbeck / pixelio.de

More available books at **www.hansebooks.com**

# SOME THINGS ABROAD

BY

ALEXANDER McKENZIE

BOSTON
D LOTHROP COMPANY
FRANKLIN AND HAWLEY STREETS

To

JOHN N. DENISON, Esq.,

*WITH GRATITUDE AND
RESPECT.*

# CONTENTS.

| CHAPTER | PAGE |
|---|---|
| I. From New York to Belfast | 7 |
| II. From Belfast to Newcastle | 28 |
| III. From Newcastle Through Norway | 61 |
| IV. From Norway to Italy | 118 |
| V. In Northern Italy | 164 |
| VI. To and Through Athens | 192 |
| VII. In and About Constantinople | 231 |
| VIII. From Constantinople to Damascus | 265 |
| IX. In Damascus | 304 |
| X. Bânîas and Tiberias | 322 |
| XI. From Tiberias to Jerusalem | 348 |
| XII. In and Around Jerusalem | 394 |
| XIII. To the End | 440 |

# SOME THINGS ABROAD.

## CHAPTER I.

FROM NEW YORK TO BELFAST.

WE were waiting for the hour of sailing when we walked out upon the bridge which joins New York and Brooklyn, and read the words of restriction and caution which were repeated for the benefit of travellers, — Keep to the right and keep moving. We felt the force of the counsel, and allowed it to settle in our minds as we turned to the unbridged sea.

It was on the Fourth of July that we really began to move. The day was as hot as it could be, and the tar melted in the seams of the deck. It was refreshing to think of cooler airs, which were lying in wait for us. Days passed before we found complete relief. Between the hot sides of the ship and the hot air of the engine, our state-rooms were intolerable. When they became comfortable, the sea became rough, and the appearance of the upper deck changed, as it is accustomed to do in the process of the voyage. Men were fewer. Ladies concealed themselves entirely, or, encased in shawls, clung to their long chairs. A general seriousness prevailed; while incipient friendships were nipped in the bud, and neighbors were interrupted in their promised intercourse, and the ship rolled with might and main. But we were at sea, with no familiar faces to remind us of the land we had left, or to recall the discussions and conflicts that had grown wearisome. For us there was more calm on the sea than on the land. The incidents of the voyage were not remarkable. Yet it takes but little to enlist attention and interest in the long leisure and the somewhat persistent languor of mind which belongs to a landsman upon the deep. Of course, a few of the company were more conspicuous than their fellows. There was one gentleman from the British Provinces who carried good-nature on his round face, and dealt it out to every one who manifested any need of such cheer as he could impart. He had his opinions upon most subjects, and illustrative incidents were at his command. He was frank, and, some might say, intrusive. He was very fond of walking with the ladies, when walking was permitted, and of chatting to them at other times. Yet he was still in the state in which he was created, because he had never met a woman who, upon his analysis of her character, answered his demands. He made no concealment of his fondness for conversation with those on whom he could not bestow a complete admiration. "They don't scrape you down to the brick," he remarked. This testimony seemed impressive and expressive. But, as I think upon it, I am at a loss to know from what department of masonry he drew his comparison, or why he should object to the intelligent scraping which removes what is superficial, and discloses the substantial character beneath.

He was an indulgent story-teller, always pointing out the point of his narratives, and doing this repeatedly in condescension to dull hearers. He liked to tell of a misguided goat who ate dried apples and drank water till he looked like a side-wheel steamer. This tale illustrated conscience, but he did not make the application clear.

He was a man of experience, and when, on one of our early days, he announced that there is a way to be comfortable in a hot state-room, we listened hopefully for the rule. The rule proved to be this: Find out how hot it is, and then adapt yourself to it. This was disappointing, and yet I doubt if he could have done better. He professed, more than once, to be shocked at the unbecoming conduct of his room-mate after a very warm night, when the poor fellow "came up to the surface of his sensibilities," and, not heeding the supposed devotions of his companion, made a brief remark which had a resemblance to swearing.

Then we had an English Nimrod who had been exploring our Far West. He told thrilling tales of his prowess. At his approach, the American buffaloes fell upon their knees, and the deer, with the piteous tears chasing one another down their innocent noses, lay quiet at his feet; while the eagle faltered in his flight and fluttered into the sportsman's hand. Possibly I exaggerate the statements, but I preserve the tone of them.

We had also a long Romish priest, who had served as an army chaplain in India and Australia, and was talkative and good natured. His geography seemed a little confused, as he plainly thought that Captain

Cook was killed in New Zealand. And he told of
a man who had seen a hundred and twenty-five different
clubs with which the murder was committed.
He amazed a bluff Scotchman with some story of a
Parsee. "Was he an Englishman?" the Scotchman
asked. "No; a Parsee." "Oh, he belongs to that
country." "No, no; a Parsee — a fire-worshipper —
a Persian." I do not think the man has yet found
out why the priest was so emphatic; he was certainly
staggered at the priest's report of Parsee wealth, and
of a hospital a mile long which one had built in India.
The priest had brought back one other tale, of a man
with whom he was once riding who refused to strike
his beast because the soul of his brother was then residing
in it. This was an inconvenient application
of the doctrine of transmigration; and it might be
asked why he was willing to drive his brother at all.

On our one Sabbath we were favored with a sermon
from an American bishop. He had a fine presence,
a strong voice, an impressive manner. He had
a good text, as they used to tell us at Andover, and
the sermon was earnest and helpful.

Our Canadian friend said that some people go
through the world "like a paper-knife," smoothly
and easily. It was in this manner our passage was
made, for the most part. On the morning of the
13th of July we saw land, and, after running
down the pleasant coast of Ireland, in the afternoon
we left the *Bothnia* for the *Jackal*. We had a
charming sail, for an hour, in the fine harbor of
Queenstown, and then our feet were on Irish soil.
The prudent custom-house officer inquired if we

had tobacco or fire-arms, and, finding that we had neither, suffered us to go on our way. We found the people easy in their habits, and very deliberate. We demurred at the needless delay, and were told that Americans are in too much of a hurry. That may be true,—I fancy that it is. But I am sure that neither the lesson nor the instruction was attractive just then. We had time for a glimpse of Queenstown, which is more of a place than we expected to find. At length we were on the train. We had a delightful ride along the Lee to Cork, where we found quarters at the Imperial. They put us at the top of the house, in recognition of our nationality or our personal worth. A fellow-passenger on the steamer invited us to drive about the city. The poor man had been greatly disturbed at Queenstown, by finding that his valise had fallen under the wheels of the dray and been crushed out of shape. He tried to obtain redress, but none was to be found. He was an old traveller, and did not let his equanimity be long disturbed. He engaged a jaunting-car, and gave us a very agreeable hour. The large, busy city, with its fine buildings, is in strong contrast to the Cork of the stranger's imagination. We found that men, women, and children had a way of walking in the streets endangering their lives and bothering the drivers, who are continually screaming "Whay!" which is understood at once and opens the way for the approaching carriage. There was an evident good-nature which was agreeable. There was a distinct recognition of America in the sign over one shop, — " Waltham Watches."

I ventured to have a strain of Irish blood added to my own timepiece, in the confidence that it would not produce any aberration.

The chief thing to see at Cork is Blarney Castle, which we visited, by an Irish boy and a jaunting-car. The castle is a fine old ruin, and well managed. There are two gates, an inner and outer; and, by keeping a man at each, they secure a double fee, which becomes a treble fee when you have gone further in. It was claimed that special favor was shown to Americans in regard to visiting-days. A woman received us at the castle, and descanted volubly on the ruins. We were allowed to wander about at our pleasure. The Blarney stone was found in its place, but, as I had little use for eloquence at that time, I contented myself with touching it. This was much easier than kissing would have been, which there does not go by favor, but by uneasily twisting and turning, thrusting the body into a window, and bending down the head till the lips press the stone in the face of the wall. The country was very pleasant as we drove through it. The little stone houses, many of them with thatched roofs, were picturesque. The trees were heavy with foliage, and the roadside flowers were pretty, as they always are. There was less evidence of care than in the hedges and lawns of England, but Ireland was green enough to justify her reputation. The children whom we met looked sleek and well fed, though their clothes were in a less creditable condition. There was an air of innocent trustfulness in the faces of the people, except, perhaps, those of the old women. It seemed queer to be in a land where Irish is the mother-tongue. It was not always easy to understand it. Donkeys abounded, and had a patient, overworked look, though they seemed to be on good terms with their owners.

On Saturday afternoon we left Cork, and, after a journey of six hours, reached Killarney. The very name was alluring, and the place at once promised to fulfil our desires. There are the finest mountains and lakes of Ireland. Walter Scott said that he had seen no grander lake than the middle one at Killarney, saving only Loch Lomond. We found a fine hotel, — the Royal Victoria, — and settled down for the Sabbath. These lakes would be thronged if they were near one of our large cities. All that could be asked is there, — delightful scenery, cool airs, pleasant drives, charming walks, good fishing and sailing. It is a place to be sought, and which will long be remembered. On many a weary day I shall sigh for the repose of Killarney. There was no church near the Lakes, so that we had leisure to commune with our own thoughts and be still.

On Monday we made the grand excursion, in company with some of the *Bothnia's* passengers. The excursion takes the whole day, and rewards the investment. Besides what one sees in the way of scenery, there are various side-shows which are thrust upon his notice. The first fact which is made apparent is that all the people live on the traveller. You bargain at the hotel for all you want, and agree to pay a good price for it. Do not think that is the end. You have scarcely lost sight of the house before gay cavaliers gather about you and almost force you to ride two or three ponies. Boys and girls solicit your money, "to buy a book, sir." As a friend of female education, I cheerfully gave a penny to a girl, who laughed and begged in the same breath, and specified the "Fourth Reader" as the book which her attainments demanded. Kate Kearney stands at the door of her hut, with a bottle in one hand and a pitcher in the other, and business in her untamed eye. She has none of the beauty of her famed ancestress, but she has goat's milk and mountain dew, which she is willing to part with for a suitable consideration. Thenceforth women attend you. They run at your horse's side, in bare feet, and beg you to buy stockings. They flourish two bottles and crave your patronage for the two kinds of beverage just mentioned, while their red shawls wave in the wind, and their fluent tongues invoke upon you long life and other blessings. From all this, if your horse is fleet, you may run away. But there is no escape from your legitimate attendants. Not a man whom you have hired is content with the price agreed upon. Each one makes his separate appeal to your compassion, and confidently holds out his hand. He expresses his discontent with your alms, and turns away like a wretch you have wronged. This unprofessional beggary is the worst of all; the hardest to satisfy and the least thankful. This custom of begging prevails throughout the island. Common beggars are not quite everywhere, but the uncommon ones abound. You run a gauntlet from the Lakes of Killarney to the Giant's

Causeway. You have almost to escape from your hotel by stealth, if you have funds enough left to take you to the nearest banker's.

The scenery was very impressivé as we rode through the Gap of Dunloe. Wild, dark, sublime, solemn were the mountains which enclosed us. We rode through the Black Valley, but saw no traces of the railroad of that name of which we had heard. There were signs that it was not far away. We passed the place where St. Patrick craftily boxed up the snakes, and threw them into the water. The work was thoroughly done, for not a snake was to be seen. The driver said only an approaching storm can awaken them, when they throw the waters into tumult. "They will come out day after to-morrow, which never comes." At Lord Brandon's cottage we took a large boat with four rowers and were carried about eleven miles. At a certain point the boat was stopped, and we were asked to solve the Killarney puzzle — how to get out of the lake. The captain promised a bottle of Irish whiskey to any one who should guess right, and expected one from each person who failed. He was disappointed. There was only one correct guess, yet no bottles changed hands.

We were then driven to Muckross Abbey, the finest ruin in Ireland. The cloister is in almost perfect preservation, with the customary yew-tree in the centre of the open space. The monuments are numerous, and the ivy is luxuriant. A young man of the company expressed a desire to see the yule-tree from which the yule-log is cut, but there was no way of gratifying him. We were ticketed in to see the Torc waterfall, which is the best in these parts. We saw Ross Castle in its decay, and from its broken wall had a fine view. It was a famous fortress in the old wars. The place was beset with women, who had for sale a variety of things made of the bog-oak and arbutus-wood. To the solicitation of one woman some one said "No"; whereupon she cried after him, "Such a fascinating young man as you to say 'No' to a lady!" We took boat again, and were taken past Innisfallen and its ruins, which we had no time to visit. Then we crossed the rough waters of the lower lake, Lough Leane, and disembarked near the hotel. It was a very pleasant excursion, very faithfully carried out.

We came northward by rail to Dublin, where, in the Shelbourne, we found "the best hotel in the United Kingdom" — so some travellers say. But "best" is a word to be used with caution. It was certainly a fine house, though it gave us rather narrow accommodations. On the side of a jaunting-car and on the top of a tramway carriage we had an outside view of the inside of the city. There is the Cathedral, dating from the twelfth century — the first church in Ireland in which the liturgy was read in the English language. And St. Patrick's Cathedral, on the site of the church built by the national saint. Among the memorials in this cathedral are the simple marble slabs which mark the graves of Swift, and "Stella" whose name and life were so closely and darkly associated with his. There, too, is the monument of Whately, with the Archbishop reclining upon it. The ancient castle has been modernized, like so many other buildings of its time, but preserves something of its old estate. When we were in Dublin, the most familiar local name was Phœnix Park, which had been recently the scene of the cruel murder in which madness expressed its hatred of English rule. We knew it was in Dublin that Tom Moore was born, and Wellington, and that O'Connell for a long time had his residence. But we could not stay even to see what has been named.

We moved on to Belfast, second in rank of the Irish cities, but had only two hours for a drive through its fine streets and among its comely buildings.

Still moving northward, we came to Portrush and the Northern Counties Railway Hotel. The house was formerly the Antrim Arms, but has surrendered that fine name for one more remunerative. The connecting of railroads and hotels has become common in the United Kingdom, and has some advantages. But it is a pity to lose the good old names. The view from our windows, which looked over the wide sea from the very end of Ireland, could only be grand even to eyes which were accustomed to the sea. Close at hand were the Skerries, with their lighthouses. The Skerries, for "Skerry" is applied to any isolated rock in the sea. We had a pleasant walk, and saw a good many of the people. There had been apparently an excursion from some other place, and we were amused and interested in watching the embarkation of the returning voyagers.

We devoted the next day to the chief attraction

of the locality. But before we saw the Giant's Causeway, we saw what was almost as great a marvel in this remote region, a horse railroad with the cars drawn by an electric engine,—I am imitating the Irish method of writing. "This is the Premier Electric Tramway," "the first in the United Kingdom, and the largest in the world." The novelty disgusts the hotel-keepers, who find their tourists spirited away from their doors, and the drivers of jaunting-cars, who find the tramway preferred above their own vehicles. Eight miles of the tramway brought us into the midst of guides and boatmen who were lying in wait, prepared to render all manner of service, desirable and undesirable. It was necessary to employ a portion of them, and it seemed best to bargain with them before setting out, though this latter part of the arrangement was of less value than a stranger would suppose. We were so fortunate as to secure the services of the best boatmen there. We knew this, for one of them assured us that it was the fact. We were taken into the smallest cave where a boy, for whose presence we had not been able to account, accounted for himself by producing an old pistol and arousing the numerous echoes of the place. We had not asked for this luxury, but we paid for it, and the boy left us for fresh victims. We were then taken into the larger cave, as the day was favorable for this, and we looked in wonder on its awful grandeur. Then we rowed and sailed past the cliffs, getting a very fine view of them, when our guides took us for a short walk over what seemed to be sunken columns. When this excursion was over, the guides announced that their mission was ended, and that the time for payment had arrived. As a matter of course, they demanded more than we had agreed upon, but we thought upon their superior qualifications, which we certainly should not have discovered, and we added to the stipulated amount. That was not all. Each guide was armed with a rough wooden box, covered with newspaper and laboriously surrounded with twine. At an auspicious moment two of these were opened in our boat, and we were asked to buy both or either. There seemed to be no partnership in this traffic. The boxes proved to be filled with specimen stones, arranged in strawberry fashion — the best on the top. We bought more than we wanted. Could we do less? After that came men with broken pieces of double-refracting spar, which has the power of making one shilling look like two. I adopt their illustration, though I noticed that they did not use the spar for this purpose when collecting their pay. All the mysterious powers of the stone were given up to the purchaser. If one should buy all the stones that are offered him, he would need to hire all the men and women who infest the rocks to carry them for him. Yet it is not easy to choose when you want none but must take some. We came upon a queer old man who was selling water from the "Giant's well." There was some variety even in his simple enterprise, for he had a cup for the well and a bottle for the still. The "mountain dew" had evidently collected in the bottle. When we asked for a drink of the water, I thought it prudent to remark that we did not desire any appendage from the bottle. "Will you wait —" he said. "But we don't want any of that." "Will you just wait —" he persisted in asking. "But I tell you we don't want anything from the bottle!" And the queer old man, in a solemn, almost reproachful tone, made answer: "Will you just wait till you're asked?" We waited. When we had refreshed ourselves from the spring, I sought to draw the offended gentleman into conversation. "Did the giants drink of this spring?" I inquired. "No, the giants drink of no spring." "But they say that when the giants piled up these rocks, they used to come to this well," I ventured to remark. "No giants built up these rocks," he answered. "Who did, then?" "The one who made these things is the One above," — and he pointed toward the sky. I found that he was getting the better of me, and I hastened to reply that we ought to try to please Him who is so great and has done such wonderful things. He assented to this, and added that he feared we do not please Him. I said that some day we should see Him. "I hope so," he continued; "I hope that we may have one look." Then we left him. But it is a strange scene even now as I look back upon it, — the grand cliffs, the vast sea, and all the strange sublimity, and in the midst this lone priest in the Temple of the Giants, standing by the spring among the rocks, with a tin cup in one hand and a bottle of whiskey in the other, turning upward his red face, and pointing with a finger, set free for this purpose, to the dwelling-place of Him who has uplifted and upholds the mountains. Well, who shall say how much he thought and hoped in his long solitude, or what he has learned in a life which must have had its vicissitudes. It may be that his ruddy cheeks will look less earthy when the hand of death has passed over them. Who does not look for some gain in that transformation?

We sat in the "wishing chair" of rock, which the guide said was also the "Giant's chair." It was a much frequented place, but the visitors did not look like descendants of the giants. Afterward we sat in another chair, nearer the sea, which is said to be the real seat of the giants. It was reasonably comfortable as a chair, and we had it to ourselves, which was a marked advantage.

I have said very little of the "Causeway." The ride to it from Portrush was very pleasant by the sea, among the cliffs, over the gorges. We passed Dunluce Castle, an old ruin, which crowns the isolated cliff where it has stood for five hundred years. The Causeway has been so often described and pictured that I need not attempt to present it here. Everybody knows how it looks. It is not quite what we supposed, but it is fully as grand and strange. To walk over the tops of huge columns sunk in the depths, to look up at the towering peaks and mountains of rock, to wander along the bays between the cliffs, to penetrate the deep caves, to gaze upon the ocean beyond whose borders lies the land we love, — this is full of interest and wonder: surprising, awakening, quieting; stirring the deep emotions of mind and heart. It would be well to linger among these stupendous works and slowly receive their inspiration. The grandeur grows as the hours pass, and the eye and the mind expand to the proportions of the place. But we had to move on. We came again among men and women. We resisted their solicitation to purchase mosses and fragments of the rocks; we had our final look at their miseries and our final listening to their complaints, and came back to the civilization of Portrush, and then moved on at once toward Scotland.

Before we leave Ireland there are a few more things to be said, which may be set together here. There is a great deal of interest attached to the people of this island. They are wonderfully good-natured and very obliging. They are talkative, but kindly. The jollity is toned down as their estate improves, but out-of-doors and along the road the wit and humor remain. They seem to take life easily, and to make the best of the seasons which are short and hard for shillings, sixpences, and strangers to dispense them. Even their extortion and vexation have but a brief existence. Plainly the people are poor. The cottages must be barren places to live in, and the national drink is somewhat expensive. We saw no signs of hunger. We were not in the right quarter for that. We saw health and length of days. Indeed, it is a fact which disturbs our estimates a little that the Irish race deteriorates on our soil. The generation born in America is not equal physically to that which came over the seas. The change in the habits of life does not work in their favor, in this regard at least.

As a whole, our first impression was sustained. There was clearly more to eat than there was to wear. Economy in dress was evidently a necessity. We saw one barefoot woman with her shoes in a basket on her head. She was waiting for extremes to meet, as in some domains they have a way of doing. Animal life was represented by donkeys and crows, with here and there a horse, and now and then a cow. A stray sheep occasionally came in sight, and there was on the hills and plains a sprinkling of goats, which called to mind the sequestered outskirts of New York. We saw men cutting peat, which they stack for drying, and we enlarged our knowledge of Natural History by learning that in a few years from the time when they are stripped, the bogs are supplied with a new crop of the national fuel.

As we went northward, the people looked better. The women in the fields wore shoes and stockings, which may be regarded as marking the boundary between poverty and less poverty. The sleek, plump children had a more comfortable aspect than those of the same class in some other countries. I asked why the people in the north were better off than those in the south, but the answers were not satisfactory. One said they were more industrious in the north, and had better land. But the land in the north is certainly not the best in the island. It is common to ascribe the advantage to the prevalence of Protestantism. But whether the Protestant faith and institutions are cause or effect, as relates to the well-being of the people, did not appear on the spot. I presume that they are both. That they are a superior sort of folk at the north was clear enough. I cannot discuss Irish questions here, but no one can travel through the island, even as hastily as I did, without feeling that the people deserve a better history than has been made for them. The men at the north were anxious to have it understood that they were not rebels and discontents: that it is at the south riot and murder assert themselves. They complain that the name of Irishman is made to bear reproach which is sectional, and from which they ought to be free. The point is well taken and easily appreciated. We were continually reminded of a past. Ruined castles were on the hill-tops, and were so numerous that after a time we scarcely troubled ourselves to look at them as we rode by. They are the witnesses to times which have gone. Rough times they were, but not wanting in heroism and virtue.

We thought of the fame which has perished: of the days when this was the "Island of Saints"; when its schools were renowned and drew scholars from other lands; when its missionaries went out with civilization and religion. We saw one sign in Dublin which seemed a relic of the more learned years. It was on a druggist's shop: *Medicæ adsunt artes, herbarumque potestas.*

Is the record of that time closed? Is there to be a coming back of renown and power? Ireland in her great cities gives an impression of wealth and strength. May there not come, in the slow process of the suns, a reviving of the light and life? The sympathy of the traveller makes him hope for this. The echoes of Dunloe are quickly started by the cannon and trumpet, and the pittance of coin which the tourist is expected to bestow. The land is full of silence which easily breaks into sound, and the voices leap from hill to hill in long reverberations. Who will not hope that the land is to be awakened from its troubled sleep, and regain the place which it has lost! Violence will not accomplish this. But time and reason and right may bring it all to pass.

There is another point upon which I am constrained to say a few words. It is the abandonment of national customs and the importation of foreign ways in hotel life. In Ireland we would like to see Irish usages at the table, that we may know what the people eat, and how it is served. A table which was characteristic of the country would have a charm of its own, even if the manner of it was not thought worthy of imitation. In out-of-the-way places the methods of the people may be found, I presume. But at Killarney the table was Parisian. The waiters appeared as if attired for a metropolitan ball, and the menu was written in French and was a list of unknown dishes, some of which retained their incognito to the close. This usage prevails through the island. At Portrush the menu was chiefly in English, but the meaning remained French. At the Giant's Causeway we found a steward or head-waiter who might have been chief-justice of the district, so far as dress and manners were concerned. He did not hold that lofty position, nor did his appearance attract us to the board over which he spread the shadow of his magnificence. This is all a mistake. Let each country preserve its individuality. It will be more honest, and far more interesting and profitable.

There is another thing which one misses in travel: that is himself. At home he has a name, a title, house, office, honors, and much which separates him from the throng. His comings and goings are noticed, and his identity and self-respect are preserved. He goes abroad and all this is changed. He passes through the process which awaits the convict in the prison and the patient in the hospital. He is numbered, and by his number he is known. The waiter has only to ask, "What is your number, sir?" When the bill is made out, it is only a number which is debtor for board and lodging. At Killarney I was No. 50; at Dublin 37. In Portrush I became 72. I sympathized with Mother Hubbard in her efforts to find out who she was. How all this shrinks the volume of complacency with which a man ventures with his merit and name into the world! There are advantages in this loss. For a time it is agreeable rather than otherwise. To have no dignity to maintain, no responsibilities to fulfil, no name to bear, is at first a relief. But soon a man wearies of being nobody, and having nobody know that he is nobody. If he has some companion to whom he can remark that nonentity is delightful, and that there is beauty in the curve that makes a cipher, even the obscurity has a charm. I had one of the best of companions in an observing and inquisitive boy, interested in everything, patient under all provocation, and wise in his estimates of persons and things. I realized that whatever is pleasant is pleasanter when a friend is at hand; the grandeur of the mountains, the breadth and verdure of the fields, the gloom and silence of the gorges, the wandering streams and the unfathomed sea. With a friend the castles can be rebuilt and repeopled; not with ghostly forms, but with veritable Irishmen, the O'Sullivans and their compeers. On the other side, there is little comfort in being miserable unless some one knows it. Grumbling lacks half its charm when it finds no listening ear and responding growl.

But come, 72! Enough of this. Call your boy. The *Gorilla* waits. "All clear, sir!" And the steamer glides from the harbor of Belfast with her prow towards Caledonia. Our quarters were close, but we had an extra man in our stateroom to make up for the want of space. It seems to be the Irish way. We slipped off the numbers of Erin, and moved on. In the morning, only an hour or two behind time, we were at the pier in Glasgow.

# CHAPTER II.

#### FROM BELFAST TO NEWCASTLE.

THIS chapter begins with Friday, July 20, and in Glasgow.

It was with confidence born of recollection that we ordered the driver to take us to the "Queen's." We found that by some law of retrogression the "Queen's" had become the "George." But it was the same house. What's in a name? I recall the answer of a young parishioner to that question, "A good name is rather to be chosen than great riches." Either of these names was good enough for the very comfortable hotel in which we settled for a few days. At once I became 52. I do not know whether that is an ascent or descent from Portrush. Poor Marshal used to say in college, that he should stand very high if the class was ever turned around.

The guide-book informed us that Glasgow is a city of very ancient origin, and the third in the kingdom in riches and people. Its growth has been in its later years. It has now a population of more than half a million, and is the seat of extensive and varied manufacturing. It has one chimney four hundred and sixty-eight feet high. With this valuable information in our hands we went into the busy

streets. George Square is in front of the hotel, and
this fact may have given the new name to the house.
There we found equestrian statues of the queen and
the prince consort, and statues of Scott, Peel, Sir
John Moore, and another in whom Scotland may
indulge a loftier pride, Livingstone. We soon made
our way to the Cathedral, which was full of interest,
as cathedrals always are. This has one peculiarity
among the great houses of Great Britain, that it belongs to the Presbyterians. This would have shown
us that we were over the border, if there had been
nothing else to remind us of it. The Cathedral has
the weight of seven centuries upon it, though it has
received additions of modern and modernizing glass.
The crypt has the deep solemnity and stately proportions which have given it high rank in ecclesiastical
architecture. We passed through to the Necropolis
which is connected with the Cathedral hill by the
"Bridge of Sighs." There we saw the towering
column of John Knox, who deserves this place of
honor; the man so strong, bold, and severe, for
whom the robes of a bishop and the dignities of the
world had no attraction, who held with a rigid mind
and stout hand to the hard realities, and was con-
trolled by an energy which submitted to no restraint
and which " put more life into him than six hundred
trumpets." There, too, is the statue of another man
of might, who will long fill a large place in the religious history of his country. As his funeral procession passed along the street, a man in workman's
attire, whose hands and arms showed that he was of
the people, gave this witness from his heart: " There

goes Norman Macleod. If he had done no more than what he did for my soul, he would shine as the stars forever." These are the men who last: the men whom we would like to have live.

There is evident in these monuments a desire to commemorate the occupation of those who lie beneath them. We read of William Miller, "the laureate of the nursery," "Author of Wee Willie Winkie," which is probably well known among those who will read the inscription. We read of other vocations, confectioner, cloth-lapper, boot-maker, seed-merchant. We know that in the highest sense a man's works do follow him, and it is not unfitting that the fact should be recognized in the memorial of him. A man's honest calling, in which he has made his chief gift to the world, has a claim to be known where he is remembered. It is a part of him. Perhaps it would be well to have this in mind when we choose what we will do.

A very good way in which to get a view of a town is to ride on the outside of an omnibus or horse-car. We adopted this method of surveying Glasgow, after we had looked down upon it from among the monuments. We took the long road by the fine botanic garden at pleasant Kelvinside.

I have spoken of the hotel tables in Ireland. Similar methods prevail beyond the North Channel and the Irish Sea. But our first dinner in Scotland opened appropriately with "hotchpotch." That has a Scotch sound. The lobster was undoubtedly native, though it presented an unhistoric appearance. One of the waiters had borrowed its livery and blazed about us in a red jacket with brass buttons for sparks. So we came on to the strawberries, which were large and early, and were given to us with their hulls on. That must be the original manner. We were not so far from nature as we might have expected.

Saturday morning was rainy. There was nothing remarkable in that, nor was it altogether discouraging. It seemed to be a feature of the weather in these parts that it seldom remained of one sort through the day. We devoted the day to the lakes. One of us had seen them before, as he had seen much of this Scotch land. An hour by train brought us to Balloch Pier, where we took the steamer *Prince Consort* for Inversnaid. Loch Lomond was gloomy under the clouds, and perhaps preferred that setting for its grand mountains. We enjoyed all we could, and that was much. But the cold and the drizzle interfered with our comfort. Yet this was Loch Lomond, with its islands and hills, and Rob Roy's prison on the banks, and traditions of chieftains in the air. We took the stage for Stronachlachar Pier, where we found a comfortable house and a refreshing lunch. Then we went out upon Loch Katrine in the *Rob Roy*. The weather had improved; the sunshine fell on the serene water; the inevitable photograph boy could display his wares on deck, while the voyagers could enjoy the reality whose images he desired to make us own. The scenery was the finest we had seen. Ellen's Isle had its own beauty, as it sat fair and green in the lake, wearing its garland of story and song. After leaving the steamer, we were driven to the Trossachs, and rested for a time at the castellated hotel where I had spent a pleasant Sabbath years before. Then we rode by Loch Achray and Loch Venachar, through a district full of familiar romance, till we reached Callander, where we found the train which took us back to Glasgow. Reflection: It would be a relief if this region were rid of speculation. To have a fee demanded at every turn, and photographs and wooden ware intruded upon the gaze which is fixed on mountains and lakes, adds nothing to the delights of travel. Where "every prospect pleases," there is a man trying to make money out of it. Possibly I should have finished that sentence by lengthening the citation from the hymn instead of writing a thought of my own. In these places one wishes to see and hear as little as may be of buying and selling. Yet monetary affairs are more obtrusive than at home. The Scotch would say, "This is a needcessity," but I wish it was not.

Our homeward journey took us through Stirling, past the old castle, of which we had a fine view. We had to think upon its wealth of historic associations, and to imagine how grand the view from its walls must be, and to keep moving. We returned to Glasgow in a crowd. There had been a fair, which had closed the workshops for ten days, and many of the work-people had improved the opportunity for visiting their friends. On this Saturday night they were returning from their holiday. A plain woman who was in our compartment was very communicative and instructive as we rode through places which she knew and we did not. Let me close the week by copying a sign which is capable of more than one interpretation. And what does it mean? "Royal Liver Friendly Society." A common sign runs, "Boots repaired while you wait." Could they be mended at any other time?

Sunday morning was very pleasant. I studied the list of churches to know whither it was best to go, and selected one with the name of whose minister I was acquainted. We were a little late in reaching the church, and found no one in the vestibule; we opened a door, entered the audience-room, and found an empty pew. We could have found many more. We ventured to take a seat. No one assented or objected. The minister was engaged in prayer. His allusion to the absent pastor made it clear that he was a stranger. I had inferred that from his general bearing, in a hasty glance. It is so strange that ministers will leave their people in this way! The good man prayed that the absent pastor might be blessed in preaching, if he was preaching, or in resting, if he was resting. That was a comprehensive statement. Few people stood during the prayer, but none during the singing, which was by the congregation, and was good. There was no organ. Then followed a psalm; and another prayer, of a wider range than the first. The sermon was from a great text: "For me to live is Christ." The preacher said many good things in fifty minutes, but he divided his minutes badly, and was hurried when he came where he needed time the most. The sermon was not commonplace, but it was not in tune with the text. He attempted analysis where it was soul and spirit which he wanted. On the heights of his theme he rambled into exposition and speedily fell into exhortation. He did not see that the apostle was revelling in the sublime consciousness of his union with his risen Lord; that he was not teaching philosophy, but opening his heart and letting his inspired passion burst into an exclamation which can no more be dissected and reasoned about than can the throbbing of the soul. He could not leave the truth where St. Paul left it. He must show how it was, when there was no "how." It just was. It was Christ, his Life, with sparkle and delight, with melody and rhythm, with a limitless exuberance of which we can sometimes, under the stars, feel ourselves partakers. Language is beggared, imagery falters. The spirit feels, and in feeling knows. Out of this feeling it puts its finger on the life of another soul and wakens it to singing, and it teaches the new song. It was a good sermon; but it was a sermon. He was a good man; but he was a man. Unction is from above. He had it in his measure. But, oh how far beyond us all was that great human heart which found its life at the gate of Damascus, and felt the oil of God and the breath of heaven, and knew "the power of an endless life!"

In the evening I went to the Cathedral. It was a "people's service," and the church was crowded. I stood with many others. The singing by the congregation, led by the choir, was spirited and impressive. The officiating minister was one who is best known as "The Country Parson." His essays were popular in their time, though no one seems to read them now; yet they are good reading. He intoned the prayers — I suppose it was intoning. It was puerile enough for that process. If any one wishes to hear this absurdity carried to an extreme, let him listen to a man who pronounces English with a local accent and brogue. Yet this was a man of gray hair, which was scant enough to have restrained him from trifling with sacred things. His sermon was from the two words, "Get wisdom." It was a much easier text than that of the morning. The sermon was in the style of the essays, bright and light, crisp and fresh. The matter was not original, but the treatment was. The style reminded me of the essay, "Concerning the Art of Putting Things." He put things well. He spoke in the language of his hearers. They could not mistake his meaning. He said that wisdom is not that common-sense which is born in a man and cannot be acquired. It is better than that, and can be gained. Some tell us that wisdom is not the same thing as knowledge. "Well, what man in his senses ever supposed it was?" To know what one ought to do, and to have the purpose to do it, is wisdom. Wisdom in the Bible concerns itself with the heart; it belongs with morals. Wisdom will be given to us if we ask it, and in it we may grow.

An American congregation would have been pleased with the sermon, but those who heard it did not appear to see its merit. Or was this only the absence of expression; a stolid way of listening? They may have felt more than they showed. But an American audience would have helped the preacher by signs of approval, by the answer of the face.

As I left the Cathedral the setting sun was casting its light through the fine west window, and the whole scene was beautiful. The stately old house is worthily used for a service especially suited to "the people." The service could easily have been better suited to their wants and tastes, and could have left a deeper impression on their hearts. But, as it was, it was something for which to be glad. The multitudinous waves of sound which rolled under the high arches had surely uplifted the great assembly of men and women. The effort to make their great churches useful to "the people" — as if we were not all people, though bearing or not bearing the marks of nobility — is to be commended. Yet it suggests the distinction at which I have just hinted, and that is not well. "The people" do not wish to be patronized, nor will they be content with the use of our best churches at the hours when we prefer to be at home. What to do for "the people" is one of the problems on both sides of the ocean. Suppose we stand with them, and regard them as children with us of the Father who is in heaven and on earth, living side by side with us in his love, hastening with us to the house which is above! But I must not preach.

As I walked home I came upon a street preacher violently haranguing a small collection of men and boys. He seemed more in earnest than his hearers. "Salvation Army Barracks" looked out from a street lantern, but none of the soldiers were visible. On the tramways when your fare is taken the conductor gives you a ticket which is not taken back, so that you amass a collection in a few days. The fire-alarm boxes in the streets look like iron banjos. With these desultory notes we enter upon Monday.

We left Glasgow at eight o'clock in the morning. We took the train to Greenock, and there embarked on the steamer *Columba*. It is instructive to notice how history and biography and nature stamp themselves, not only on their country, but even on the names of conveyances by land and sea. At Ardrishaig we landed and walked to the Crinan Canal, where the *Linnet* waited to carry us through the canal, when the *Iona* took us up for Oban. It was a wonderful day's sail, as the maps will show. The scenery was fine and varied; the islands had their own special interest, — Bute and Arran and Mull and Kerrara, and the rest, — while the Kyles of Bute and the Bay of Crinan and the Sound of Luing opened up a way among them where they were arranged in forms of grandeur and beauty. But the air was cold and the wind was high, so that we had to take the scenery in instalments, and to shelter ourselves in the saloon between our observations. In the canal the lochs were numerous, and we amused ourselves in watching the operation of them. Quite as exciting was the gathering of boys and girls at the first loch. Each had a tin pail and a tumbler, and each voice kept up the one cry, "Any milk, sir?" They ran from loch to loch, crying as they ran, now and then securing a customer, for whom they seemed grateful,

and a penny, which was their objective point.
They wore only Nature's attire on their locomotive
arrangements, and there was not a pretty face
among them. Very appropriately a bagpiper appeared at one place and played us a welcome to the
Highlands. It was a very graceful attention, but
it marred the romance of the greeting to have him
pass round his hat afterwards. Perhaps he had that
in view all the time. But he did not get much.
We left out our side of the attention.

Oban is finely situated on the curving shore.
The houses are near the beautiful bay, for the most
part, while a few creep up on the hills which shut in
the little town, but as a recompense give a beautiful
outlook to any one who will go up to their summit.
Oban has become a place of considerable resort, and
must be very pleasant through the leisure weeks of
summer. It has large hotels, but we declined the
polite offers of the liveried suitors, and walked
quietly to an attractive little house called the "Argyle." A neat Scotch landlady stood in the door
and readily agreed to furnish all we desired in the
way of bed and board. She kept her word. The
pillows were hard and the fare was simple. But
everything was neat, and there was a primitive
method of management which was pleasing and inexpensive, two qualities which are seldom found
in combination where tourists abound. Very quiet
and restful were the streets of this village as we
strolled through them at night. It was refreshing
to be far away from the noise and bustle of the
world we had left. But we were to keep moving.

On Tuesday morning we left Oban in the *Chevalier*, and we landed at Iona, or Icolmkill. It was famed in its day. There the Druids had their principal seat, but it is more than thirteen hundred years since the Pictish king gave it to St. Columba, whom his own people called Columbkille. It is a good place to recall the story of his life. He was an Irishman, born of the royal race of O'Donnell on his father's side, while his mother was a princess of Leinster. He was trained and ordained in the Church of Rome, and became one of its most zealous sons. Using his wealth and his influence, before he was twenty-five years old he had founded thirty-seven monasteries in Ireland. We are getting back into the grandeur of the island we have just left, as we think upon such works. At length, trouble found the good man, as it is apt to do, and he was involved in a suit concerning a choice manuscript of the Psalter, and the king decided against him. The king's men put to death a prince of Connaught, who had sought asylum in the saint's monastery, whereupon in revenge Columba led his kinsfolk against the king and defeated him. Then followed excommunication and a final expulsion from the island of his birth. With twelve companions who were monks, he went to Iona, and ministered to the wants of the people there and in the region round about. Prince Connal, to whom the island belonged, gave it to Columba, who devoted himself heartily to his Christian work, so that churches and monasteries multiplied. Thus early did Iona become the flourishing seat of Christianity. When the Scotch Parliament abolished religious houses, in 1560, that established at Iona fell with the rest. The island came into the possession of the McLeans and then became the property of the Duke of Argyle. Its length is three miles and its breadth is a mile and a half. There are some three hundred people on the island, who rear black cattle on the land, and draw the fish from the sea, and thus, with the help of potatoes and barley, pick up an honest living. It is scarcely necessary to confess that I did not learn these historical and statistical facts on the spot, but have since gleaned them from books. I confess this the more confidently because a great New England philosopher and writer has said boldly, "Every book is a quotation; and every house is a quotation out of all forests and mines and stone-quarries; and every man is a quotation from all his ancestors." Originality is hardly to be expected after that.

We landed at Iona in a large boat. We saw little except the island with its moorland and hills, and the ruins which are the memorials of its better days. We went to the nunnery first, because it was nearest. It bears the name of Mary and dates from the twelfth century. There was at the gate the girl of the present century. On this occasion she was selling pebbles, or, more correctly, offering pebbles for sale. Within we found sheep who were not of the original fold. They fled at the approach of a stranger, for they knew him not. If the women we saw were nuns, or had any special character, they wore only an every-day look. Then to the Cathedral, which is also St. Mary's but is in desolation, both spiritual and material, and has fallen from a house of prayer to a house of merchandise. The boy was there. The photographs were with the boy, where most of them remained. The old Cathedral is an impressive ruin, with its large square tower, some seventy-five feet high, and the walls, which are nearly complete, and the wealth of traditions and memories. Outside stands the famous Iona cross, the oldest of the four which now remain of the three hundred and sixty stone crosses which were erected on the island. Not very far away is the McLean cross. We saw also St. Oran's Chapel, which is older than the Cathedral, and that of St. Mary, which is nearer the shore.

We should have been glad to linger at Iona, to go into the cottages which stand in a long row looking towards the sea, to talk with the simple island folk and gather up the stories of departed times, and to bring again to the sacred houses those who once filled them with song and prayer and many a saintly deed. But we turned away. We left behind us the grave of Columba. It is known to be his grave, because when it was opened his bones were not found in it. This may seem an Irish method of reasoning. It is not quite so illogical as it appears. For, by the tradition, the bones of the saint were taken to Ireland. So there was good reason for believing that they would not be found in Iona. And they were not.

We left also the graves of kings of Scotland and Ireland and Norway, and of holy abbots and Highland chieftains. The island was a famous place for the repose of the great. They liked to lie down under its sacred sod. There was, too, an ancient prophecy that when the second deluge should come, seven years before the end of the world, and all the nations should be submerged, the island of Columba would float securely over the waste of water. It is not strange that kings took possession of the added years, though they were far distant. Yet how little it really mattered where the royal dust returned to dust, or where the coming deluge left the ashes which had been dethroned. Not for this reason was Iona made the last resting-place of sixteen American sailors over whose graves rises the granite monument which our government has set to mark the haven into which they passed through storm and shipwreck. King or sailor, it is a peaceful spot to find when the reign is over and the voyage is done.

Iona and its conspicuous Cathedral afforded very pleasing sights as we steamed towards Staffa, where we landed in a large boat. There was no difficulty in recognizing the island as we approached it, for the school-book pictures had given us an idea of it. The tall columns of rock mark the place beyond mistake. When the wind and water permit, small boats make their way into Fingal's Cave, which is the chief place of interest. This was not one of the days when such permission is given. We landed at Clam-Shell Cave, which was entered by some of the company. We all made our way laboriously over the irregular tops of the massive pillars to the cave which is called after the old hero of Gaelic poetry. Fion na Gael, or Fingal, furnished the name for Ossian's epic of six books, and also for this great grotto. He was of royal blood, the son of Comhal, who was the son of the King of Morven, and Morna. He married the daughter of Cornac I., the third King of Ireland, and Ossian was their son and the successor to the throne of Morven. All this is in the books, but not in the rocks. It may be well to take from the books also a few dimensions. Unfortunately the books do not agree. But the cave is two hundred and twelve or two hundred and twenty-seven feet long, and its width at the entrance is thirty-three or forty-two feet. It is sixty feet high, and the water is about twenty feet deep on the floor. Immense ranges of columns support the high arch which forms the roof, and stalactites of many tints hang between the lofty pillars, which dash back the rushing, foaming waves that are thrown upon them. We found a wire railing which guided and protected us as we advanced in the cave towards the dark. It was a sombre and awful place to be in. Not long after we were there, several persons were washed from the ledge where we walked by the fierce incoming of the sea, the treacherous and resistless sea. The construction of Staffa suggests the Giant's Causeway. But there is more variety there, and the pillars are more regular, though some in Staffa are larger than any we saw in Ireland. We ascended a long wooden stairway, and climbed to the top of a hill from which there is an extended view. Our stay was too short because the day was so short.

Perhaps the most remarkable thing about Staffa is that nothing is there offered for sale; not a photograph, not a piece of wood or a fragment of rock. I doubt if there is another place of interest in the

United Kingdom of which this can be said, or a place of equal size where no beggar puts in an appearance. I do not find these facts mentioned in any books to which I have access, and I am gratified that I can bring them to the attention of travellers. Columns of rock may be seen elsewhere. We had a glimpse of a set of pillars on one of the islands which we passed. I read not long since that similar columns have been found on one of the Pacific Islands. But they are so rare that they are worthy of a visit wherever they are to be seen. It was a rich day's excursion which ended in the Bay of Oban. Yet much of the day had been cold and windy and cloudy, yielding at last to the sunshine. The scenery which we saw was equal to any in these parts, but it would be much more convenient if the weather would coöperate with it in the interest of strangers. The air was mild on the land. The linen sheets on the beds were a trifle too cool, but we had an abundance of blankets. Our little hotel was very comfortable in all respects. I am constrained to mention the rarity of attractive faces here at the North. The common people have a hard look, as if the shadows of their mountains rested on them. There are signs of poverty, though these are not numerous where we have been. We took on board the steamer that day a wretched-looking man and woman with their bare-legged children. They drew out our sympathy, perhaps further than was necessary; for they were all on the forward deck at once, the woman with a pipe in her mouth, and a baby in a shawl hanging on her back, Indian fashion.

Life seemed to have no perplexities for her or hers. After a time the man took the pipe, which seemed to be a family luxury. Whether it descended to the brood, to whom comfort would not have been amiss, I did not see. The burden and the back often get fitted together as the years roll on.

We left Oban very early on Wednesday morning. The "boots" of the "Argyle," who acted also as clerk on this occasion, had some difficulty in making up his accounts for us, and would certainly have defrauded the worthy woman whom he represented if our arithmetic had not been more accurate than his. But he was a novice and we were not. The steamer *Mountaineer* took us to Banavie, where we were transferred to the *Glengarry*, which was better adapted to the journey before us, and in this we entered the Caledonian Canal. From Banavie there is a good view of Ben Nevis, the highest of the Scotch mountains. An ungracious cloud did all it could to hide the mountain from our view. The canal is more than its name denotes. It is sixty miles long, reaching from the Atlantic to the German Ocean, from the Firth of Lorn to Moray Firth, thus running across the county of Inverness and dividing the island. In more than half its length it makes use of lochs and rivers, which are joined by the artificial stream. The water is seventeen feet deep, and the canal is wide enough for large steamboats. The day was cold in the first part, with occasional showers, and grew milder as it went on.

But no weather could destroy this romantic journey, from loch to loch, among mountains and hills, past castles which were laden with story. There was Tor Castle, where the Camerons ruled in the old days; and Invergarry, where the "Lord of the Isles" mustered the clans which followed him. We had bought the poem at Oban and were able to read it among the scenes which it describes. By falling in ruins the castles have preserved themselves from the hand of improvement, and have thus retained something of the character which was their strength, and now constitutes their attractiveness. Between Loch Oich and Loch Ness is a series of seven lochs, extending through two miles and taking an hour and a half of time. Many persons prefer to walk while the steamer is slowly making her way down the hill to Fort Augustus. At Loch Lomond we were beguiled from the stage into the ascent of a muddy mountain, under the flimsy pretence that our little walk would relieve the horses. No such inducement of mercy was held out to us at the lochs, and the walk was not only voluntary but agreeable. We were not left to ourselves. Women and girls who were native to both manor and manner attended us, carrying milk, the visible and staple refreshment of the region. They received but small pecuniary encouragement. Probably this was not entirely a disadvantage to them. For it is to be presumed that the less they sold, the more they had for their own evening repast.

At the Pier of Foyers we were allowed time to visit the fall of that name, which is sometimes changed into the "Fall of Smoke." It was a tiresome walk, over a steep and rough path. I do not think we should have been repaid if the walk had been a thousand miles, to take Wilson's estimate, but there was compensation for the walk which we did take. A leap of a hundred feet is not very much for a stream in a land of mountains. But the surroundings here were picturesque, with their grandeur and beauty, their roughness and grace, while the waters plunged from sparkling sunlight into the shadows below.

We may properly here recall the lines which Burns wrote with a pencil as he stood by the Fall of Foyers, the lines beginning : —

> "Among the heathy hills and ragged woods
> The roaring Fyers pours his mossy floods."

Our day's journey ended at Inverness, "the capital of the Highlands," where we took up our quarters at the Imperial Hotel. The old name of the town had a more metaphysical look than the present one. It was Innerness. The River Ness runs through the town. It is a very old place, and once had a castle near by, in which it is thought Duncan met his death at the hands of Macbeth. There was a later castle, in which, in the times of James I., Parliament was once held. In 1746 that castle came to an untimely end, and now the court-house and county buildings occupy the site. Three miles away is Culloden. The town has a flourishing trade by means of the canal, and its imports and exports run into large figures. We strolled through the streets for a little time, and looked into the shop windows, which were well supplied with goods. We ventured into the open door of the Town Hall, a large stone building, with a fine hall for public meetings. The coats-of-arms of the Scottish clans were in the windows.

The next morning we left Inverness, and found that we were ticketed to Edinburgh by a very long way. But this enabled us to have an hour in Aberdeen, which we improved by a stroll, and a survey of the very fine new market-house which was abundantly furnished with good things. It was a weary day's ride, and we were glad at night to enter our names at the Royal Hotel in Edinburgh.

Edinburgh is so often visited, and has been so fully described, that I need not give much space to the brief time which we spent there. We saw what everybody sees, and what I had seen before. Yet these places were worth far more than we could give to them, and their relics are their own. We went to the castle, and looked from the high, peopled walls down upon the city. We saw the old regalia, and we went into Queen Mary's room and Queen Margaret's Chapel; and expressed the usual wonder at the size of Mons Meg. We went to Holyrood palace and abbey, wandered among the pictures, and through the rooms, told again the sad story of Mary, and saw where Rizzio's blood had stained the floor. The ancient tapestries, the antiquated royal bed, the furniture of other days, the little trifles and treasures which association has made valuable, all these we saw and talked about. What a wonderful place it is! And how the heart warms up to Scotch story and the things which have had a place in it! The broken walls of the Chapel Royal show what a fine structure it must have been in its glory. Why could not these wonders of architecture have lasted to our day? We went to St. Giles', where we were admitted for three-pence each. I remonstrated with the ticket-seller on the impropriety of asking a fee for admission to a church. But my words made no impression. He took the money just the same. I presume that was the whole of his office. This is the old parish church, with restorations. They were still restoring or decorating when we were admitted.

We drove through the old city, through its narrow and dark streets, peered into its dismal closes, looked at the dingy buildings, watched the human life which in its poverty and dirt swarmed into the streets, marked the attempts at cleanliness as they hung from the poles which projected from every story of the tall houses, and thought on the days which are no more, and the events of which these crowded thoroughfares and antique buildings were the scene.

A sixpence from each of us gave the right of entrance to the house of John Knox. We saw the rooms which he occupied, and the study in which he wrought great works. It was made plain that the size of the room has little to do with the quantity of the study or of the learning which results from it. We looked from the window of this small room, from which he preached to the multitude on the streets below him. A chair is the only thing now in the house which confesses him as its owner.

It was a fine drive which we had on Arthur's seat, where the "Queen's drive" is the public road. The monuments had their share of attention, Nelson's,

Burns', and chiefly the magnificent pile of stone which commemorates the name of the man who has added even to the renown of Scotland, and has done more than any one besides to preserve the song and legend of its ancient life, and to make a journey under his guidance rich in such pleasure as he alone could impart.

It is a delightful afternoon excursion from the great city to quiet Hawthornden and Roslin Chapel and Castle. The chapel is beautiful beyond any power of words. It is a gem of architecture. The Gothic period has left nothing more elegant. It is four hundred years old, and more. For only a shilling one can cross its antique threshold and listen to the recitation of its wonders by a man who probably knows little of them beyond the piece which he speaks. He is an encumbrance; but he will go on and on, though life is short. It would be hopeless to attempt to escape from him, or to look for a few leisure moments after his declamation. It will then be time to leave. But as his story spins itself out, the eye wanders through the church, examines its exquisite tracery in stone, admires the columns and arches, takes in the whole symmetry and grace, while once again the story of the twisted pillar is told and heard. Who has not heard it? Of the master who vainly tried to create the column, and who went to Rome to learn the art; of the apprentice who wrought out the marvel in his master's absence, and paid for his cunning by his death when the envious master returned? A legend? Yes; but the pillar is there. It might all have happened.

Read it as legend or parable, and it has happened scores of times. We turned from the chapel to Roslin Castle, or to what remains of it, hanging over the river. It was cheaper than going to church, for the proprietor demanded only a sixpence of each visitor. An amiable guide represented the proprietor, and escorted us through the dungeons, which are nearly all that is left. The fact which he labored most to impress upon us was that he had the lumbago in his back. This was not particularly valuable as an item of history, but it had a certain local interest, and was a specious appeal to our sympathy. He did partial service, and on account of his malady excused himself from more. But he had enough strength to take the shilling which we felt obliged to add to the legitimate entrance fee. After all, the dungeons were no better than the church, even in a monetary view.

We followed a footpath along the Esk, through a romantic glen, and crossed the river on a small bridge. A lonely guardian of the bridge demanded from each a shilling toll. We remarked upon the excessive charge. He admitted that it was rather hard on us, but declared that it was not his fault. On this walk we explored the cave where Bruce is said to have taken refuge. We saw his sword, so called, and John Knox's desk. A woman was in charge of the place and its treasures. I fancy that she expected a shilling in return for her courtesy; but she made no sign to that effect, and we did not run the risk of offending her by offering to pay for what had been pleasantly rendered. We thought, too, that the landed proprietors had made enough out of us for one afternoon. At Hawthornden we waited for a train and were returned safely to Edinburgh.

Saturday afternoon we came down to Melrose and found a most comfortable home at the Abbey Hotel, hard by the abbey. I found that the house had been enlarged since I was last in it, which was a token of prosperity. Its situation is perfect, and all its arrangements are excellent. We had the house almost to ourselves, and the quiet was very restful. It was delightful to be so near the abbey; to have the ruins before our windows, where we could look upon them as the day glided into the evening and the shadows of night crept over the walls, and to hear the ancient bell ring out the hours of day and night. There were none to answer, but the bell maintained the fidelity of its more useful years. "Melrose Abbey (admission, 6d.) was founded in 1136, but was destroyed in 1322,"—so runs the book. Not long after the walls were reared of the house which now stands desolate. It was one of the finest of the class of fine houses to which it belonged. The stone was hard enough to preserve some of the carving which embellishes it. The graves of kings and other mighty men are yet to be seen, and the place where tradition says the heart of Robert Bruce was laid when it had ceased to beat with love for his country and his people. It was a good place for the last slumber, and as safe as Icolmkill. The waves of time have already swept over island and abbey, but the sleepers have not been wakened.

Melrose is a very attractive place. The old monks liked a fair, well watered country about their houses, and they had it here. The abbey was worthy of the place which they selected for it. Even in its despoiled estate it is majestic and beautiful, with its massive pillars and lofty arches, the delicate tracery of its capitals, where constructive and inventive skill labored to one end, and the graceful and grotesque figures which look down from the walls, and the empty framework of its great windows. The venturesome boy, with an instinctive desire to stand in high places, wished to go up to the gallery where of old the monks walked, and from which they looked down into the sacred courts. But visitors were not allowed there. Perhaps the regulation is wise; it certainly can be made remunerative. I had a friendly chat with the motherly dame who was in charge of the abbey, and she represented to me the perils of the high promenade. She said her son had forbidden her to go there; but I so far ingratiated myself that she finally said the boy might go if the woman who serves as guide would attend him. The woman was more than willing. She knew there was reason for yielding a cheerful consent. So the youth passed along the dusty path once trodden by feet which long ago rested from their wandering and turned to dust in the field beside the house they loved and served. It is an interesting old burial-place where they are lying with many of later days.

How much charm there is in the very name of Melrose! What house awakens more tender recollections! For this we are doubtless indebted in good measure to him who chose his home on the banks of the Tweed. But the house and its history have their own choice interest for us. The house has its heroic annals: —

> "For Branksome's Chiefs had in battle stood
> To fence the rights of fair Melrose:
> And lands and livings, many a rood,
> Had gifted the shrine for their souls' repose."

But who shall tell the tales of love and devotion, of gentle charity and gracious ministry, of hope and desire, and holy communion even with those who had gone up into the excellent glory? So many of the best things never get written! The bones of Michael Scott and the heart of Bruce may not be there. Alexander and the Douglases may not be found. The saints have left their niches empty. But the lives remain, and it is not very hard to bring back the men who once had here their home, and received those who came for rest in life, or for the rest which follows after.

> "More meet it were to mark the day
> Of penitence and prayer divine,
> When pilgrim-chiefs, in sad array,
> Sought Melrose' holy shrine."

We looked upon the scene "so sad and fair" when

> "The gay beams of lightsome day
> Gild, but to flout, the ruins gray," —

and when

> "The broken arches are black in night,
> And each shafted oriel glimmers white;
> When the cold light's uncertain shower
> Streams on the ruin'd central tower;

When buttress and buttress, alternately,
Seemed framed of ebon and ivory ;
When silver edges the imagery,
And the scrolls that teach thee to live and die."

You who read this may think there was no need of copying lines so familiar. If you do think so, will you try to write of Melrose, and leave them out?

But when one indulges his imagination by moonlight, he must be prepared for the disillusion. I looked from my window at night down among the graves, and saw the figure of a young woman in the arms of her lover. Not far off was the stately figure of her mistress, as I conjectured. She was very prim, and her skirts were scant and straight as they fell to her feet. As she was watching, and I feared with no good intent, I felt at liberty to share her vigil. My sympathy was with them as against her. Of the little group no one moved. The spell which was upon the abbey and the graves seemed to have fallen upon them all. At length I was forced to suspect that there was a lack of reality in the vision. The morning showed that it was even so, and that my fancy had been playing with the monuments. Well, it might have been true. In that field, or some other of the fields, it has been true.

It was a fine place for the Sabbath. What could be better? It was a pleasant walk to the churches. I selected the Church of Scotland as best adapted to my condition. Could one choose any other, being there? The building had an old look, though it has not closed its first century. The watchful bird upon the spire looked aged and weary. Indeed, I have seen no one of these sentinels in the United Kingdom who could be compared with the dignified, vigorous bird who so long presided over Boston streets and Boston harbor, and now looks down upon the Cambridge parsonage. The pews were unpainted, and had very high and straight backs, with very narrow seats, whose severity was not relieved by cushions. I was given a place near the high pulpit. The pulpit and the gallery were of oak, so far as the genius of the local painter could transform pine into oak, and, to the same degree, the supporting pillars were of elegant marble. Decorative art could not have gone much further, at least in that direction. After a time the sexton, if that was his title, made his appearance with the Bible and hymn-book, which he placed in the pulpit. He descended and the minister came in, a short man with a long beard. He marched down the broad aisle, holding up his gown as if he was passing through deep water. When he was fairly in his place, the sexton, if he was the sexton, mounted the stairs again and closed the door. He had the preacher safe till he chose to let him out. All the ceremony was amusing to a foreigner, but not without impressiveness. Yet when I try to imagine all this done by the sexton and minister with whom I am most concerned, I can never make it work well. I fear they would not fit into these arrangements gracefully. But they might come to it. The manner of the preacher was dignified and serious. "Let us solemnize our minds by singing the eighty-ninth Psalm, beginning with the fifteenth verse." Then a man in a black gown stood at the end of the broad aisle and raised the Psalm. There were a dozen boys in front who appeared to be the assistants of the leader. There was no organ, but the singing was hearty and good. I shall not report the sermon. "All things work together for good," was the text, with the rest of that helpful verse. If the good man had stopped with the words of the apostle, he would have done well. But he proceeded to show how much of the spirit and life of a grand sentence he could take away in thirty or forty minutes. No man could fail to say good things on such a theme. But he dwelt so carefully on the latter part of the verse that there was small comfort left in the former part. I could not avoid the feeling that the man of Tarsus and Damascus wrote larger and better things than the man in Melrose described in his name. The people did not listen as if the increasing words had added much meaning to their own first thought, though now and then the girl who sat next me brushed a tear from her eyes. I fancied it was more for some memory of her own than for the sentences that fell upon her ear. At the close of the service I asked her if this was the stated preacher there, and she answered with a pleasant smile and the bewitching Scotch accent, "No; it is a strange minister."

I am coming to feel that to preach is more difficult than I have supposed. The preacher's message is so great in itself, so noble in its tone, so gracious in its spirit, that it is hard when a man has spoken it to speak about it. I wonder if it would be better to start with ourselves; with the human thought and want and longing and experience, and work our way up to the mount where we may hear the voice which comes to every man according as he has need. When one wants the word he waits for it, and listens while it is speaking to him. I am more and more persuaded of one thing, that preachers ought to let God's word to the soul have its full meaning and force and speak for itself. When we keep close to him whose messengers we are, and speak as we are bidden, we shall have more authority, and therefore more influence.

"Then the Lord answered Job out of the whirlwind, and said, "Who is this that darkeneth counsel by words without knowledge?"

All this is a soliloquy and not a criticism. It is addressed to only one man, and I hope he will profit by it.

Monday was given up to that to which the day belonged. Its occupation was easily determined. We had a delightful drive to Abbotsford. It was not merely the residence of Sir Walter, but his home, the house and home of his own making. Castles and abbeys furnished stones for it, and the history of the Highlands was enshrined in and within its walls. I doubt if there is another house in the world where so many people would feel at home. The form of it is known to everybody. Who does not know the ample hospitality which dwelt in it? Who has not sung the songs and read the tales which issued from its heart? Who has not roamed through its garden with the master and his companions? We were fortunate in the time of our visit, as we had the genial cicerone to ourselves and he seemed in no desire to hurry us. So we lingered in the rooms, among the arms and the books, and the gathered relics of many days, and the abounding memories which were more than recollections.

The drive lost none of its charm when we turned towards Dryburgh. We had to leave the carriage at some distance from the Abbey, and to cross the bridge on foot. Then we walked on till we stood among the remains of magnificence, and communed again with vanished glory. Melrose and Dryburgh were founded in the same century, and were both destroyed by Edward II. Dryburgh had two centuries more of life, but at length fell again and has found no one to restore it. We could easily erect the walls and divide them as of old; and there was enough of the former work to serve as a pattern for the restoration. But the chief attraction of the place is in St. Mary's aisle, where, in a broken corner of the ancient pile, with that of his wife and son, and of Lockhart, is the tomb of Walter Scott. An iron gate shuts out the visitor, but he can stand near and easily read the modest inscription. A better memorial are his own words, which are in all the world. What a life it was; industrious, incorruptible, patient, courageous, simple, and gentle, full of friendliness, rich in love of his country — doubly his — and of all which ever belonged to it! He illuminated the land, opened its secret treasuries, told its tales, and taught others to sing its melodies, until, more than any other, he has given Scotland its place in the hearts of men.

This is remembrance worth having, when it comes unsought, when it has to come, when a man compels it by virtue of his manhood and manliness. It may be long a-coming, but such a career and name as his make us trust that the day will dawn when it shall be seen that not before thrones or titles or estates is the truest and most loyal homage paid, but before men and manhood. I cannot feel that the place for his grave was well chosen. Why should he lie in the past who inhabits the present, and whose name is the most common one and the most honored one in his land? Should he not lie in his own home, or on some hill-side over which his Highlanders wandered, or by some lake whose waters he brightened and widened, rather than with the dead, in the midst of a ruin, among the grim and broken stones of a fallen house to which he never belonged? So I thought when I stood by the grave. I wished that he was in the sunlight, where the minstrel's song might seem still to charm him, and he could "feel the daisies growing over him." But even that would be his grave, and he is not dead.

We drove back through Newstead and took a last, long look at Melrose.

"Was never scene so sad and fair!"

In the afternoon we moved on, bidding farewell to Scotland. At ten o'clock we were at Newcastle-upon-Tyne.

# CHAPTER III.

## FROM NEWCASTLE THROUGH NORWAY.

NEWCASTLE once held the new castle which was begun by Robert, the eldest son of the Conqueror, in 1079 or 1080, and finished by his brother, William Rufus, and had an important part in the wars of that period. A hundred years later Henry II˙ erected the castle of which the Edwards made much use when they led their armies into Scotland. The castle has been restored, and is a fine representation of the military architecture of the Normans. But the town reaches into an earlier time, when the Romans had a camp there, which they called Pons Ælii, which was one of the forts which defended the wall of Hadrian. The deserted camp of the Romans was taken up by a colony of monks, and the town thus acquired the name of Monkchester. Not for these things, but for its vigorous modern industries is it famed now. It stretches for two miles along the river, which furnishes a natural dock for the shipping. Artificial docks have been added to this for the accommodation of the multitude of vessels. Ship-building is carried on upon a very large scale, and we found the river studded with iron ships in the process of construction. A familiar saying reminds us that Newcastle has coals enough.

Indeed, its extensive trade consists largely in coal and in such things as coal helps to make. It is an ancient traffic, reaching back to the Henrys and Edwards. The railway system had its origin here, and here the Stephensons wrought upon locomotives and civilization.

We drove about the town in a leisure hour, and had a passing view of its fine streets, its large buildings, and the signs of its earlier and later life. The place deserved — what place did not — a longer time than we could give to it.

At one o'clock on the afternoon of Tuesday, July 31, we left the pier at Newcastle on the tender which was to take us to the steamer at the mouth of the river. The name of the tender was *Providence*, which had a pleasant suggestiveness. It was an interesting sail down the Tyne, between the shipyards and the factories. Where the river widens into the sea we passed through the "graveyard," and looked with a sense of pity at the old ships which have "outlived their usefulness," and are now abandoned together there for the elements to break them up. We found the *Norge* waiting for us. She belonged to a new line of ships running between England and Norway, and promised more comfort than the ships whose English port is at Hull. The new line fulfilled its promise, and it is much to be regretted that it has been discontinued.

We were allowed for this northern journey to join two of our countrymen whose plans were like our own. With one of them we had crossed the ocean and rambled about Killarney. I think they will allow me the pleasure of mentioning their names, for they were the most genial companions, and greatly enlarged the interest and happiness of the weeks which we spent with them. They were the Rev. Dr. Williams of Baltimore, and Mr. L. M. Blackford, the master of a noted school for boys near Alexandria, Va. There were but few other passengers on the steamer, and conspicuous among them was a learned and courteous canon of the English Church, with whom we kept company for some time in Norway. There was but one lady among the passengers. The North Sea, which is capricious, and at times most violent, was very quiet during our voyage, so that we could enjoy it to the full. The staterooms were small but comfortable. There were so few of them that our two friends were put into the smoking-room, which was not in all respects comfortable. They could not have it till the smokers had gone from it, leaving the lingering fragrance of their presence. There was no key in our door, and a watch-case hung over each berth. It was clear that we were among honest folk. The table was good, and was abundantly furnished with cheese, which we found to be a staple article on sea and land. We had at least four kinds, so that we could give to our meals something of an experimental and comparative character. One kind, which resembled an obelisk in shape and color, and gained that name, seemed to be the main reliance. The service was rather primitive, but generous and good-natured. It was not without difficulty that we managed to make return for the extras, which we enjoyed without knowing that they were extras, so that memory and imagination were taxed to sustain our integrity and the ship's finances. When we had conscientiously given in our personal statements, there came the added difficulty of paying for what we had received in a currency of which we were ignorant, and to men who were ignorant of our language. But I fancy that they were reimbursed, as they deserved to be; for all of the men and maidens of the ship, from the captain to the table-girls, were eager to minister to our comfort.

In forty-four hours from the time of our starting we were in the harbor of Bergen, on the south-west coast of Norway. The approach was very pleasing. The coast-line was not unlike that of Ireland, although the hills were more rocky and barren. Bergen has a picturesque look, with the red roofs of its houses, which are mostly clustered at the base of a high hill, and on a sort of promontory stretching into the fjord. The people count seven hills back of the town, and a stranger in the land can readily count four. He has a suspicion that the balance must have a classical rather than a natural existence. The steamer stopped in the harbor, and boats at once came around to take us to the quay. We were landed in a fish market, though the market itself was chiefly in boats which were massed together and formed the scene of a busy traffic, carried on by both men and women. Besides fish, we saw potatoes, pottery, cheese, and other commodities. The women were bareheaded, or wore a peculiar peaked cap. Some of the men and boys had wooden shoes. We found no carriage or van to take us and our belongings to a hotel. But there were porters for the baggage, which was loaded on the back of an old man to an incredible degree. We moved in procession behind him, and soon found ourselves at Holdt's, which is one of the several hotels of the town. The porter shook hands with us when his duties were over, and went his way. We found then, and afterward, that politeness is a strong point among these people. The house was crowded by the time we reached it. The register was kept on a blackboard fastened to the wall, and there the enterprise of Dr. Williams had placed our names against vacant numbers. We were thus well provided for, and we found the house very comfortable.

Our introduction to Norway was most fortunate. We had been commended to the consul of the United States at Bergen and to another gentlemen of prominence in the country. They were both members of the Storthing, or national Parliament, and were able to give us much trustworty information in regard to public affairs, as well as those of more local interest. Nothing could have exceeded their attention, and no men could have made kindness more serviceable.

Bergen is one of the oldest of the towns of Norway. It has some thirty-four thousand inhabitants. The climate is mild and damp. Bergen has been called "the fatherland of drizzle," but the weather was good while we were there. It had been an exceptionally dry season. The town has suffered much from fires. But these have opened the way for placing modern buildings among those of more antique design. The people are said to be more social and vivacious than in other parts of the country, and their holidays are merry ones. But they are industrious and frugal; a very pleasant people to live with. The language is very musical. There is a peculiar inflection at the end of a sentence which makes speech almost like a song. It is a delight to listen to it when it is spoken by a refined, musical voice.

The consul took us out to a fine country house which he was building. It was a charming drive. We found that the construction of the house was very substantial. The timbers were heavy and were well set together. No plaster was on the walls, but above the wainscot they were covered with brown linen. This could be covered with paper, if one chose to have it so. But as it was, it was much more pleasing to the eye than bare white walls would have been. Many of the houses are fine structures. The town house of the consul was so much admired by an English traveller that he procured a copy of the plans, and had the house reproduced in England.

Bergen is a town of a considerable trade. The leading article is fish. The northern fishermen make this their market, which is the largest in Norway. There are also yards for shipbuilding, and steamers and vessels of many kinds frequent the port. We made some small purchases, but found that we could do this more easily under the guidance of one of our friends. The language offered some obstruction, and it was not so easy as it might seem to make ourselves understood, even with a vocabulary in our hand. I wanted a knife, and, coming upon a store where I thought I could obtain one, I boldly repeated the Norwegian word "kniv." The kind woman stared, but did nothing to gratify my desire. Yet I was sure of my word, for I had it in my book. Failing in the department of words, I resorted to the sign language, and asked my boy to exhibit his cutting utensil. The woman was enlightened, and, repeating my word, giving a peculiar click to the *k*, she produced the knife.

We went into the Exchange and saw the busy merchants of Bergen, who appeared very much like those in Boston. We went to one old house, rebuilt in the last century like an earlier one in which, in the time of the Hanseatic League, a merchant lived and did business. It was a very quaint building. The staircase of the living-room was very steep and narrow; the bedrooms were extremely small. Yet once a stirring life was content to have its home in these contracted quarters. Now the house is a sort of museum, containing many objects of the period to which it belongs, and all curious and instructive. We visited the public museum, which is a fine building, with collections of many things illustrating the natural history of the country, and many others which are connected with the methods and history of the people. There is a good library on the lower floor of the museum. But nothing interested us more than the grave of Ole Bull, to which we were taken by one of his old friends. It stands in a central spot in the cemetery, in a position of especial honor, and is a rectangular mound with ivy running over it. There were fresh flowers lying on it. The scene of the funeral of the great artist, whose home for so much of the time was in our own land, was described by his friend, and we thought we could imagine something of the intense interest of that day when all the people gathered to pay him sincere honor, and to mourn for one who had long carried them on his heart. We were told that a monument was to be erected to his memory in the town. His name and his work will not be dependent upon stone, but will live in many hearts on both sides of the sea.

On Saturday morning, the 4th of August, we left Bergen in the steamer *Lyderhorn* for a day on the Hardanger Fjord. The steamer was not large, but she was comfortable and well arranged for an inland voyage. It is a peculiarity of Norway, made evident by the map, that it is penetrated by fjords, arms of the sea, which reach far into the country among the mountains, and form broad highways for the traveller. It is of surpassing interest thus to journey through the land. Our sail down the harbor was very interesting. Boats were gathering for the the market-day, laden with enterprise and expectation, and more salable products. Women rowed in the boats with men and seemed quite as strong, and quite as well used to the work. Indeed, men and women seemed to share life along this coast, at least on business days. They had joined in producing, and came with a common interest to the disposing of their goods. We passed among islands of many shapes and sizes. We thought of Lysö, the island which Ole Bull had loved from his boyhood, where at length he made his home, among the tall pines which caught and repeated the melody of the wind which blew across its rocky shores. There in his double loyalty he would give our own flag to the breeze with that of the land of his birth. There he rested at the close, when his fingers lost their cunning and his heart grew still. From its seclusion he was borne to the grave amid the homage of rulers and people. We did not pass within sight of the island, but a Norwegian gentleman, at my request, pointed in the direction in which it lay.

It is too early to be weary of the attempt to describe wonderful scenery. But the pen falters even now. We had seen nothing to equal that which was about us that day. There is more variety in the views on this fjord than is found on the others. The quiet waters lie between rough and steep mountains, where trees contend with rocks, and have a measure of success, while along the banks are grassy fields. The coast-line winds gracefully into bays which are the seats of hamlets nestling at the foot of the hills. Over hill and sea the light and shade play with continual change, making the whole scene both grand and delightful. It was a sunny day, but clouds were on the mountains, and the Folgefond, that mass of ice and snow, thirty-five or forty miles long, was covered from our sight. We knew it was there, for we saw it on the map, where it lies like a vast lake among the hills.

The steamer stopped at various places along the way. Sometimes she went up to the pier, at other times only waited for a boat to come from the shore. These were all forlorn-looking settlements, with a few lone houses, and in the largest places perhaps a mill and a church. Life must have an even flow in such retreats. Once a cannon was fired for our entertainment, and the echoes had a striking, but familiar, sound. Echoes seem independent of national tongues. We had the usual amusement in watching the passengers, who were of several classes, and were to a considerable degree possessed of the same purposes as ourselves. The eating arrangements of the steamer were not on a lavish scale, but the steward and his assistants did what they could, and were always patient and obliging. There was an unusual amount of consideration shown in assessing the fares. Persons travelling in a family had family rates, as I found at a later time. Our distinguished church dignitary was easily the most important personage on board, and he was always courteous, and ready to use his fund of knowledge for the common good. He had studied the language of the country for his own convenience, though the Norwegians seemed to get on quite as well when he used his mother-tongue. He seemed to have given some attention to our country, for he remarked while we were at Bergen that he had no doubt the English language was well spoken in Boston and the more settled parts of the country, but that it must be more rudely used in the wilder portions, as Cincinnati and Oregon. His repetition of that phrase indicated that it stood for all our wide West. Yet I have seldom met a man to whom it was so pleasant to listen in his familiar talk. I am confident that he adorns the high position which he holds, and he seems like one who has deserved even a loftier place.

By slow degrees the day wore on and the darkness gathered. We all grew dull as we sailed down the Sörfjord. We even grew anxious. We knew that we were bound to a very small place. The guide-book was not encouraging. It told of Ole Prætsgaard's, near the pier, and Baard Aga's, two hundred paces off, and the Vetterhus. But we were a large company, and how could so many find quarters late on Saturday night? It is to be confessed that we were more especially concerned for four of the company. Our excellent friends at Bergen had marked out our route through the country, adding their suggestions to the plan made for us before we left home; and the consul had also telegraphed in our behalf to Mr. Baard Aga. We had expectations. But who could tell whether a line over the wires would give us precedence among so many who had shown themselves equal to securing the best places on the steamer? It was about eleven o'clock when we drew up to the pier at Odde. It was dark. Many people were on the quay. But to which of them were we consigned? We called, " Mr. Aga! " and had no response. With increased emotion we again shouted " Mr. Aga! " He appeared at our cry, and we found that he had received the news of our coming, and that our rooms were in readiness. We followed him to his house, which was not an imposing building, although it was very attractive at that time. We were received by a woman who could speak English, but could hardly be called proficient in the accomplishment. She may have learned it in Cincinnati or Oregon. But she knew as if by instinct what we wanted. She fairly read our thoughts, late as the hour was, and dark as it was out-of-doors. It is an inestimable aid when travelling where there is no common tongue, that the pressing wants of men are very few, and can be quite accurately determined by the time when they present themselves. This woman knew that we wanted rooms and beds. She offered two rooms to our party of four. They were on the same floor, and opened out of the dining-room. The room assigned to my boy and myself was about eight feet square. The walls and ceiling were nicely painted. There were two beds, which were short, after the manner of the country. My own bed was apparently modelled after a bread-tray. The sides were some four inches high, and the floor of the bed was exactly my length. It was very comfortable, and difficult to roll out of. It was good for sleep, and for that purpose it was wanted. We had two pitchers and bowls for personal ablutions — one set on a washstand, and the other on a chair. Everything was wonderfully neat. We always found neatness in Norway. We proved the table in due time. It was excellent in the abundance and quality of that which it set before us. That was a matter of the next day.

Sunday brought its disappointment, for we had expected to attend service in the village church.

But there was no service on that day. Only one Sunday in three is the minister in this village of forty houses. We saw the humble house in which he makes his home, and wished we could have seen him. I think there is a Sunday-school in the neighborhood, where some good man instructs the children who are sent to him. We should have been glad to have worshipped with these plain country folk in their Lutheran Church, and could have joined in the songs and prayers even though the language was strange. It would have been interesting to see the peasants as they came from their scattered homes in their gala costumes up to the house which was a home for them all. But we were left to ourselves. We went for a little time into the empty church, and sat in its silence and communed with our own hearts. We looked up to the hills and out upon the stream, and far above us saw a part of the Buarbræ, a portion of the Folgefond, all of which had been hidden on Saturday. A visit to the glacier makes an excursion of four or five hours. This includes the Gaarden Jordal, with its elms and birches, a garden shut in by a precipitous wall of rocks. Some of our fellow-visitors made the excursion. Some went fishing and came back with very creditable trout. We passed the day more quietly; but it was a pleasant pause between the weeks, and it was a fine place in which to have it come to us.

It was very early on Monday morning when we returned to the steamer and resumed our voyage. We went from Odde up the fjord, turned into the Eidfjord, and landed at Vik. We made haste to the inn of the town, which was kept by the brothers Næsheim, and was reputed to be a more expensive stopping-place than some others; yet nothing in the outward aspect of the building or in the furnishing of the rooms presented any sufficient reason for this. But we had not come to see the village, and there was little to see if that had been our design. Like many a large place, this derives its importance from the independent fact that it is near certain natural attractions. People stop at Vik in order to go further, as a tourist from Killarney might properly remark. We wished to see the Vöringsfos, which ranks among the very best of the many fine waterfalls of Norway. We made a very short tarry in the house, but one long enough to secure the services of a guide. He was not promising in appearance, but it seemed a good fortune that we found any one unemployed. We had learned that at Vik we should take a boat for the falls. We learned more when we were on the spot, for there was a walk of two English miles across the neck of land which lies between the fjord and the Öifjordsvand, — there is a real pleasure in writing these names from memory and Baedeker, — which is a lake fifty-four feet above the level of the sea, and bordered with high rocks which are adorned with waterfalls. The boatman lives at Gjellero, and when he is there may be addressed in shouts which will bring him to his boat in due course of time. When he was obtained, it became clear that the boat in which he proposed to ferry us across had absorbed too much of the lake. Bailing out was a slow process, but our time was not of much account. At last we embarked. It was a fine boat-ride, and it ended where we were to take horses — that is, a further walk of half a mile brought us to the place where it was fabled that there were horses. We made the walk in haste, as there were plainly more persons, in different boats, than there were likely to be horses. Our fears were not groundless. We thought our speed was considerable, but it was not immediately rewarded. One of the brothers had remarked that he did not know whether we should find horses or not. He was correct. We came to a small house with a large sign, and there we halted. Other persons were doing the same thing, and apparently for the same reason. The sign was somewhat remarkable: it was rectangular, and in the lower right-hand corner was a small table, on which stood a bottle and tumbler. The bottle was very much higher than the table, which was about as high as the tumbler. On the top was the legend

HERE ARE HORSES AND GUIDES
AND GOOD LODGINGS.

Of the lodgings I have nothing to say. We were then running up a bill at Vik. But there were no horses. A woman appeared, and to her we addressed ourselves with some embarrassment. Her ideas on the subject of horses, or hests as she called them, were vague. From the humble, very humble, dwellings about the natives speedily appeared. No species seemed to be lacking. Men were in the mustering group and women; boys were there and girls. The aged grandmother tottered out on her bare feet; the matron with her arms full of a baby and agricultural implements came squarely to the front. The freedom of the city was evidently at our disposal; but from the whispering of the natives one with another nothing came. They stood and they stared, but they produced no hests. We partook of such refreshments as the unassuming hostlery offered; but this brought us no nearer to the stream which was leaping over the remote cliffs. To us and to the other tourists there seemed to be an uncertainty attending the outcome of our expedition. Now and then a hest appeared, and there were rumors of men seeking more among the mountains. Our own peculiar guide disappeared. After a long absence he returned with two hests. We learned from him, through a friendly interpreter, that a third would soon be along; of the fourth he was more uncertain, as he was supposed to be grazing on an island. He came at last, and proved to be the best of the lot, and he fell to me. We mounted, grasped the rope reins of the rope bridles, and moved off in solemn procession. We were the last in the line. There were ladies before us, the most favored of whom had the national side-saddle, which was the ordinary saddle with a curving back on one side and one stirrup or step.

It was a serious two hours which followed. The road was narrow and stony, and often so steep that we dismounted and led the horses. In one part we left them to find their own way for ten minutes, while we clambered on as we best could. There were paths before two of us which make these seem easy in the retrospect; but then they were hard. We rode up and down stairs, crossed bridges, and forded a considerable stream. Much of the way ran by the side of the rapids, which roared and rushed in their descent. It was rarely possible to hear the voice of a person at hand. Then we heard the deep roar which told us that we were drawing near to the cataract which we were seeking. It was a stupendous journey. I had never so deeply felt the sub limity, the immensity of mountains; the grandeur and the awfulness which belong to them in their highest estate. To move slowly, silently among them, yielding to their sombre and weighty control, was the most impressive experience of the day.

We left our horses when we could go no further, and made our way over the wet and slippery rocks till we stood opposite the falls. It was certainly a fine sight which was before us. The water falls by a single perpendicular leap of four hundred and seventy-five feet into a basin of rock. It breaks into spray as it descends, and the spray rises from below like smoke. We could see this long before we saw the falls themselves. We went further on into the mist till it was like a thick, fine rain and we could not face it. We were drenched by it almost as if we had been under the stream. Then we turned back, regained our horses, had a bit of the poor lunch we had brought with us, and returned by the way over which we had come. Now and then we found peasants who seemed to be interested in

us and ready to serve us. Once a woman gave me
a drink of water from a large bowl which she held
in her hands. We reached the hest station in
safety, where we paid for our steeds, about eighty-
six cents each. Then we walked to the boat, re-
crossed the lake, and walked back to the Næsheims',
which we reached at half-past seven. We had done
a good day's work for novices. There was some
difference of opinion regarding the profitableness of
our excursion. Dr. W. said that he was glad that
he had seen the Vöringsfos, but that he would not go
again. He affirmed that he desired to see no more
waterfalls. Mr. B. seemed chiefly impressed with
the danger of the ride on account of the roughness
of the road, and more particularly of those portions
over which we passed on our own feet, where we
might easily have been crippled. The boy thought
it had been a very good day, but regretted that he
had not enjoyed a fleeter steed. For the remaining
member of the party I can only express my satisfaction. The expedition to me was remunerative. I
knew that I should remember it and feel its
power.

I must add a few words more touching the mountains through which we passed. They were so great
that they made us feel very small as we crept along
the narrow path which they gave us. In such a presence one feels carried beyond himself, and brought
close to Him " which by his strength setteth fast the
mountains; being girded about with might." Life
dwindles, till a man remembers that he is greater
than the hills, and shall live when they have been

moved out of their place. It is grand that we can know we are his children, and that "the strength of the hills is his also."

On our return to the inn we found that other guests had come while we were away. One of them I knew as an Andover student, then studying at Berlin, and another was the son and associate of the famous geographer Kiepert. We travelled with them afterwards. Then, there were many strangers, too many. We had come home hungry. But on the subject of dinner or supper the landlord could give us little comfort. He heard our statement of our case, and recognized our prior claim to places at his expensive table. But that claim he did not enforce. I do not know at present whether he could have done so. It seemed then that something should be done. It was done only by the later comers to the house, who were the earlier comers to the table. It seemed probable that our time might arrive. So we waited, but not patiently. Finally we found seats at the table. We found little besides. Raw beef and fried eggs were proffered us, but not accepted. The fish, a salmon, had been finished. We remonstrated in the language we understood best, and at last somebody brought forward a very good trout. Then we made our supper. We followed this by a conference, after which we climbed into our boxes, and over a very smooth road glided into sleep.

There were clouds and showers in the morning, but the day promised well. We visited the very old church of the place, which stands on a moraine conveniently placed for this purpose. The house bears marks of its age. The seats were very narrow, with high backs, and were unfavorable for ecclesiastical napping. The pulpit was high and gaudily painted, as were portions of the walls. The artist was probably a resident of the region. There was a painted crucifixion over the communion table. A partition divided the church. There was a brass alms-plate, and an iron frame for it to rest upon. Small boxes for money were on the walls. The contribution-box was a small leather bag affixed to the end of a pole six feet long. Just behind the bag was a bell, like one of our sleigh-bells, which gave timely notice of the approach of the collector. By the side of the church was the yard where "the rude forefathers of the hamlet sleep."

As the regular mode of conveyance was not at hand, and there was no more to detain us at Vik, we chartered a boat and four rowers to carry us on our way. Nothing could have been better. The air was soft and the water quiet, the hills were friendly, and the clouds were considerate. We had leisure for a long talk, with no stranger to understand or interrupt. We discussed matters of church, in regard to which we had diverse opinions but one spirit. Then we passed to the war and the questions connected with it. The two members of our party who were from the South were able to speak from that side of the matter, which we considered. One of them had been an officer in the Southern army. Both could describe the spirit of the conflict, and its causes and issues. Both could open up the life out of which the war came, and in which it ran its course.

I shall not attempt to repeat their words or thoughts. But their sincerity and intelligence and earnestness were manifest. It is like a dream, that long boat-ride on that summer day in Norwegian waters, where we were in perfect repose and leisure, far separate from the wide world, thinking and speaking of events which seemed to belong to another age, in times which were remote from those we were living in. We talked of conflict in that impressive peace, and told of the strife of armies as we moved on an unruffled sea, where we heard none of war's alarms, but only the sound of our own friendly voices, and the continuous plash of the heavy oars which were held by men who knew none of the things we said. Yet, doubtless, among those who fought for the old flag were some men from Norway. There was an old alliance of blood which must have made itself felt when the Northmen rose up in the name of freedom.

Thus two hours were passed, making a serene memory, and our boat touched the pier at Ulvik. This was a finer and larger village than any which we had seen. It was charmingly placed on the rounding shore among the high hills. It was rich in hotels, and was clearly a place of summer resort. It was admirably situated for this. It was a spot on which we should be glad to linger for rest. I may say here that "vik" means creek, and for obvious reasons is a common appendage to names in this land of streams. We thought it expedient to patronize the nearest hotel which promised what we desired. Baedeker assured us that Vesterim's Hotel was the house of the Forbrugsforening. We saw no reason to call his statement in question, but it was more convenient for us to seek the Sjur Brakenæs, which he called "unpretending." We were soon in doubt whether it was not too unpretending for four American travellers. Could the deaf and dumb boatmen have said anything to our discredit? Our arrival created not so much as a ripple of excitement, though we came by private conveyance, in a boat and four. We boldly entered the house, but even that aroused no one. We dropped our luggage in the narrow hall, and awaited developments. There were none for a time. At last there was a movement. Twenty people, more or less, appeared and hurried into the dining-room. We knew what that meant, and attempted to join the procession. We succeeded in this perfectly, but when we reached the threshold of the door every seat at the table was occupied. We came and saw, but left the quotation incomplete. We deliberated, and no one offered us so much as a word of encouragement, or a scrap of the advice which is usually freely given under such circumstances. We made no remarks to the company or to the proprietor; I do not know that we even saw a proprietor. We were not fluent in the Norse, and if we had been there was no one to listen to our appeal. With the help of our red-coated friend, who went with us everywhere, we could have inquired, *Hvad kan jeg faa at spise?* Some one could have replied, *Vent lidt! Bi lidt!* But there was no use in talking. We walked out and took an outside view of other hotels. There was the Skyds Station; and Villemsen's, which had an attractive look. But we saw no encouragement, and we had grown distrustful of ourselves and of the world. We went back to our luggage, quite as hungry as when we set out, and waited to see what would happen. Nothing happened for a long time. Finally, a woman emerged and drew near to us. Her face indicated good-nature, with a touch of curiosity. Her manner hinted a suspicion that we might be in want of something, and it was barely possible that dinner might meet our views. She looked an inquiry till one of us ventured upon speech. "Middag?" She replied, "Ja." "Fisk?" "Ja." "Örret?" "Ja." Our conversation was entirely satisfactory. The woman went off pleased, and we remained pleased and expectant. As soon as could be expected, the trout were on the table and we were summoned to our repast. It was good, and our patience, if it was patience, had its reward. When we had paid the proper charges, there remained an hour in which we contentedly surveyed the landscape, and then we left the house as unnoticed as when we entered it. This is all characteristic of the people. They are kind and hospitable; but they are at the farthest remove from sycophancy, while they abound in politeness. Hence the arrival at a house and the departure from it are without ceremony, and the guest is allowed to care for himself and to use anything which he can find. When you do come upon anybody in authority, you are treated with deference, and no one is so poor that he will not shake hands with you. This simplicity is attractive.

I now see four travellers descending the steps of the Sjur Brakenæs, each of them bearing his own impedimenta, and the sight is pleasant as a memory. One of us left a hat behind him in the house, and the same is probably doing duty on the shore of the fjord to-day. We nearly missed the steamer for which we were waiting. There was no one to instruct us, and we went to the nearer pier. Presently the sharp eyes of the boy discovered that the steamer was coming to the other pier. We seized our bags and hurried off, and were just in time to embark.

From Ulvik we went to Eide. The pier at Eide was crowded with soldiers who had broken up camp and were on their way to their homes. The boisterous manner of some of them indicated that not far from the camp had been the cup which both cheers and inebriates. The sale of liquors had been the subject of legislation, but perhaps the old rule, that in the time of war the laws are silent, applies to a military encampment in time of peace. Later in the evening we saw a young fellow, with a fine fresh face, lying in deep slumber on his dray, while his contented horse nibbled the grass at the roadside in lieu of the hay in the manger from which he was detained. We touched the man as forcibly as it is proper to prod a gentleman with an umbrella, but we made no sensible impression, and we left him to his shameless sleep and shameful wakening. We looked into the crowd on the pier and inquired for Mr. Mæland. He presented himself, and we mentioned the name of the consul at Bergen. It was enough. He took charge of us and our belongings and escorted us to his house. This was under his personal care, and in its management was not unlike a good American hotel. We had seen nothing like this, and it was refreshing. Eide is pleasantly situated at the base of the mountain, and is more resorted to in the summer than any other place on this fjord. But the views are not so good as there are at Ulvik. In the morning, at ten, we were off again in a carriage of our own. We had an interesting drive. Shall I say once more that our way was among mountains and waterfalls, over roads which were often steep and rocky, through plains which were green and fruitful? Early in the afternoon we reached Vossevangen. Two hotels had been recommended, but neither of them without qualification. We hesitated, but settled upon Fleischer's. Here was a Norwegian who had been in our Northern army, and a Confederate officer had come to be his guest. But neither was disturbed by the military affiliation of the other. Mr. Fleischer was a stout, good-natured man, and seemed to take life as easily as he could. His house was a busy place, and not so well ordered as Mr. Mæland's at Eide. We were in time for dinner, which was a very slow meal. The chief article presented was a compound of meat, bones, cabbage, and potatoes. Mr. B. insisted that the foundation was ox-tail, but we could not see that he had sufficient ground for that opinion. Then came sausage and potatoes, followed by cherries, nuts, and raisins. Cherries were plenty at this season, and I should think that sausages in different forms were always in season. It was a very fair dinner. There was in the house a rather extensive collection of national costumes, and trinkets, chiefly of silver. These were for show and for sale. The silver was left unguarded, and was a witness to the national confidence. The girls who were in attendance showed us the dresses, and with them an elaborate crown such as is worn by a bride. We asked the younger of the girls to put this on her head that we might see how it looked. She laughed and declined; but she afterwards set it on the head of an older woman, and also the cap which is worn on the way home from church, after the crown has been taken off. There is a pointed and most becoming white head-dress which only married women can wear. It is an art to put one on properly. We saw it done at Odde. Unmarried women wear on their heads a handkerchief, or nothing, while their hair hangs in long twisted braids. All the costumes are certainly pleasing, and it is a pity that they are now so little worn except in the most retired parts of the country.

Vossevangen is at the eastern end of the Vangsvand, a beautiful lake with several towns around it. We devoted a few hours to an examination of the town and its surroundings. The country about is finely cultivated, and has been significantly termed "the kitchen-garden of Bergen." But it is surely much more than that. The farms are well conducted, and are more extensive than are usually found in this land of mountains. The most interesting building is the stone church, which is six hundred years old.

A venerable dame admitted us to the ancient precincts. We found the church very neatly kept. A very young child was the companion of the very old woman, and probably the solace of her age, if not the assistant of her labor. The woman seemed properly impressed when she learned that we were from America, though it was not without difficulty that we conveyed that information to her somewhat sluggish brain. She cordially extended her right hand after we had generously put something in the left. There was an old altar-piece, a candelabrum of 1733, and an antique Bible, with memorial tablets in honor of long departed worth. The font was a pewter basin held by a plaster angel, who was suspended from the ceiling by an iron rod fastened in his back. We went into the high gallery, where there was an old and infirm organ, and a music-book published in Cleveland, and a copy of Bliss and Sankey's hymns and tunes.

They have prizes for something of a sportive sort even in this remote town: for in a window we saw two silver cups, and this inscription upon a paper which was lying on them: —

<blockquote>
Central foreningers<br>
Premier<br>
Ved<br>
Konkerrenceskydningen<br>
paa Voss 5te August 1883.
</blockquote>

At nine o'clock on Thursday morning we resumed our seats in our carriage and left Vossevangen. The clouds were heavy, and it soon rained hard; but we were protected by umbrellas and rubber coats. We dined at a small house by the Opheimsvand, upon the customary trout and sausage. The rain was over when we started again, save for an occasional sprinkle, and we greatly enjoyed our drive. The mountains and valleys in the latter half of the day surpassed any which we had seen. The sublimity of the one and the profundity of the other are unequalled, at least in this part of Norway. The valleys were a picture of quietness as we looked down into them. "Vang" means meadow or pasture, but we saw more rocks than grass. Far up the hills we could see patches of green which it seemed well nigh impossible to reach. It looked as if the grass there must be cut with scissors, and the grain measured in a thimble. Small buildings — *sæters* — showed where herdsmen have their summer homes, and where sometimes the sportsman is glad to find refuge, and to be refreshed on fladbröd, with milk and cheese, and to rest in a mountain bed. From lofty fields the hay is sent down on a wire. In the fields below we saw the grass hanging upon a sort of fence made by poles and strings running across a line of posts, where it could quickly be dried. Where the showers are frequent, haste in haymaking is very necessary. We saw grass growing on the roofs of many of the poorer houses and sheds. In some cases trees of considerable size were firmly rooted on the roof. The roads were excellent. In some parts they were marvels of engineering. We were reminded of the Swiss passes and their wonderful winding roads. Waterfalls were of constant occurrence, from the impoverished rill to the affluent *fos*. The fine cup which a Cambridge friend had given me was very useful. We came at night into a narrow valley between awful mountains. The gloom was oppressive. Never had we been so completely shut in and overpowered. For sixteen weeks in the year the sun does not reach into these depths, and it can never linger there. Our road led into the valley and through it. There was no other. On one side of the fjord was a path at the base of the mountains, by which the little church could be reached; for there was a church there, and a few houses and two hotels — Helland's and Hansen's. This was Gudvangen, at the head of the Närö Fjord. The attentive canon had arrived before us, and, fearing that we might not find accommodation for the night, had engaged rooms for us at Hansen's, and he came out to tell us that he had done so. We were made very comfortable for the night, but it was a fearfully lonely place. How life must shrink and thought die out, and the whole man be crushed, in these sombre recesses of the earth!

We left Gudvangen at six o'clock the next morning. The rising sun changed the aspect of the mountains, and the cloud effects baffled all description. Think of the light stealing down the long slopes, creeping slowly into the valley, and casting the shadows of the clouds it sported with over the long ranges of rocks! The steamer came out into broader waters and under a more open sky. We passed through the Aurlands Fjord into the Sogne

Fjord, near its eastern end, and, running into the
Lärdals Fjord, landed at Lärdalsören. The consul
had telegraphed to Mr. Lindström, the proprietor of
the hotel, and he had a carriage in waiting for us.
We completed the process of bargaining, and resumed our travel by land. We were in a carriage
with seats for four persons. It was very much the
same as one of our barouches; but it was rather
shabby, and the two front seats were much more
uncomfortable than the others. This seemed to be
the best mode of conveyance for us. It was not the
only one. We could have taken the public stage,
or diligence; but in that case we should have been
subject to such horses and such company as might
be provided. We could have hired a *stolkjærre*,
which is a light wagon for two persons, or a *kariol*,
which is a kind of gig for one person. Then the
luggage would have been tied on behind the seat,
and somebody called a *skydsgut*, or *gut*, would have
had his seat upon the luggage. The traveller could
drive for himself and run the risk of accident, or the
attendant would take both reins and risk. The *gut*
might be a man or a woman, a boy or a girl. In
either case there would be little conversation with
the traveller. At intervals along the road are stations where horses can be procured or changed.
These are regulated by law, and are of two kinds.
At the *faste stationer*, or fixed stations, a certain
number of horses must be kept in readiness. In the
parts of the country where there is little travel,
there are the *tilsigelse stationer* — stations whose
keepers are required to send out to the farmers in

the vicinity and procure horses when they are needed. This is the origin of the name, for *tilsige* means to tell to, or send to. The period of waiting may be prolonged for hours, so that tourists naturally make a name in antithesis to the former, and call them "slow stations." The proper thing to do is to send a *forbud*, or message, in advance, that the horses may be on hand when they are wanted. Of course, when there are many travellers it is not an easy matter to provide horses for them; and, while the first comers are promptly supplied, those who are later may have a long trial of patience. But there is a book kept at every station, called a *dagbog*, or day-book, in which the traveller can make a record of his orders, and can also enter his complaints. This may help the next man, and may bring an offending master to a reckoning; but it cannot be of much immediate advantage to the complainant. It is to be supposed, however, that those who are engaged in the station business will do all in their power to "speed the parting guest." They also welcome one who comes, as the station is usually a modest house of entertainment, where the traveller also finds bed and board. At the season of the year when we were passing through the country the arrangements of all kinds were ample.

We did not wish to move in a string of four *kariols*, or even of two *stolkjærres*. Neither method would be favorable to friendly intercourse. Riding alone must be lonesome, and the person behind the traveller could not break the monotony. There was an attractiveness about the national conveyance, but we adhered to our instructions and our shabby barouche. We moved on without delay, and at noon stopped at Husum, a *faste station*. We were in the Lärdal, one of the grandest of the valleys of Norway. The station was at the centre of its best scenery. We had the usual dinner and rest, and then moved on. At night we stopped at Maristuen. Our plan set down Nystuen for this night; but our driver had declared before we set out that he could not go so far, and he proved this by his slow driving. We muttered as we came along, and when we stopped we reasoned. It made little difference where we were that night; but we wished to reach our allotted place on Saturday, and to lose a station on the first day meant that we would be a station short on the second day. We prevailed on a friendly stage-driver, who knew enough English for this purpose, to express our views to our driver, and to offer him a pecuniary inducement to take us through to the right place on the next day. The man stubbornly refused. We resolved to remember his obstinacy when we meted out his gratuity. It was plain that, while we travelled in our own carriage, we were not our own masters.

We were in a very lonesome place, but the kind woman in charge gave us a good supper of cheese with other things. The station-house proper was full, and my boy and I were taken across the road, where we had a good room and beds. We were on good ground, for six hundred years ago, almost, a hospice had been founded here by pious men, for the comfort of travellers through their mountains. Their house was gone, but the hospitality remained, to be enjoyed by men from beyond the sea.

I have not mentioned the most interesting part of the day's journey, our visit to the old church of Borgund. No one knows its age, but we may call it seven centuries and not be far out of the way. It is one of the very few surviving specimens of an ancient and fantastic style of architecture, and is in better condition than any other. Nothing but a picture can give any idea of its peculiar construction, and a picture at once suggests China and its pagodas. It was built of logs laid horizontally and strongly fastened to heavy posts. Upon the walls is a high roof, from which rises a clerestory, out of which rises a structure resembling a belfry, in three diminishing stories, surmounted by a very slender spire. There are many gables. Some of them are adorned with a cross, while from others spring the most curious projections, which have the look of serpents attempting to escape from the influences within the house by a sudden flight into the open air, though never able to free themseves from the imprisoning roof. Within, the church is extremely dark. The builders made scant provision for the admittance of light and air. There is a nave, which is nearly square and very high, and encircling this are low aisles, with round pillars sustaining arches of wood. The choir is at the east, but appears to be cut off from the church proper by the aisles, which run aground the central portion or nave. The walls and roof are shingled. There is no paint in or on the church, but the exterior looks as if it had been coated with tar for its better preservation. It is almost black. About the lower story is an arcade, or covered passage, with small columns of wood. This may have been designed to protect the house against the severe cold and the snow. The doors and their frames, the capitals of the numerous columns, and other parts of the building, are decorated with strange carvings, dragons twined together, and animals in various eccentric forms, with foliage and elaborate scroll-work. It needed a lively fancy to produce such marvellous ornamentation. On one of the doors are Runic inscriptions, which are translated : —

> Thorer wrote these lines on St. Olaf's fair.
> This church in the church-ground.

I do not know what meaning these lines may have had when they were traced. But now the former reads like inscriptions which are painfully common in public places, and as if Thorer had sought fame in an easy way; while the latter seems to be the work of a thoughtless knife in an idle hand. But it is very likely that they had a higher significance in the forgotten century which gave them to the world. Entirely separate from the church is the old *Klockstapel*, or bell-tower, a lofty structure of wood with sloping sides, and a clerestory with an ornamented roof. There are two bells in the high belfry. These buildings now belong to the Christiania Antiquarian Society, and will thus be preserved as a memorial of the elder days of art.

The church is not used for public service. It would hold about a hundred persons. The altar and font are of stone and very rude. The pulpit, which is dismounted, and the altar-piece are of more recent times, I think. It would be pleasant for the people to raise their psalm and prayer where their ancestors worshipped. This would not be convenient. Yet a stranger would much prefer an hour within its gloomy, venerable walls to one in the modern and well appointed church which is near by, and is now the meeting-place and sanctuary.

We left Maristuen at nine o'clock on Saturday morning. The day was cold in the first part, but grew warmer and brighter. We found the road hilly, so that we walked much of the way. In portions the road was quite under the cliffs out of which it was cut. At one place a shed had been built to protect the traveller from falling stones. We dined at Grindaheim, where the landlord, Ole For, speaks English, if the book is to be trusted. But he did not present himself, and we derived no benefit from his linguistic talent. We had parted company with the accomplished canon, but a pleasant German and his wife kept along with us, and there was also a young Lancashire man, whom we called "Kariol" because he journeyed in that vehicle. In the afternoon we met a funeral procession. A low cart carried the black coffin, on which three men sat astride. Then came eight small vehicles, of different styles, filled with men and women who showed no signs of grief. It might have passed for a festal company but for the coffin. The end of the line was decidedly of this character. As we came up, the last two carriages were in trouble. One of these was a kariol, but on its single seat was a woman with a man in her lap. This was probably regarded as an improvement on the inventor's design. In the other carriage were a young man and a woman with a gay handkerchief on her head, which showed that she was unmarried. These two vehicles had collided. Evidently, one or both of the men had partaken too lavishly of the funeral refreshments. Locked in the step of the kariol was the hub of the wheel of the other carriage. Words attended the entanglement. The brilliant head-covering made a flying leap, and the maiden who wore it landed at the side of the road, where she stood and expressed her feelings. She expressed her feelings in Norwegian, which seemed equal to the exigency. Her man pulled his wheel clear, while the other man kept his seat. At length the extrication was complete, the freed carriage fell into line, and the sad procession went on its way and was soon lost to sight. The impressiveness of the occasion was marred by the incident which I have described. Yet the ending of a life is always solemn, even when one knows nothing of him who has passed away. There were sad hearts at the front of this little company, and some home was darker for want of the life which had gone out from the hills of Norway to the land which is not very far off. We noticed that the graves which we passed were usually marked by a wooden cross on an upright board. The inscription was chiefly on the cross-piece. We saw white stones at some graves. We passed this afternoon a Lutheran minister on his way to his Sabbath service in some one of these scattered hamlets.

At night we reached the station at Löken. We expected a great deal here, for the landlord, Mr. Ördgaard, was a member of Parliament. We thought that this fact and the commendation which we brought from two other members of Parliament would secure for us all the luxuries of the place. Perhaps it was so. The M. P. was a man of good appearance, and his house was superior to those we had before seen. The building was large and somewhat adorned. If the proprietor spoke English, we did not find it out. Mr. B., who prided himself on his ability to talk English to a foreigner, labored hard to convince him that more covering was needed on his bed. At last he resorted to pantomime, the universal language, and the proprietor expressed himself convinced and enlightened. The supper was rather ordinary, all things considered. " Will you have supper? " " Yes." " What would you like? " " Fish." " No fish." " No fish ? " " No fish." " What ? " " Eggs." " And meat ? " " Yes, meat." So the bill of fare was constructed — eggs and meat, with tea. The meat proved to be the inevitable sausage-balls. After a time one wearies even of such dainties. The German lady wished to " command shicken." We knew that would be hopeless. " Kariol" arrived late, having experienced many delays. He had a woman for a *skydsgut*. Four Norwegians arrived in a carriage, and the house was full. Beds were on every side of us. In the morning I heard the voice of birds and fancied we were to have "shicken." The voices ceased, and the hope grew towards an assurance. Then the voices were heard again. I wondered if there were any fowls in those parts. A lonesome hen which I saw afterward made it probable. The word for chicken is *kylling*. Was there ever a greater misnomer? The chickens of Norway must reach an old age. The eggs gave out at breakfast, so that a hen's life cannot be laborious, which would secure longevity. I believe that up to this time we had seen fowls on the table but once, and that was at a private house in Bergen.

We found that there was no service in the Löken church on that day, for which we were sorry. We passed the time very quietly. The view from the house was very fine, including a lake and the mountains standing around it. The whole scene was restful and refreshing. The lone hen was cackling out a frivolous existence, and no one was hurried or troubled.

We found it necessary to pass the night a little farther on, at Fagerhund, the fair grove. It was a delightful spot. Artists and sportsmen resort to it, and many others find it attractive. It was well appointed for the pleasure of the guests. We found a very bright girl who spoke English remarkably well. She gave us an admirable supper, late as it was when we arrived. She also gave us a fire in the parlor, for the night was cold.

We had an early awakening, and were faithfully cared for by the English-speaking girl, who did herself credit at the table. Then we took our carriage.

The way soon brought us to a high hill, — a mountain, in fact, — and we made most of the ascent on foot. This was largely a pedestrian journey. At noon we halted at Sveen, a well placed station in an interesting part of the country, with good views and pleasant walks. The day was sunny and warm. The scenery was less bold than that we had left, but the fields looked better. We passed large farms, which were well tilled, with good houses and various farming machines, which were the signs of a more prosperous condition. We drove through forests of spruce, and saw many weeping birches, very handsome trees. We were pleased with the children whom we met. Many of the boys took off their hats in our honor, and the girls dropped a courtesy. The men and women often greeted us with respectful salutation. At night we reached Odnæs, and our long drive was ended. It had been very pleasant, and we had been prospered in all our way. We had come through a wonderful country, to which no words can do justice, and we had seen much of the people and their mode of life, and had made a good store of things to think about on the other side of the sea.

We paid our driver his hundred *krones*, and added the six which we had been told would be a proper gratuity. This part we had talked of withholding when he refused to carry out our plans; but he had been a good-natured fellow, and had brought us through very comfortably, and we felt amiable and generous. He shook hands with us, and went off highly contented.

The hotel at Odnæs was forlorn so far as eating went, and that is a long way in a hungry land. We struggled hard for bodily refreshment, but there were many engaged in the same work, and we had but moderate success. We left the town early the next day, and had a dreary passage down the fjord. It rained and rained, and the boat was crowded; but we reached Randsfjord before two o'clock. We saw a hotel at some distance off and made our way to it and took our seats at the table. No one objected; no one did anything else. A waiter paid some attention to other guests, but spared none for us; so we left the table and walked through the sand towards the railroad station. Soon we found that a woman was following us, and beckoning us back with abundant gesticulation. But we gave no heed. She had lost her chance. We found a table at the station, with coffee and cakes, and we helped ourselves, after the manner of the country, and paid our reckoning upon our own statement. When the train was ready we took our seats, and at eleven were in Christiania. We needed a conveyance to the Victoria Hotel. A man offered his services, and we accepted them. We took him for a cab-driver. It was a mistake. He led us through the station and out-of-doors, past all the carriages. Whither was he taking us? That was our inquiry, to which he made no intelligible reply. With wild motions he disappeared, and we stood on the pavement with our luggage. He soon reappeared with a hand-dray, upon which he placed our goods. Then he started rapidly down the street. We followed him, for there was nothing else to do. Now and then we lost sight of him, and realized the absurdity of our position as we rushed blindly through the streets of a strange city at midnight. We finally came up with him, and soon stopped at the friendly door which we sought. The excellent consul at Christiania had engaged fine rooms for us, and had left a good pile of letters which had come to his care, and we had a very home-like feeling as we ended the day in the delightful house which was to be our home while we remained in Norway.

Christiania, the capital of Norway, is a city of seventy-seven thousand people, according to the last reckoning which I have seen. It has a fine situation at the head of the fjord of the same name as the city. Its appearance is modern, for it has been renewed by fires from time to time, so that the most of the old houses have disappeared. Those were, naturally, built of timber, while their successors are usually of brick covered with stucco, which gives them a very neat look. The wide streets, the great buildings, the well furnished stores, were especially impressive to us who had just come from the simplicity of the interior. It was evident that we had come into the life of the present, with its novelty and its eagerness. Here there was, eight centuries ago, the town of Oslo, or Opslo, founded by Harald Hardraade. That was burned by its own citizens, that it might not fall into the possession of the Swedes. Fifty years later the town was again burned, and then the king, who was Christian IV., set up a new town about his fortress of Akershus, or Agershus. About this a wall was erected. It suffered fearfully from a plague soon after, but a little later it profited by the misfortune of its London neighbors, whose great fire made a demand for the lumber of Norway, and thus created a foreign trade. The town has felt the vicissitudes of the years, but it has prospered. There the Storthing, the national parliament, holds its annual sessions. The one university of Norway is there, where Frederick VI. established it in 1811. Its lecture-rooms were in various places in the town, but are now in one large and handsome building. The last report which I have gives five faculties, with fifty-three professors, and more than a thousand students, and a library of two hundred and fifty thousand volumes. There are various museums connected with the university, for the illustration of the natural and social history of the country. Near by is the Art Museum, in a building presented to the town by the Savings Bank, and containing the galleries of sculpture and painting.

At the time of our visit the National Exhibition was open, and we were surprised to see how extensive and excellent this was. We saw what the people were doing, and with the greatest interest. There was wonderful work in silver, in designs of surpassing beauty and with the greatest delicacy of execution. There were elegant carriages, from the stately brougham to the more characteristic *kariol* or *carriole*. Furs were there in large variety, and woollens of fine quality. The exhibition of books and of photographs and of paintings was most creditable. The building itself was an attractive specimen of architecture, and admirably adapted to its purposes. It was a delight to wander through its departments, to listen to the fine music, to watch the people, and to know that this was the Norway among whose mountains and hamlets we had been wandering. Here we saw the commodities and elegancies of the life of the nation; the furniture of the houses, the pottery and crockery, the gloves and shoes — even the cod-liver oil and punch and beer, which were in proximity to whale-meat, which seemed to be a new article for hardy fishermen whose earnings are not enough for luxuries.

Through the great courtesy of our excellent consul we saw a little of the best home-life of Norway. We visited his own place, Frogner, which is a little way out of the town, and preserves its character as a country home. The buildings make up an extensive establishment. We could hardly believe that we were in private grounds as we drove up between the outstretched buildings to the long house which is the residence of the family. There we found the hospitality which has no national limits, which gave to us the best of two nationalities. It was more pleasant than I can tell to have these hours in a home; to look down upon a fair garden, to sit under the majestic trees, and to renew a friendship formed beyond the sea. If the eyes of Consul Gade should ever rest upon these lines, I trust that he will pardon me that I have spoken so familiarly of his house and household.

I was permitted to go still further into the country and to get another glimpse at the home-life. This was at a summer house, a neat, attractive building, where the handsome wood was allowed to show its color and texture untouched by paint within or without. The hospitality was in keeping with the house, and was generous and genuine. Some sixteen or eighteen persons were at the dinner, which was in honor of a gentleman who had formerly been the British consul at Christiania. It was a very pleasant party, and I was able to learn many things through eyes and ears, and to get what seemed a fair idea of the Eastern feeling upon the disturbed political affairs of the country, and to balance that which I had received at Bergen.

I cannot describe all that we saw in Christiania, or give an adequate impression of any of it. We visited a large new hospital, which we saw to advantage under the guidance of Dr. Gade, one of the surgeons. It was very complete, so far as we could judge. Our sympathy was drawn out by a poor sailor for whom some of our friends had been caring, to whom he seemed to be grateful. He had lost an arm on one of our national ships in a Fourth of July salute, and was waiting till he could return home. He had every attention, and appeared to deserve the care; but I have since learned that he turned out to be a worthless fellow. The kindness was right, nevertheless, and will not lose its reward. We went also to see the viking's ship, or the viking's ships. One of them is in very good preservation. There is some personal interest in these vessels; for, if these particular ships never reached our coast, others which were like them certainly did so. It is judged from their shape that they were good sea-boats. The viking was a venturesome man; his name has a distinguished sound in it; but he was in truth a sort of sea-rover or adventurer, not to give a harsher epithet. One of these old wanderers, dead for a thousand years, has been betrayed at this late day. He made his ship his tomb, and rested quietly through stormy centuries. Then curiosity opened the mound which was over him, and tomb and tenant came to light. It was at a time when Science could reconstruct him. He was not more than fifty years old, and he was over six feet high, and in those distant and forgotten days he suffered from rheumatism. His life on the rough seas wrote its story into his bones in hieroglyphics which we can read, and at last, in the height of his years, the stout sailor made his last voyage, but did not give up the ship. "Then I said, I shall die in my nest." We saw also the bones of horses and dogs who had sometimes kept him company. We could readily construct a tale of adventure which might not be very far from the truth, while we were near the man who made it a real thing. We have not yet done justice to those old Northmen, upon whose history our own abuts on our shores. Perhaps we shall know more and do more by and by.

The visitor to Christiania brings away a few pieces of old silver, in addition to the new works which he admires. Men are going about the country with their wares, which the peasants are glad to buy with their old-fashioned spoons and cups and brooches.

So this old ware, sometimes bearing a date and a name, finds its way to the silver-smith's, where it is preferred above that which is new, and with good reason. We were able to examine a notable collection of bric-à-brac in a private house. The house itself was of rare interest, and it was filled with relics and wonders, and was rich in wood-work, beatifully carved, and in china, glass, and silver, and pictures. There were great treasures in a small place.

We went out to Oscar's Hall, which is in a fine park on a high hill. It was built for King Oscar and is left for the use of the reigning sovereign. It has many fine paintings, and affords extensive views of the surrounding country. Many royal dresses are to be seen, standing as stiff as if their elegance still enclosed the royalty which they once covered and adorned. It was a vision of pageantry without the life. It was the viking's ship without the man. We wanted to try the kariol, and for this purpose the boy and I chartered two in which we drove to the Frognersæter, where there is the summer residence of Consul Heftye. The vehicle proved an easy one, but our experience confirmed our impression that it must be a lonesome method of travelling. One does need another one with whom to talk, even if he has not much to say. We could not go into the house, but as it was not occupied, and the windows had no closed shutters, we seemed to be invited to look in and see where undoubtedly comfort and plenty have their seat, where we should have been glad to find them that day. We admired the grand views which the height opened before us, and went up beyond the house, where we could have a still wider range over sea and land, and out to the mountains of snow. It was a profitable excursion in all respects.

Our little company broke up at Christiania. Dr. Williams and Mr. Blackford were going to Stockholm and Finland. We saw them leave us with regret, for we had been very happy with them, and we wanted to see the countries which they were to visit. But our way led towards the south. On Saturday, the 18th of August, we said our *Farvel* to our kind Christiania friends, and on the large steamer which bears the name of the city we sailed away.

But I must say a little more of Norway before we go further. One cannot be in the country without becoming interested in its political condition and relations. His inquiries may not take him back to Ynglingar, or Olaf Trœtelje, or to Halfdan Svarte, or even to his son, Harald Haarfager, the fair-haired king. But he will surely wish to know the connection between Norway and Sweden, which seem to have been destined by nature to make one kingdom, and which are one and not one. There is no occasion to multiply names and dates in these pages. At the very end of the fourteenth century, Norway, Sweden, and Denmark were united under Margaret of Denmark as regent. This union, which was little more than nominal, lasted for a hundred years and over, when Sweden withdrew. That was the time when the Vasa line began to rule in Sweden. The other two countries maintained the union until 1814.

During this period Sweden attempted to get control of Norway, and did not succeed. But the purpose was not abandoned. A national spirit was rising in Norway. The people were encouraged by the result of their conflict with Sweden, and by their wealth and independence. They were becoming separated from their allies, the Danes, whom they regarded as inferior to themselves. In 1810 a society was formed for the welfare of Norway, and by some persons it was urged that this end would best be secured by a union with Sweden. In 1812 Russia gave Sweden permission to annex Norway, and in 1814, at the Peace of Kiel, Denmark ceded Norway to Sweden. Thus Norway and Denmark were separated. In these transactions the party chiefly interested had little share. It is not a solitary instance of this in European politics. But Norway was not ready to submit to this chess-board treatment. The spirit of independence was rising, the old Norse temper. What had been done in the name of liberty in France and America fostered the desire for a free country. The Swedish king promised a liberal constitution, but the Norwegians preferred one of their own making, in which the neighboring king should have no part. With fasting and prayer and preaching and vows of fidelity, they met by their representatives, and made their declaration of independence. They set up a temporary government, and framed a constitution which was adopted on the 17th of May, 1814, at Eidsvold, a small town forty miles above Christiania. The farm-house in which the meetings were held has been purchased by the government, and on its walls are portraits of members of the famous assembly. The Seventeenth of May is the Norwegian "Fourth of July." The day deserves its honor. It was a brave deed which these men wrought, a bold stand which they took for independence, when a people few in numbers and with scant resources asserted their right to liberty, in the face of all the nations of Europe. They did not accomplish all their purpose, but they served and advanced their country. They proclaimed the Crown Prince of Denmark, Christian Frederic, King of Norway. Then the great powers, Russia, England, and the rest, came to Christiania to carry out their plans and enforce their bargains. War was declared against the brave people, and they could only submit to the forces they could not resist. They fought well and with success, but they could not hope to prevail. The outcome of it all was, that Christian resigned his throne and went back to Denmark, that the Storthing which had been summoned confirmed the union with Sweden, that the new constitution was modified, and that Charles XIII. was proclaimed king. After him came the Bernadotte family, Charles XIV., Oscar I., Charles XV., and Oscar II., whose reign began in 1872.

The union of the two countries is peculiar and not very close. There is one king, who resides at Stockholm, but passes a portion of the year at Christiania. The Council of State consists of two ministers of State, one of whom resides in each capital, and at least seven councillors, of whom five are in Norway and two in Sweden. On his accession to the throne the sovereign is crowned at Drontheim as King of Norway. Norway has a separate Parliament, — the Storthing, — which holds the legislative power. Its members are chosen by deputies who are elected by the people. One-fourth of the members constitute the Lagthing, or Upper House, and the remainder the Odelsthing, or Lower House. Except in the foreign relations of the kingdom, the two countries are practically distinct. Each has its own language. The language of Norway has long been the Danish, although this is enriched by words from the old provincial dialects. The people prefer to call it the Norsk, and dialects derived from the old Norsk are found in the more secluded parts of the country. The currency has been made uniform in the two countries. One hundred *öre* make one *krone*, and eighteen *krones* are equal to one English sovereign, or five dollars. But each country has its own coinage. Each country has its own flag, and in one corner of each is the "Union mark" which constitutes it a national flag. But there is a deep unwillingness on the part of many to have the yellow of Sweden in the flag which floats on the Norwegian breezes, except when it is used for purely national purposes. Ole Bull was one of these, and would never unfold any but the Norwegian colors. We noticed that the boys in Bergen, when they played soldiers, marched under the banner of Norway. In Christiania the union flag was much more common. Indeed, we found that the political sentiments of the two sides of the country were further apart than their coast-lines. It was a time of unusual excitement, and we had no difficulty in obtaining information. So far as we could understand the position of affairs, there was a contest between the king and the Storthing touching the royal privilege. In ordinary cases the king has the veto power over the decrees of the Storthing. If, however, the Storthing passes a resolution three times, it becomes a law, even if the king refuses his sanction. The Storthing claims that this provision relates to all matters, even to the fundamental law of the land. The king, naturally, denies this. For if this is conceded, some day a Republic may be proclaimed and the king be deposed. He would hold his office at the will of parliament. It is claimed, on his side, that the Constitution is a compact between him and the people, and that it can only be changed by the consent of both parties. There seems to be reason in the claim. The king had in this contest thirty-two members with him and eighty-two on the other side. The majority of the Storthing claimed the right to have a militia, and voted supplies for this purpose. They also voted that the Ministers of State should be members of the Storthing. These were grave matters affecting the Constitution. The king refused to give his consent, and declared that these measures could not be passed without his consent. In this view he was sustained by his Council of State; therefore the Storthing impeached the ministers and councillors. They did this, it was asserted by the king's friends, at a time when they had secured a court after their own mind. The trial was to be before the Lagthing and the Judges of the Supreme Court. The decision was not doubtful, it was said. But it was not clear how a new Council could be obtained if the men in office were to be removed. The king would not want men who agreed with the Storthing, and the Storthing would have no others. The Conservatives claimed that they had the greater proportion of the intelligence and property of the country; the office-holders would side with the power which appointed them, and the clergy would feel that they and their cause were safest on the royal side. But the numbers were on the other side, and there were certainly among them men of the highest intelligence and of large property. There seemed to be, also, in the general contention, some who sought an extension of the liberty of speech on matters of religion; but we did not find that this was prominent in the discussion. Whatever was the result of this movement, we had little doubt that the authority of the people would prevail, as it has done elsewhere. The popular movements of our time set in one direction and with one result. It is not likely to be otherwise in Norway.

As I write now I have before me the result of the trials which were impending when we were in Norway. The trials lasted nearly a year, and eight ministers and councillors were declared unworthy to hold office, and each of them fined eight thousand *krones* and the cost of his trial. Their friends rallied to their assistance; over twenty-five thousand dollars was raised by private subscription for their aid, and a public dinner was given to the deposed statesmen. The king filled their places with other men similar to those who had been removed, while the opposition were consulting over the expediency of trying to remove those whom their former efforts had not convicted and deposed. The end has not been reached. The king seems to have yielded something to the Radicals, and to have made up a Cabinet which is not entirely Conservative. But the popular movement will go on. Old claims will be asserted. At last the people will be in power, and will put their own meaning into the terms of the Constitution which declare that Norway is "free, independent, indivisible, and inalienable." To sojourners like ourselves there did not seem to be grave causes of complaint against the government, or evils which demanded severe remedies. The present king appeared to be administering the government quite as well as kings in general do, and the country seemed to be improving upon itself, and increasing its material and intellectual wealth; but larger things are sought, and we must hope that they will be secured.

The Lutheran is the State church of Norway. There are six dioceses, or *stifts*, each of which has its bishop, who is appointed by the government. On account of the connection of this church with the government, and its natural sympathy with the appointing and sustaining power, many of the people are not well inclined towards it. There are many other churches of different denominations, and these seem to have more spiritual energy. They have been very active of late, and their work has had a large and deserved success. There is a generous distribution of religious literature among the people. The temperance reform has engaged the attention of the rulers and the people. The legislation is based on the principle of local option. The authorities in each district may grant licenses for the sale of ardent spirits by retail, or may refuse to do so. They may, if they think it best, grant to a company a monopoly of this trade, with the condition that after the expenses of the business are paid, and five per cent interest on the investment, the rest of the profits shall be paid to the municipality. The latter method is more common in the larger towns. On Sundays and saints' days, and on Saturdays and the eves of festivals after five o'clock, the sale is forbidden. The sale of wine and beer is carried on with restrictions which are less stringent. By these arrangements intemperance and its attendant evils are much less than they were but a few years ago. We hardly saw a drunken person in Norway.

I have, perhaps, said enough of the general character of the people. They are marked by their honesty and sincerity, and by the simplicity of their life, especially when they are living by themselves, out of contact with the wider world. They bestow and respect confidence. They are polite and helpful. Their hand-shaking and their *God nat* and *Farvel* are pleasant to the visitor. Their ways are often clumsy, and there seems to be a lack of enterprise; but the stranger would be slow to change their methods lest he should mar them with his improvements. Their thoughtfulness is sometimes startling in its simplicity. When we were on the Rands Fjord, a German lady carelessly allowed her shawl to fall into the water. No one of us saw any way of recovering it. We knew only the manners of other and prouder lands. But the honest Norwegian captain stopped the steamer, reversed the screw, and we all went back to recover the property, which was then at quite a distance from us. A boat was lowered, and the shawl was recovered and restored to the owner. That may have been an extreme act of courtesy, but it may stand as a sample of Norwegian kindness.

The physical structure of Norway must have affected the character of the people. It has left them to a good degree isolated, and allowed their native virtues to flourish; but, beyond this, the stern mountains and the dark valleys must have put their impress upon those who have lived for generations among them. This may be seen in the stories of the ancient faith. One cannot be surprised at the grandeur and sternness of the Norse mythology who travels through the land in which it was conceived, and sees where the gods were born and where their deeds were done. This was no place for sportive divinities, or for the light fancies of a sunnier clime. The sombre and solid character of the land entered into the making of the people and the construction of their legends and their faith. The stories of Norway should be read in Norway. The sagas need the mountains.

The emigration from Norway to our own country has become large. The Norwegians are excellent colonists and settlers, as we know. But in their own land we could not help asking if so many stout-hearted and stout-handed men and women could be spared. The instinctive answer was in the negative. But to ride through the country, to see how much rock there is in proportion to the soil, and to mark the evident poverty and hard struggles of the peasantry, removes all wonder that men seek a new home for themselves, — and especially for their children, — where life can have a larger hope under more generous conditions. The land is likely to have enough sowers and reapers for its narrow fields. A country which offers so little bread cannot blame those who seek a land of prairies and harvests. In a new land the character of the people will be modified; but we may hope that they will preserve the virtues which are their honor and strength. We shall still be able to see the true Norwegian in his own home. Travellers will carry in their strange ways and corrupt the simplicity of the people. But it will be long before the charm disappears. The attractions of Norway are very fresh and great. The country is easy of access, and travelling is inexpensive and agreeable. In the years to come, Norway will be more frequented by the English, who are already there in good numbers, and by Americans, who are now rarely met. The continent will be the roaming-ground for its own inhabitants. The Germans are on foot, and are flocking into Switzerland in the summer months. But Norway remains for travellers from beyond the narrow and wide seas. The North Cape and the midnight sun will allure them in growing numbers. But many will be content with nearer things, and will pass a few weeks delightfully upon the southern fjords, and in the wonderful scenery about them, and in the cities and villages of the land ; while for the pedestrian, the sportsman, and the artist the resources in every direction are almost without limit.

## CHAPTER IV.

#### FROM NORWAY TO ITALY.

THE passage from Christiania was without special incident. We ran down the fjord, across Bohus Bay and the Skager-Rack, and in the early morning touched at Gothenburg, or Göteborg, the capital of the province of the same name, and in commercial importance the second city in Sweden. There was only time to go a little way up the quay, and with this step on the border of Sweden we were obliged to be content. Although it was Sunday morning, there was quite a stir around us. As usual, people gathered about the steamer, and some of them joined us as passengers. Other steamers were preparing to leave the harbor. A boy was busy selling papers, which appeared to be of a secular character, but which, whether sacred or secular, could be of small advantage to us. Far away a church bell was ringing in the day. But our path led from the church door, and we were soon on our way down the Cattegat. These days at sea were very restful after the hurried life in strange places, where we were compelled to make the most of every hour. They gave leisure for thought, for gathering up the threads and fastening them together, and for adjusting ourselves to the new scenes which were soon to open upon us. About six o'clock in the afternoon we reached Kjöbenhavn, Copenhagen, the "Merchants' Haven." There was the usual bustle of the Custom House officials, which resulted in nothing but delay and annoyance, and then our luggage was put upon a dray which a man pushed along the streets. They gave us a very lofty position in the Hotel d'Angleterre, but we found a fine house, worthy of its reputation. The capital of Denmark is on the large island of Sjeland and the small one of Amager. The approach to the city through the narrow gateway, which is guarded by Elsinore and its castle of Kronborg, and then along the Sound, is very interesting. The capital itself is full of interest. The city is rich in public squares, and in churches, palaces, and other buildings. When we thought of exploring the great city, we were painfully conscious that we had lost not only our pleasant companions in Norway, but also the friends there who had done so much to guide and assist us in a strange land. We were alone, and we knew neither the people nor their language. But we were able to get some advice, and we had the ingenuity which had served us a good purpose on previous occasions. First we visited the Church of Our Lady, where we saw Thorwaldsen's statues of the twelve apostles, and other works from his hand. The church is large, but not especially attractive in itself. The exterior is very plain. Trinity Church is famous for its round tower, which was intended for an observatory. The ascent is by means of a wide road which winds its upward way inside of the tower. It is said that Peter the Great went up this road on horseback, while Catharine went up in a carriage. We had a fine view from the top of the tower, and were able to form a good idea of the city. We walked in the Rosenborg Park, a place so much frequented by young children and their guardians that it is popularly termed the "Nursery." The university is four hundred years old, and has twelve hundred students and a body of able professors. But we saw very little of academic life. We spent some time in the extensive Botanic Garden, with its palms and ferns, and many other appropriate treasures. At night we mounted to the top of an omnibus-horse-car, which sometimes ran on the track and at other times on the pavement. This double arrangement seemed to be desirable, as it surely was practicable where the road lay partly in the city and partly in the country. We went out to the "Tivoli," a public garden much resorted to by all classes of the people, and affording ample materials for a pleasant evening. The lonely citizen could there meet his neighbors, while the father of a family could give his household an outing at very small cost. There were a great many persons there at the time of our visit, but there was good order everywhere. Many sat in the open halls and listened to good music; some watched the acrobats and bicycle riders in their performances. There were various exhibitions of various kinds, and each engaged the attention of a portion of the throng. Nothing was more novel to us than the Rutschbanen. A double series of wooden hills and valleys had been built, over and through which the traveller glides, as the book calls it. He first climbs a flight of stairs to a high platform, where he is placed in a car whose seat is wide enough for two or three persons, and is provided with a leather apron for the security of the passengers. The car glides swiftly down the first hill, and thus gains enough impetus to carry it to the top of the next hill, which is a little lower than the first. This process is repeated till the end of the route is reached, at the top of the fourth or fifth hill. The car is then drawn up to a higher level, which the passengers reach by stairs, when the journey is repeated in the opposite direction. The motion is exceedingly rapid, and one can hardly breathe as he rides. He wonders what would happen if anything should break. He wonders whether he is enjoying the ride or not. But on the whole the performance is exhilarating, and might form a profitable addition to our American picnics. This description is tame, but the thing itself is sufficiently exciting.

There are two other places in the city which are of great interest. One of these is the Ethnographical Museum, which has large and finely arranged collections illustrating the history and customs of many lands from remote times. Stone weapons, ornaments of bronze, and articles in iron and silver and gold abound, while there is a great quantity of coins from many countries and periods.

The other place of special interest is the museum which bears the name of the sculptor of whom Denmark is so justly proud. Thorwaldsen was the son of an Icelander, and was himself born at sea, between Iceland and Denmark. But his name and his work belong to Copenhagen, where he studied when a boy, and which he enriched by his genius and generosity. He bequeathed to the city his collection of works of art and the greater part of his large property, to establish and maintain the museum which is called after him. The museum was opened in 1846. The building is large and fine. On the lower floor are Thorwaldsen's own works in marble and plaster, and on the upper floor are other works which belonged to him. There are also personal memorials, which are of value from their association with him. There is seen, also, the work which he left unfinished. It is a bust of Luther, who was a fitting subject to engage the skill of the master. The head seems complete, but this has not wholly freed itself from the marble. In its condition it is like the man, for the work of Luther is not complete. It is further from perfection than we have been inclined to believe. The work is grand, and the head of it stands out in strength and beauty. But more is to be done before the spirit can have rest. The Reformation must advance until all things are free and true in the domain of religious thought and life. We honor the Reformers and their achievements when we carry forward what they left unfinished. As I think upon the stone which the sculptor left I am not sorry that it is incomplete. It is the better presentation of the man who wrought so mightily for the moulding of human thought and the widening of human life.

In a court within the walls of the museum is the grave of Thorwaldsen, a rectangular mound enclosed at the sides and ends with stones which tell his name and the date of his birth and death. The top of the mound is covered with ivy. Thus the great workman rests among the works in which he embodied his life, and which remain to do him honor. It is a good resting-place, and he is worthy of it.

We left Copenhagen in the afternoon and were to be in Lübeck the next morning. A thin mist was hanging over the islands, and a beautiful light was shining through it upon the city and the water. The effect was peculiar and recalled Turner's Venice, and others of his dreamy pictures. Sea and shore seemed a fairy-land, serene and distant. We did not know what the splendor portended. We found out. Such scenes can be trusted to declare themselves. Soon the radiant mist thickened to an unsightly fog through which the steamer slowly groped her way all night, while the shrill whistle reached our narrow quarters to remind us that we were moving in the dark. When morning came no land was to be seen, but how near or how far the shore was no one could tell. Seaman or landsman, we were equally lost. The lead and line were freely used, and at length they warned the captain that he was as near the land as it was prudent for him to go. Accordingly, at his word the anchor went down, the fires went down, and the skipper went down for a nap after his long and anxious watch. The forenoon wore away, but the fog did not. The whistle had lost its voice, and the tongue of the restless bell took its place and rang out its appeal. I suppose this was intended, like the blind man's lantern, to keep others from running into us. The hours were leaden. I thought of absent friends, and multiplied letters to them. We had simple amusements, but there was a dulness in all our play. Late in the afternoon the fog lifted, and we saw that we were very near to the shore. We had not stopped too soon. The land was very attractive just then, though I fancy it was a very common piece of ground. The captain came up, and the anchor and the fires followed his example. The steamer started, but before we went down to supper the fog had returned and the anchor had dropped into its old place. Eating had become a matter of uncertainty. We were not provisioned for a long voyage. The good-natured German girls did their best, but there was a lean look to the table. White bread was scarce. There was an egg here and there. Melting the butter restored it to its original state, and gave us milk for our coffee. While we struggled through this miscellaneous meal, we heard the rising anchor once more. Then we moved on. After a time the boat stopped at a village and allowed any who wished to take the train and finish their journey where no fogs could interrupt it. We would not give up the ship, and early the next morning we were in Lübeck, twenty-four hours late. A day had dropped out and left no sign. There were few people astir, except money-changers and their clerks. These offered us inducements to give up our money for theirs, but we had arranged such matters with the captain on the steamer. We found our way to the railroad station, which was very dreary at that hour, but we managed to get a cold repast, and then devoted ourselves to the study of the best route for our journey. Advice was freely offered us, and we made our decision. We had satisfied the customhouse officials that the treasury of the empire would not be defrauded if we were allowed to pass on, and we took the train for Hamburg, and then again for Cologne. It was a long day's ride, but it was over at last. At Cologne the Hôtel du Dôme was in doubt of its ability to receive us. Pending the settlement of the question we turned into the cathedral. It was a good time for our visit. We looked up the majestic pillars and along the high arches in the twilight which gave an added mystery and grandeur to the place. The shadows deepened the solemnity as they crept through the stillness. The whole impression was enhanced by the service which was going on in a chapel, with the monotonous reading of priest and people, the singing of boys, and the rich, full tones of the organ filling the gathering gloom with melody. The next morning we went again into the cathedral and saw in the brightness what we had seen in the gloom. How grand it is, by night or by day! Gothic architecture has its culmination in this church, which has been six hundred years and more in rising to its wondrous majesty and grace. It was a large faith which consented to toil so slowly for what was to last so long, whose completion generations of builders were to believe in and not to see. There was a service in the morning and in the evening. The beadle or sacristan — I do not know what his title is — properly warned us from the precincts where the few worshippers knelt about the officiating priest, but was not so much absorbed in the sacred rites that he could not sell us tickets which would admit us to the foot of the stairs which lead up into one of the high towers, and allow us to work our way upward as far and as fast as we chose. It was a wearisome ascent, and we were not repaid for our trouble. The glory of the house is not seen from above, but as one walks through its long aisles, and wanders about it on the outer ground. We paid afterwards a liberal fee for the poor privilege of passing along the lofty gallery and looking down into the interior of the church. But we were able to resist the demand for a larger gratuity which would have opened to us the Chapel of the Three Kings, and have brought us a few feet nearer to the shrine containing the bones of the Arabian kings, who were not kings so far as any one knows, but wise men from the East, whose relics probably do not rest in this gorgeous enclosure. We confess to a slight struggle between good sense and a desire to see all which we were told that we could see. But prudence turned the scale. We lost the imposition, but we kept our francs. Yet we were prepared to give our tribute of respect to the faith and desire of the Magi who have gained a place in sacred story: —

"For Gaspar and for Melchior and Balthasar, who from far
Found Mary out and Jesus by the shining of a star."

We yielded to the spirit which we had resisted in the cathedral, and went to St. Ursula's — "the bone church," as I heard a child call it. The house is old — so much is certain. The walls are crowded with bones which are wrought into many ingenious figures. Whether they are the remains of eleven thousand virgins whom the Huns killed is very uncertain. We had a priestly guide, who had no doubt or no belief on the subject. His manner would indicate either condition of mind. After all, what did it matter? Very likely, these relics never belonged to the women for whom they are named. But they belonged to men and women, — or most of them did, — and they served a useful purpose in their time, and bore their part in martyrdom, it may be. There is always a pathos about the form which a living man has used and deserted; the dust which he has laid aside. But life and the living are more attractive and helpful. In a steady and easy flow of words, with a scant use of periods, our attendant called our reverent attention to the skull of St. Ursula, and to other relics of the saint and her chief companions; to a stone water-jar in which the water blushed into wine that a bride might not blush at her wedding-feast in far-away Cana of Galilee. Nobody knows where Cana was, or what befel the six water-pots of stone. It is not easy to think that this was one of them. He showed us thorns from the Saviour's crown, and assured us in the same tone or monotone that two francs and a half would be a suitable reward for his services. We saw other churches — St. Gereon's, which commemorates the martyrs of the Theban legion who suffered under

Diocletian; St. Peter's, with the crucifixion of that apostle for its altar-piece; the work, it is claimed, of Rubens, who is said to have been born in a house near by. We marked the multitude of Farinas whose names stare from the front of so many stores, presenting the perpetual conundrum, which is the only genuine and original maker of the perfume which has made the name of the city a household word. But among these things we could not linger. We passed the long day upon the Rhine. The weather was very pleasant, the steamer was large, and it was delightful to glide along the curving line of the shore, under the high hills, below the ruined castles, among legends and songs of war and of love, stopping at some of the towns on the banks, watching the people as they were coming and going, enjoying every hour with its new scenes in new lights, till in the darkness, at nine o'clock, our voyage ended at Mayence.

I cannot continue to trace our steps from day to day, but there are a few places, seen then or afterwards, of which I may make a brief record here.

Strasbourg "is a place that the tourist should not fail to visit," — so runs the guide-book. There were certain monetary reasons which enlarged the necessity that we should pause at this ancient city on the Ill. We found that the banker had locked his door and gone to dinner. It was the custom of the place, and had not been found susceptible of modern improvement. We made a vain effort to persuade somebody to help us. It was an unheard-of thing to deliver money out of hours, and there was no help but in waiting. Indeed, our difficulty began earlier than this, when we chartered a guide to take us to the bank without loss of time. He too was under the influence of the hour, and led us promptly to the door of a restaurant. Our French seemed a long time in making an impression upon his preoccupied sensibilities. So we lost the train we meant to take. It was to no purpose that we had disregarded the advice of the Mayence porter and made a very early start. We were stranded in the middle of the day. But it was in a very good place. We readily found our way to the cathedral, which stands around the Strasbourg clock. It was not Cologne: but it was a house full of grandeur, one of the finest of these fine Gothic buildings. It stands where there has been a church since the days of Clovis, the son of Childeric. This house was founded eight hundred years ago and more. The lofty spire, with its uncertain height but its unquestioned beauty, has a lonesome look without the mate which should have been placed beside it. It has the more interest in that, when its designer had left it incomplete, the work was carried on by his son, and afterwards by his daughter. Some of the fine work of Sabina is also found within. What wonderful results can be produced in stone, if the workmen or workwomen have skill and patience ! Those old builders were as noted for their patience as for any other quality. They used time over their designs. They were sure of the centuries, and in this assurance laid out their work. If the generations passed away, the plans remained, and other hands could move them slowly towards their fulfilment. If money failed, as it had a way of doing, the years would last, and more money would grow. But patience only comes with age. It needs not a little absorption in one's work to be willing to commit it to other hands, desiring only that it should be done. Work for the work's sake ranks among the higher laws of building, whatever the material may be. The old minster illustrates and enforces the principle. The unfinished cathedrals are a witness to a large purpose, and one which could wait. There were many persons moving about while we lingered in the sacred sublimity and elegance. Some of them were peasant women with the Alsatian ribbons on their heads. The long black bows seemed in keeping with the ancient house. It was interesting to watch them as they came in. Their first resort was to the font of holy water. We saw two sisters enter together; we judged them to be sisters. One dipped her fingers into the water, and then touched the hand of the other. It was a simple and natural communication of grace.

Whatever else may be seen at Strasbourg, the ordinary visitor will be certain to see the famed cathedral clock and to give to it a full measure of wonder. The present clock is only about forty years old, but it has the place of one which was constructed three hundred years ago. The puppets march and divide the hours, and their appearance and disappearance are waited for, albeit their motions are not quite life-like. The noon, when the full procession appears, is a time of high importance. The staring company wait and watch and deem themselves rewarded. This is all vulgar, of course. Why should grown-up men and women care for a senseless show like this? The question is asked with a sneer at the popular taste. Well, let it pass. Whatever be the æsthetic judgment, the people will look at that which interests them. The Strasbourg clock does interest them. They can appreciate it. Doubtless there are more visitors who can take in the mystery of the moving figures than there are who can detect "the amalgamation of the German and French manners" in the architecture of the cathedral, or properly estimate the splendor of the glorious wheel window with its forty-two feet of diameter. But some can do all this. For the rest, people have some right to know what pleases them, and to enjoy what is suited to an innocent taste. They may be trained to something higher. Meantime let them possess their pleasures in peace. To us there was not much illusion in the high structure in which the planets hold their place. There was even less when we had seen two men ascend the stairs and enter into the clock, and heard the Saturday windings by which suns were to rise and men were to move. But it will be long before the traveller fails to seek the huge wonder in the corner where it has so long done its work.

In the ceiling of the cathedral we noticed many empty holes. There was no one to tell us their meaning, but we conjectured that they once held the standards of the French banners which the German war had removed out of their place.

From Strasbourg let us pass to Baden. They call this Baden-Baden, because there are other Badens.

It is on the border of the Black Forest. We had a long ride among the dark trees, in a car which allowed us to look freely upon the district through which we were passing. The tops of the hills have few trees, but lower are pines, and maples, and beeches, which are supported by the thick, dark groves of fir. Among the rocks are found gold, copper, iron, and other minerals, while mineral waters spring up generously for the invigoration of the visitors who resort to them. The manufacture of wooden clocks and music-boxes and similar things has formed the leading industry of the people.

Baden-Baden has been a place of fashionable resort since the time of Antoninus and Aurelius. The Romans seem to have enjoyed the springs. They left behind them tokens of their presence, which have been placed in a museum for the delight of later generations of health and pleasure seekers. I do not know that there is any natural connection between mineral springs and gambling, unless it is the leisure which is afforded by the one and employed by the other. There is high authority for believing that idle hands readily take to mischief. Baden-Baden had the most renowned gaming-houses in Europe. But these were closed in 1872, with other institutions of their sort throughout Germany. The town remains, and throngs still resort to it and enjoy its pleasures; but its power and occupation are gone, which is for the advantage of everybody. It is a very attractive town, with its fine streets and noble trees. The Kursaal, a large park in the centre of the town, is a charming place for a leisure hour. A small admission fee is charged, and then the visitor is free to wander where he will. There is good music in the day and evening, and it is very restful to listen to it while sitting before the showy stand or strolling over the grounds. There are many stores in the park, and these are brilliantly lighted at night, so that their windows present a dazzling array of goods of many kinds. Gold and silver ware, and glass in many colors and more designs, allure and tempt the passer-by. There is something in all this, — in the place, the people, the music, the gay shops, the absence of horses and carriages, the general air of quiet and sense of pleasure, — which constantly reminded us of Venice and the Piazza of St. Mark. What can be said more of the luxury and delight? The large Trinkhalle suggests its purpose in its name. It had a deserted appearance at the time when we were at the springs, but in the season must be full of life and of the effort to make life more desirable. The Conversationhaus is more than would be inferred from its prolonged title. It has an immense assembly room, though we saw none flit over its polished floor; and a very inviting library and reading-rooms, which drew many persons among the books and papers. There are very pleasant drives about the town. The Lichtenthale Allee is a long avenue, shaded with tall trees, and bordered with groves through which run winding paths leading to charming places of rest. This road is a special feature of the town. As we went along this avenue, we came upon a fragment of our home life. We found the flag and the name of our own country, commending to the people of these foreign parts "The Great American Circus." It may have been American: it certainly was not great. There were two elephants, two forlorn camels, a meagre array of horses, with gayly caparisoned riders, and an immense car on whose perilous summit rode the bespangled queen of the enterprise. I do not know whether the pageantry impressed the people of Baden with the magnificence of the republic, or not. But it drew after it a long train of men and women, boys and girls, even as it would have done in its own national domain.

Castles are not a rarity in the region where they are the remains of a different order of things from that which now prevails. Baden-Baden has the ruins of the old castle where the Margraves lived and ruled. The broken walls stand on the summit of the Schlossberg, and afford a wide view over the town and country beneath. The ruins are open to all travellers and without price. This is a fact deserving of notice. The peculiarity is in some measure balanced by a neighboring restaurant, for which patronage is requested but not demanded. Furthermore, when the visitor has ascended as far as he cares to go, he sees, leaning over a railing above him, a man. There can be but one reason for his presence there. It is possible to mount to his level, and on this possibility he evidently depends for his livelihood. To venture higher is to pay for his useless presence and worthless services. The wise do not disturb his meditation on the beauties of the landscape. But he shows no signs of regret, or of anything else. It is not hard to fancy him a part of the ruin: one whom time has forgotten and left behind, and who now lingers on the poor stage which a living creature would desert; or, if he did not desert it, from which he would descend nearer to the victims, who could not then escape him. At the new castle, which dates from 1479, there is a venerable keeper who is more alert. He is so dignified and courteous that a novice would either shrink from offering him a fee for his pompous attentions, or else make the gratuity so large as to disturb his equanimity. The experienced traveller commits neither mistake. The new castle, as it is termed by comparison, is not so high an elevation as the old. But it is high enough. In this castle the Grand Duke sometimes resides in summer. In his absence the stranger may see where he dwells when he so elects. He will be much more impressed by the parts of the castle which are now untenanted, but which forcibly suggest the misery, the agony, once endured within their narrow walls. These dungeons are small but dark and awful. Hope must have been left at the outer door when the prisoner entered their chilly gloom. There is the small room in which the secret court sat to condemn its victims. The places of the judges' seats remain. From that relentless tribunal the condemned were led away, often under the pretence that they were to be released. They were brought before a small figure of the Virgin, and told to kiss the image. While they pressed their lips upon the form which represented their sole reliance, perhaps their deliverance, the floor dropped from beneath their feet, and they sank into a deep well upon the knives which were not more merciless than those who appointed them to their office. All that is over, so we say standing there. No; all is not over. "There is a God."

We came up from the caverns, our candles were extinguished, and we returned into the light of day. The gay throng was moving through the pleasant streets. We were in the present, which has broken from the past, — the light-hearted present from the oppressed and oppressing past.

The Villa Solms is a fine house in the town, somewhat castle-like in its architecture and furnished in the style of the middle ages. We found an obliging man in charge, and enjoyed roaming over the whole building, and seeing the attempt of a family of our age to reproduce the surroundings of another. A little further up the hill on which the Villa stands is a Greek church, or chapel, containing several fine monuments. The marble anticipated the need of it in some instances. There was a beautiful statue of a mother who was then living, which was hung with black in memory of her son. This was carrying realism further than we had before seen it, and opening the household grief to the public compassion. One or two priests whom we saw appeared to be having an easy life on this height, where they could read and meditate, with no cares to vex them and few duties to interrupt them.

The last word which I can write of Baden-Baden

must be in praise of its beauty and its many attractions.

A very different place is Nürnberg, Nuremberg.

"In the valley of the Pegnitz, where across broad meadow-lands
Rise the blue Franconian mountains, Nuremberg, the ancient, stands.
Quaint old town of toil and traffic, quaint old town of art and song,
Memories haunt thy pointed gables, like the rooks that round them throng."

It is getting into the past to enter this old town. It was a conspicuous place in its day. Emperors resided there, and patrician families administered its affairs. It was the seat of manufactures and the home of art. It has been termed the "Gothic Athens." This glory has largely passed away. The trade in lead-pencils and toys is extensive, so that the town has a commercial importance. But too much of the antiquity has already been rubbed off. This is a pity. Yet much remains. The mediæval architecture preserves its peculiar attraction, and many of the newer buildings have copied the old and picturesque style. There is an ancient look upon the town, and upon the separate parts of it, — the streets, bridges, churches, fountains, castle, houses, — so that it stands as a well preserved fragment of the middle ages. The river, which has been already named, divides it in two parts, which are nearly equal. Each of them has its great church, and its saint, from whom both precinct and sanctuary take their name. St. Sebald and St. Lawrence share the honors of the divided municipality. Each has his "side." The churches are both in the hands of the Protestants, so that ecclesiastical rivalry does not bring in confusion.

St. Lawrence's Church is the largest and finest in the town. It boasts six hundred years, and stands in its Gothic nobility unmoved in the passing of the centuries. The mullions in its towers present the symbol of the saint whom Valerian laid upon the gridiron. The front is rich in sculptures. The Virgin and the Child are on a pillar between the doors, while around and above them are represented various scenes in our Lord's life, while Adam and Eve, with prophets and apostles, illustrate the sacred story. We noticed that over the head of the Christ in the Crucifixion and in the Last Judgment a dove was hovering, the sign of the Spirit which was and will be upon Him. There are two other doors of wonderful workmanship, elegant in form and rich in decoration. One bears the name of the bride's door. The interior of the church is adorned by splendid windows. One, which is called after the Volhauser family, is hardly surpassed in Europe in its marvellous coloring and admirable design. But there is nothing more striking than the tabernacle, the sacramentshäuslein, where the wafer of the sacrament was placed. Shall I quote again? —

"In the church of sainted Lawrence stands a pix of sculpture rare,
Like the foamy sheaf of fountains rising through the painted air."

It is a structure of stone which, tapering as it rises, reaches a height of more than sixty feet. The top bends over, as the top of a tall fir-tree bends in a strong wind, and the end turns under in a graceful curve. The plan is perfect, and the execution faithful to the last detail. The light form of all the parts, and the open-work with its delicate tracery, give a charming grace and beauty. Around the base is a low gallery, or platform, where the officiating priest could stand. Above the recess for the bread the chief events of the Passion are appropriately represented. The Christ is seen taking leave of the mother whose soul is soon to be pierced. The Eucharistic Supper, the Agony in Gethsemane, the Scourging and Crucifixion, and the Resurrection, are all portrayed in the almost living stone. Under the whole fabric, as if bearing it upon their shoulders, are the kneeling figures of Adam Krafft, the sculptor, and the two apprentices who wrought with him. Five years of thought and skill are enshrined in this notable creation of human genius working with high purpose for a sacred end. The work was completed in the year 1500. Seven years later, the old artist died in great distress in a hospital at Schwabach. But in his work he lives in honor.

St. Sebald was distinguished among the German saints of early times. The legends make him the son of a Danish king, and his English name we know as Siward or Seward. He went through Germany as a missionary, and finally made his home in Nuremberg. This is not the place to recount his miraculous deeds. Indeed, I have not many to recount. He came one day to a hut where he had often rested, and found the family freezing. He had icicles brought in and cast upon the scanty coals, when the room was filled with warmth. When the lord of the city had put out the eyes of the saint's servant, who had obeyed his master but disobeyed the lord, the saint gave the poor man his sight again, as he seems to have been bound to do. The church on the north side of the Pegnitz bears the name of the saint. It is a superb building without and within. It carries five centuries and more, and bears the weight of heavy and elegant sculptures. At the west end, on the outside, is a colossal bronze statue of Christ, which is one of the oldest works of its kind in the city. In the interior architecture may be seen the transition from the round to the pointed style. The windows are narrow and high. In a chapel is a very old bronze font in which Wenzel the Emperor was baptized, and which is more noted as being the oldest Nuremberg casting now remaining, if fame is to be credited. It would be expected that the shrine of St. Sebald would be a prominent feature of his church. Peter Vischer and his five sons constructed it, with thirteen years of labor. It is of bronze, in the richest Gothic. Slender columns sustain a canopy of fretwork, and underneath, in a chest of oak, encased in silver, are the relics of the saint. At the sides of the columns, standing on brackets, are statues of the twelve apostles. The figures are much admired for their naturalness and expressiveness. Over them are twelve fathers of the church in smaller figures, while over these are leaves and flowers, with cupids and mermen, and living creatures of different sorts. In bas-reliefs under the sacred chest the miracles of the saint are set forth: the burning icicles, the broken kettle mended by a blessing, the stone which was changed to lead, and the rescue of a man whom the earth was swallowing for his unbelief. At one end is a figure of Sebald, and at the other of the artist in a mason's dress, with a chisel in his hand. In the statue of Sebald the saint is represented as a pilgrim with shell and staff, rosary and wallet, and holding in his left hand a model of his church. The entire structure has a fantastic support upon the backs of snails.

Near the church is the parsonage-house, whose chief attraction is an oriel window of singular beauty.

The Church of Our Lady, the Frauenkirche, has a great treasure of sculpture and a façade of great beauty. The Gothic portal, with its elaborate ornamentation, is the notable feature presented by this ancient edifice. This is the Roman Catholic Church of the town.

Back of this church is the goose market, where enough copies of this bird can be bought to save any number of Romes. The geese are alive at the time of the sale, and are fastened with withes of straw to the baskets in which they have been brought from the country. The market was in good order when we saw it, and the selling was chiefly performed by women who were in the peasant costume, which it is always a pleasure to see. We were drawn to the market by the fame of the "goose man." He turned out a much more insignificant fellow than we expected to see, — simply a small figure of bronze, having under each arm a goose from whose open bill the water was spouting in a feeble stream.

But near by stands the "Beautiful Fountain," which is really an imposing affair. It is a pyramid of stone, eight-sided, Gothic in style, and rising to a height of fifty-six feet. It is very old, and was originally covered with painting and gilding. It has been restored and is still an interesting work. It is surrounded with twenty-four statues, full-length, seven of which are for electors of Bavaria, nine for heroes, Christian, Jewish, and pagan, and eight for Moses and the prophets. The town has many other fountains, each of which has its own merits and its own patrons.

Portions of the old walls and towers of the city remain, a witness to the military strength and consequence which have passed away. Between an outer and inner wall is a deep, dry ditch which makes a very good place for gardens. We drove out of the town to St. John's Churchyard. Along the way, at regular intervals, were seven pillars of stone, each of which presented in bas-relief an event in the Passion of the Redeemer. A citizen named Ketzel, four hundred years ago, made two journeys to Palestine, and brought back the necessary measurements for reproducing in his own town the Via Dolorosa of Jerusalem. The sculptures were made by Krafft, but they have been defaced in the course of the years. Some have been restored, and traces of the original beauty of the work can still be seen. We found a kind woman in charge of the churchyard. She would have known our errand if we had not told her, and she led us promptly to the two graves which we had come to see. We had seen the houses in which Dürer and Sachs had lived, and would see the places where they were laid when life was over. We stood by the grave which is called Albert Dürer's, and are now told that it is no longer tenanted by his dust. It was a great life he lived. He reached what we should call his majority in the year that Columbus reached these Western shores. He was architect, and painter, and sculptor. His works abound and are his monument. He was devoted to his profession. It is a pity that the daughter of Hans Fritz, to whom his father wedded him, should have worried a man who had cares enough without her. In his last portrait the flowing hair in which he took an honest pride is wanting, and the lines of care are drawn over his face. At last he died, and now no man knows his grave. But a monument, with a bronze statue, has been erected by the people of Nuremberg, who delight to preserve his name and fame. There is also a monument to Hans Sachs. He was born in 1494, and became a cobbler. He went to Munich, where he learned to make verses and to sing them. It is said that he wrote six thousand poems of various dimensions. He was one of the meistersingers. These were an association of master tradesmen whose object was to revive the minstrelsy of their country, which had fallen with the decline of the minnesingers, the low minstrels. They chose subjects for the most part of a religious or moral character, and pursued their art by fixed rules. The three chief meistersingers were Hans Rosenblüt, an armorial painter; Hans Folz, surgeon and barber; and Hans Sachs. He died in his eighty-second year, having gained the name of "Honest Hans Sachs." He had done much to help on the Reformation by his writings. It will be noticed that the men whom Nuremberg holds in special honor were men who served their town by their useful lives. Not high birth, but high service, made their lasting renown. It speaks well for the place. Can I do better than to copy familiar lines once more? —

"Here, when Art was still religion, with a simple, reverent heart,
Lived and labored Albrecht Dürer, the Evangelist of Art.

" Here Hans Sachs, the cobbler-poet, laureate of the gentle craft,
Wisest of the Twelve Wise Masters, in huge folios sang and
laughed.

"Not thy Councils, nor thy Kaisers, win for thee the world's
regard;
But thy painter, Albrecht Dürer, and Hans Sachs, thy cobbler-bard."

We paid the requisite fee for admittance to the German Museum. No reluctance was shown in receiving it. It was hardly out of our hands before we were told that the time had come for closing the building. Why? It was the time when they closed. There was but one course to pursue — to see what we could in a few minutes, and to return another day. There is the usual collection of antiquities in their accustomed variety. These are always interesting, and often more. We saw abundant illustrations of the land and its history. You would expect to find many of Dürer's paintings, but they are not there. One of his best works remains, in the portrait of his patrician friend the Burgomaster Holzschuher. There is also a striking painting by Kaulbach — " The Opening of the Grave of Charlemagne by Otho III."

The highest position in the town was naturally given to the castle. It is a rambling collection of buildings which have survived their usefulness. Some rooms are occasionally used as a royal residence, but the buildings as a whole are on exhibition. There is no lack of attendants, and there is no danger that the gratuities which they accept will be less than they are entitled to. The inhabited rooms are commodious, and there are, of course, fine views from the windows. No one knows how old the castle is. In fact, it belongs to no single time. It grew as it was needed. A portion of it is thought to be older than any other building in the town. The castle has a double chapel, or two chapels one above the other. The upper one was used by the seigneur and his family, the lower one by his retainers. They date from the eleventh century. The chapel proper is small and bare, but sermons must be imbedded in its stones, and some things besides sermons. There are fine pillars which, if legend is to be trusted, were brought from Rome by Satan himself, who was outwitted by a monk who said the Litanies with unparalleled rapidity, and was honored with an effigy in testimony to his success. In the castle yard is a lime-tree whose straight trunk reaches a height of thirty-four feet from the ground, and has a diameter of five feet. The tree has a historic interest, for tradition tells that it was planted more than eight hundred years ago by Cunigunde, the daughter of Siegfried, and the wife of Henry II. of Germany, Emperor and saint, founder of schools and monasteries. The Empress had once proved her innocence by walking on red-hot ploughshares, and in 1201 she was canonized. Her tree has received great care, and is still flourishing in its old age.

In one building is a famous well. A venerable woman is in charge of this, and on her authority I give its depth as three hundred and thirty-five feet. She did all in her power, short of a personal descent or actual measurement, to impress us with the truth of her figures. She poured water from a dipper and bade us listen till it struck the water below. It was a considerable interval. She lighted candles and lowered them into the darkness and then with a mirror threw the reflection of the lights upon the surface of the water. We were convinced that it was a very deep well. It must take the truth a long time to come up from such depths, and this may explain some tales one hears. We found the water refreshing, and, having recompensed the attendant for her pains, passed to less pleasant places. In different rooms connected with the castle are kept the instruments of correction and torture which have come from cruel times. Some of them are not without their merit, rude as they were. We could not use them now, yet every one must have seen a person on whom he could consent to have them tried, gently and briefly. Such were the head-pieces for scolding men and women, and the ducking-cage for incorrigible beggars, and the pillory in which the contentious man and wife stood side by side, eating with one spoon from the same dish. We have so far eliminated the element of shame from our punishments that the penalties we inflict have lost half their proper terror. We would not bring back the curious devices by which quiet and peace were sought. But we looked with horror upon the inventions by which men sought to torture others, oftenest better men, to their own purposes. If cruelty has any monuments and memorials, they are in the dungeons which were built not very long ago, and the instruments which were the ally of the prisons. We saw them at the old castle. They are curiosities now; yet, as one thinks upon their uses and their powers, he almost hears the groans which went up to heaven but found no resting-place on earth. We saw the rack on which men were stretched and beaten; the wheel on which they were broken; the sword by which they were beheaded, and even the chair in which they sat to receive the stroke. Ingenuity had labored that tyranny might grow fat on blood. Most cruel of all, in appearance at least, was the Iron Virgin. It is of wood, lined with iron, and roughly represents the form of a woman. It is seven feet high, and its front is divided into two doors. The interior is pierced with long, sharp spikes, or iron poniards. The bed where the condemned person, man or woman, passed the last night stands in a corner of the room, and on the wall is the crucifix which received the last kiss of penitence and appeal. The dread doors of the Virgin opened, and the victim was thrust within, where all the space was thus filled. Then the doors were shut upon him, into him; pressed in and held in place by a bar of iron. The end could not have been long delayed. Then a sliding door was drawn from under his feet, and the mangled body sank into a deep well, where its destruction was completed, and the pieces found their way into the river. The cruel woman will never be used again. But it is well for us to see of what men have been capable.

Not far from Nuremberg is Bayreuth, the home of Wagner, where, in the building which he prepared, his music is performed. Many resort to the place to hear the music in its home. The story of Percival, or Parsifal, was presented to throngs of listeners at the time of our visit.

While we were in Nuremberg we stayed at the Baierischer Hof. It is an old house, and lacks many things with which a more modern hotel is furnished. But the table was good, the company agreeable, and there was a general desire to make the guests contented. We passed a Sunday there. The reading-room of the hotel was transformed into a chapel, where service was held after the English form. The congregation was small. So was the sermon. It is not well to be critical of preaching. It is a rare discourse which does not have something helpful in it. But the summer chaplains who are sent from England to the hotels of the Continent are seldom very edifying. They have the impressive church service in which it is good to join. There seems to be little reliance placed on the preaching. Yet there is no reason why the two should not be combined. There is certainly admirable preaching in many of the English churches. This is so common that it cannot be claimed that the sermon is of small account. The wonder is that men of thought and reading, with a knowledge of the world and its affairs, who are very interesting and instructive in conversation, can consent to be so stupid in the pulpit. The Nuremberg discourse was on the net which was cast into the sea and gathered of every kind. In a manner which would have prevented any success in fishing, so lifeless was it, the bearded preacher described the way of using the net, and pictured the conduct and emotions of the entangled fish. The lessons were serious ones, but it must have been with greater powers of persuasion than he employed that the saint drew the fishes by his call. This man was quite animated afterwards at the table, where his conversation indicated more of spirit and truth. He may be a diligent man in his parish and a model to all the country round. But why does he not carry his enthusiasm when he goes upon his travels? It may be that some found in his words the spirit which we missed. Let us trust that it was so.

From the old to the older. We left the train at Schaffhausen and were driven in an omnibus to

Neuhausen, and the Schweizerhof, which we found a most attractive house. The large dining-hall has one side of glass, through which the falls of the Rhine can be seen. The broad piazza affords a broader view, and one which is enchanting. An extensive garden, or grove, is below the house, and through this there are pleasant walks to the shore. It is delightful to watch the river as it breaks upon the rocks which divide it. There is not the volume of water which is found in some places, nor does the stream descend from so great a height as some others. But the rush of the swift waters is full of energy and grace. We crossed the river by the bridge and were received at the Castle of Laufen for a consideration. We saw what the house had to present in the way of armor and paintings and curiosities of various kinds. We found the customary souvenirs in ivory and wood, penholders and pencils, paper-cutters, match-boxes, and photographs; with the usual microscopic pictures which are calculated to amuse the youthful mind. We found that even this tumultuous nature was fenced in for private emolument, but we responded to all demands, and encased ourselves in rubber coats, and stood where the spray was thick about us. We returned by a rowboat which took us nearer to the leaping stream that we might better see and feel its force. We could have climbed to the top of an island which stands firmly in the midst of the waters. It did not seem desirable to do this. We had many views of the falls. At night they were illuminated with lights of several colors, and their appearance was very novel and charming. The stranger wonders at the unaccustomed generosity which provides for him this glowing scene. His admiration is somewhat chastened in the morning when he finds a practical reminder of the display in a single line of his bill, where the scene is sketched by a master hand. The illumination is less brilliant when set forth in black and white. But he paid for looking out of the castle window, and he pays for the splendor which he has enjoyed but not ordered. These are the trifles of travel. There is a sameness in them as one journeys from place to place. There were, however, two novelties at this hotel. One was the waiter-girls, who were dressed in the becoming Swiss costume, and made a simple but pleasing feature of the place. The other was the special request that no fees should be given to the servants. We fancied that as much as we deducted from the usual payment, so much they deducted from the usual attention. But we fared very well. The brief visit is delightful in the retrospect. This was one of the places where we longed to linger for days and days in the quiet, amid the beauty, with everything to minister to eye and heart. But we kept moving.

We gave more time to the Lake of Lucerne, the Lake of the Four Forest Cantons. Lucerne itself is a place of much interest. Two of four bridges across the Reuss, which here leaves the Lake, belong to another time. The roof of each is decorated with paintings. In the one these represent scenes in the life of the patron saints of the town, and events in the history of the country. In the other they illustrate the "Dance of Death." It is not very easy to see the pictures, but they deserve examination. Joining the historic bridge is an old tower where the archives of the town are kept, and where the fabrics which belong to the place can be bought. Lucerne abounds in hotels, and in those of a superior character. They are finely situated, where they overlook the best of the Swiss lakes with its fair waters, and beautiful banks dotted with pretty villages, and the stately mountains which shut it in and keep guard over it. The old Hofkirche, with its slender twin spires, the fine organ and pulpit and windows, and the churchyard by its side, fits into its place perfectly, and makes a convenient landmark by which the town can always be recognized, even in the little pictures which find their way abroad. The marketplace of Lucerne is full of life and stir. Almost everything is for sale in the booths, and around them are the contributions from the farms. The winged creatures cackle and struggle in their baskets, and wait, with the fruits of many kinds, to be bought and consumed. The traffic is to a large extent carried on by women, who are as worthy of notice as their goods. This is the every-day life of the people. We were amused in watching a rustic belle who had on the back of her head a long showy pin, much ornamented, and in shape very like a flattened spoon. Something, — it looked like cotton, — was braided into her hair. She was neatly dressed, as she knew, and she also knew that she was pretty. So did the young soldiers whom her charms drew in her train. It would have made a capital sketch; the background, the girl, the martial admirers. These bits of genuine life are charming. But the most noteworthy thing in the city hardly needs to be mentioned. Everybody knows the Lion of Lucerne, who is alone in his peculiar renown. Since 1821 he has stood out from the rock of which he is a part, without " pawing to get free." His rest is of course appropriate, seeing that he is the representation of the soldiers of the Swiss Guard who fell while defending the Tuileries. In his vast proportions he is the symbol of courage, devotion, heroism even in death. The broken lance is at his side, but his spirit is not pierced. The inscription underneath tells the meaning of the monument. It is in a retired and lovely spot. Trees and vines overhang the rock, and at its base is a pool fed by a stream which runs down at one side. The lion needs to be seen from many points, that his grandeur and beauty may be appreciated. It was a happy thought to construct it directly opposite a large store where models and photographs of all sizes and qualities can be procured, with the endless variety of forms into which the cunning hands of the Swiss carve their wood. The street which leads to the Lion is bordered with shops which are devoted to the same purpose. The country is lavish of its trees, and certainly transforms them into lovely shapes. Near the Lion is a garden to which admission can be gained in the usual method, where there are wonderful memorials of the ice-period. The great rocks are worn smooth by the glaciers, while there are numerous deep holes which have been cut into the rock by the stones which the waters have driven round and round, in strength and patience. There is a chance, also, to see a fine relief map of Central Switzerland, which gives a clear idea of the mountains and lakes. Photographs of everything are amiably dispensed by the young woman in charge of the exhibition. If the visitor wishes, he can examine relics from the lake-dwellings, and walk among the animals of the Alps where they are arranged in natural and unnatural ways in their stuffed and harmless condition.

It is a pleasant sail upon the lake, when it does not rain. Many boats are steaming up and down, touching at the various ports all the way to Fluelen. A few days can be spent agreeably at any one of these lake-side villages. From the houses which are on the hills, as at Axenfels and Axenstein, beautiful views are obtained, and pleasant walks are easily taken in the fine air. The regular thing is to stop at Vitznau. The little town itself has an inviting look. We strolled into the village church. It was plain and humble. But before the altar stood a bier covered with black cloth, decorated with the cross, and over it the skull and cross-bones. Around the bier were unlighted candles. It seemed that the archer whose arrows are more certain than Tell's was haunting even this quiet retreat. Vitznau is chiefly important as the lower terminus of the Rigi railway. The station is very near the pier. A train usually consists of one car and the engine. The car goes ahead in the ascent and the passengers usually ride backward as they go up. One side of the car affords much finer views than the other, and there is a scramble for that side. There are many impressive sights on the ride. The point of chief interest is where the road crosses a ravine seventy-five feet deep on a bridge which rests in the middle on two iron pillars. They are quiet moments when the train is creeping over those deeps on that frail structure, and the traveller looks far down into the abyss over which he trembles as he moves. Through the projecting rock is a tunnel eighty-two yards long. There is a great deal of travel on this road, and the cars are often uncomfortably crowded. But most persons are good-natured, and as they are thrown together from many lands they form interesting objects for the survey of one another. There are fragments of conversation which are entertaining. We were amused at hearing a young soldier, whose knowledge of the English language and literature could not have been extensive, declare his preference by saying, "I do not like Shakespeare. I like Mark Twain." Plainly, there are different avenues into the world of English letters.

The first station of any consequence on this Rigi railroad is Kaltbad. There is a hotel at the station, but only a little removed is the Rigi Kaltbad Hotel, which is the fashionable house of the mountain. The house offers the attractions common in a place of popular resort, and at rather high prices. The nobility make it their headquarters. The Prinz Georg von Preussen was occupying a goodly portion of the large building at the time of our arrival. But we were taken in, and allowed to hover on the coast of aristocracy and listen to the band in one evening and morning, when we flitted off on a branch of the railroad and found a much more agreeable house at the Rigi First. No one seemed to regret our sudden withdrawal from the fashionable world, and we were certainly gainers by it. We entered a fine house, charmingly situated, with elegant appointments, and a landlord who cannot be excelled. The courtesy and attention of Mr. Humbel left nothing to be desired. It was a real pleasure to us when, a year afterwards, we could again put ourselves in his care.

It is not common for American travellers to stay long upon the Rigi. Yet few places hold out more inducements. The name is more inclusive than is usually supposed. The Rigi is a group of mountains between the Lake of Lucerne and the Lakes of Zug and Lowerz. The circuit of the group is about twenty-five miles. The height of the peaks above the Lake of Lucerne varies from forty-five hundred to nearly six thousand feet. There is, however, one member of the group to which the name Rigi is commonly limited; and this is the place of chief resort for those who would gain the extended view, and especially the glory of the sun-rising. To witness this daily phenomenon is the restricted idea associated in the popular mind with the ascent of the Rigi. For this purpose every night during the summer raises a throng of visitors to this commanding spot. Something is expected of the sun in his setting, when the whole stretch of hill and plain is bathed in glory. But the interest culminates at dawn. The Alpine horn summons the expectant sleeper from his bed, and the houses are soon full of hurrying men and women. A unanimity of purpose and sentiment prevails. In all kinds and degrees of attire the visitors hasten from the doors to stand upon the brink of the summit, or upon the small tower which lifts a few persons a little nearer to the sky. There they wait, cold and impatient, yet eager and hopeful, for the spectacle. They see the darkness grow thin and roll away. The stars disappear. The light begins to glimmer in the east, and to brighten the multitudinous peaks through a circumference of three hundred miles, and to make them resplendent with its "orient pearl." When the sun has ascended, the whole expanse is full of his splendor. Within the cordon of mountains one sees thirteen lakes, large and small, with towns and villages in every direction: each a cluster of white objects, with one larger than the rest raising its humble roof and spire among them — the church among the homes. No one can ever describe this scene or depict its surpassing grandeur and beauty. The watcher feels repaid with usury for his untimely rising, and treasures up what he looks upon with the vague intention of telling what he has seen. This is the region of vain hopes. But the reality is enjoyed and remembered. All this at which I have hinted may be. It has been. Sometimes it is all found. Yet there are few things that speak more confidently to the ear, and treasure more frequent disappointments for the heart. The impenetrable clouds do not always look kindly upon the intruder,

and they have a sullen way of saying so. They are
quite in the habit of spoiling the picture they could
not paint. They settle down upon all the country
around, and quietly defy the sun. There is no help.
The pilgrim who has squeezed from his mortgaged
days this one morning hour for doing the Rigi has
little to show for his lavish expenditure of time,
unless he can find it in staring at a mass of vapor
and grumbling at the failure of his enterprise. He
cannot wait for a happier time, and he turns his
frowning face towards the waters which he left in
expectancy. He may be able to draw some pleasure
from the sellers of wooden ware; but it hardly pays
to come up so high for what can be found in the
valley. The truth is that the Rigi demands time.
It simply refuses to be hurried. Wait on its leisure,
and it will be gracious. When the sky is clear the
broad top of the mountain offers attractions which
will employ many hours and repeated visits. I do
not refer to the place itself, but to the opportunities
it presents. I do not mean the opportunities which
are nearest and most clamorous, which cluster around
more stalls and stands than one wishes to count,
and hide out of the sunshine under the huge white
umbrellas, and keep company with the men, and
women, and youth whose entire interest is in you
and in their minerals, flowers, pictures, paper-cutters,
stamp-boxes, watch-cases, and thermometers, jewelry
and trinkets of ingenious device, all bearing the sig-
nature of Rigi. I do not forget that these centres
of traffic receive a disproportionate share of attention, and that travellers from the far West turn away

from the wonders of nature to the marvels of art — if this is art — and linger too long around the money-changers who have ventured into the temple. Everybody does it. But there are finer and rarer things waiting on every hand. The hours pass too rapidly as the visitor swings around the circle, and studies with his glass the scene which is outspread beyond and beneath him. The snow-covered Alps lift up their peaks which crowd one upon another, each with its own name and worth, while they stand as the strong guardians of the valleys, which are so far below that high hills sink to the level of the fields about them and the lakes which nestle and glisten among them.

The Rigi Kulm, which is the place most frequented, is but one of the attractive points. From other places there are different but hardly less impressive views. Indeed, it is only by standing in many positions that any complete idea of the surrounding country can be gained. The scene varies as the spectator moves. Mountains come in sight that have been concealed. The light falls at ever varying angles as one passes from height to height, and the shadows pass on with him. Besides such changes are those which the clouds make, as these constantly change. Whether the sky is clear, or the light clouds are floating in deep blue, the vision is full of delight. While there is discomfort in being quite shut in by mist, there is a peculiar charm when the clouds lie beneath you, and you look down upon them from an uncovered spot. Sometimes the valley will be so completely filled with the vapor that it looks like the Mer-de-Glace, and one almost fancies that he could walk upon the frozen sea. The traveller will be well cared for at the large hotels at the Rigi Kulm, or in the others which have been mentioned, from which there is easy access to the summit of the railroad. The branch road on which the Rigi First stands runs to the Rigi Scheideck, which is a place much resorted to, especially by the Germans. The position is isolated and lonely, but the views are very fine. Connected with the hotel is a small chapel which is used by both Catholics and Protestants. There may be seen the altar of the Romish Church, and the Prayer Book of the English, with the Bible. The place is high enough and far enough out of the world for this outward friendship.

In a basin among the mountains, reached by a short walk down a steep road from the Rigi First and other points, is the Klösterli, a humble monastery of the Capuchins with a corresponding hospice. The number of monks in residence seemed to be very small. We noticed that one venerable ecclesiastic, when he had entered the door of the hospice, or sanatarium, looked through the window at the side upon the ladies who were visible, with as pleasant a smile as if the joint vows of sanctity and celibacy were not upon him. It must be a lonesome life they lead in this valley from which nothing can be seen but the surrounding hills. It must be more comfortable in the winter than places further up the hills. Pilgrimages are made to the chapel, and the herdsmen have special recognition in the services. The sacred house was well furnished with the usual votive tablets and the waxen effigies of arms and legs which have been restored. There are two hotels, the Schwert and the Sonne, but there was nothing inviting about them except the probable cheapness of board.

A more interesting chapel to us was St. Michael's, which is near the Kaltbad. It is a very small stone building, standing among immense rocks, boulders perhaps, which almost hide it from view. A narrow path between the rocks leads to its door. The chapel was erected by two sisters, who found refuge at this spot from a persecuting ruler when Albert was king. Before the door is a spring, which used to be called Schwesternborn. There are votive tablets, one of which tells the story of the two pious women, and there are other memorials of a humble but expressive character. Yet that which arrests attention, and especially interests the English or American visitors, is the marble tablet placed in the wall by Dean Stanley in memory of his sister. The tablet has her medallion portrait upon it, and bears her name and her brother's, with a brief recital of the circumstances which placed it there, while her grave is in England. She spent much time on the Rigi and derived good from its pure air, and was blessed as a worshipper in this modest temple. At the bottom of the tablet are these sentences from the Vulgate : —

Levavi oculos meos in montes, unde veniet auxilium mihi.
Requiescat in monte sancto tuo.

Beyond the chapel is a pleasant park, with the Känzli, a pavilion which is finely placed for a survey of the mountains and lakes.

We had the Rigi weather in most of its varieties. It cannot be said that it is pleasant to be on a mountain through successive days of rain. A very congenial company might make it tolerable. We had our fine house filled for the most part with strangers and foreigners, regarded from our point of view. They may have regarded us as interlopers. We had little to do with them, for several reasons. As usual in such places, the evenings were the hardest to dispose of. Our associates tried to amuse themselves but seemed to find it hard work. While they were sufficiently noisy at other times, they carried much solemnity into their play. One night they had a New England game, spinning a plate or cover, and imposing a forfeit when it was not caught before it fell. There was some levity while the cover was passing from hand to hand, but the forfeit was adjudged and paid almost as if a magistrate was administering the statutes of the canton. Even the dancing was performed with the gravity which usually attends more serious affairs. Yet they seemed happy and kind, and probably supposed they were having a very good time. The liveliest person of all, the leader, was an Italian lady, who did her best with her more ponderous followers.

Sunday was as other days. Men sat over their beer. Chess and checkers held their place; at night there were fireworks and dancing. Everything was done naturally, apparently. It seemed to no one that there was a more appropriate way of celebrating the Lord's resurrection. The fire-balloon from our house responded to the fire-balloon from the Kaltbad. There was no excitement; no excessive mirth: and no further recognition of the day as separate in meaning from other days. There were services in the parlor of the Kaltbad, but there were few in attendance. It was not New England — may New England never be like that!

We did not see much of the natives at home. One night a few Tyrolese musicians entertained us with national songs and other musical devices, including the yodel, and quite as much by their personal appearance and deportment. Even upon these something of the wide world had passed, and had done them no good. They would have been more pleasing to us, and perhaps to themselves, in their native simplicity, and the habits of their mountain life. But doubtless they esteem themselves profited by the glimpses of society which they catch in their professional tours.

We left the Rigi First with regret. A man and boy carried our luggage on their backs, and we attended them on foot down the declivity to the Klösterli, where we took the train which runs on that side of the mountain, and came down to Goldau, where we took the train from Lucerne, and at night we were at Locarno, on Lake Maggiore.

# CHAPTER V.

### IN NORTHERN ITALY.

WE had come by the St. Gothard Railway, that wonder of engineering, and the ride was one of surpassing interest. We were much crowded in our small car, but nothing could destroy the pleasure of the ride. The long line of rails winds up and down the mountain, within and without, winding through covered tunnels, turning upon itself and making loops with the tracks, and thus surmounts the height and descends into the valley. Only a drawing could make this plain, and that could do it but imperfectly. The road illustrates the changes by which the Alps of other days are passing away, and travel surrenders its romance for ease. Is anything really gained? The old St. Gothard pass was famous in its time, and the grandeur is still there. But "Europe in sixty days" prefers the iron road.

We were at the Italian Lakes. They are called Italian, yet some of the villages among them belong to Switzerland, though even these have the Italian character. The boundary between the two countries, which is often crossed, is made evident by the scarcely ornamental encumbrance of custom-house officers, who examine by intuition whatever comes in their way, and cannot collect enough in tribute to pay for their worthless services. I would speak more emphatically were it not that the traveller has more trouble at the American custom-house than at any other. We shall outgrow this in time. Photographs of Swiss mountains cannot seriously endanger American art, nor will our silk-looms be made idle by the stray dress patterns from France.

Of the shapes and sizes of the Italian Lakes the maps will give much better information than any writing. It may be well enough to say here that Lake Maggiore is about thirty-seven miles long, and four to five miles wide according to the place of measurement. It is nearly seven hundred feet above the sea-level. Locarno is one of the Italian towns that belong to Switzerland. It has some two or three thousand people. The streets are quaint and interesting, and the lemon and orange trees and luxuriant vines make more beautiful a place which is beautiful for situation. My walk in the early evening brought me to the door of an old church in which I found a few persons at their devotions. The house was dim, almost dark, with the three lights which were burning. A distant voice, which sounded like a woman's, was reciting the prayers, which elicited a faint response. The place, the hour, the gloom, and the few voices speaking when the persons were nearly or quite invisible, made the service very impressive.

The next morning we came by steamer down the lake to Baveno. We meant to stop there for an hour or two. We were taken captive. The beauty of the place, the perfect serenity of lake and land, the charming influences of a charming spot, were more than we could resist. We confided our feeling one to another, and the desire to remain was found to be common. The air was very soft, the clouds had their most delicate beauty, the hills were green in hospitality, the lake was sparkling in greeting. A man could not work there, but for repose nothing could be better. The one stately building of the town is the Villa Clara, which stands in a fine park. A park may well be fine in such a climate. The Villa has its special interest in the fact, found in other places and never concealed, that it was for a few days a royal residence. In April, 1879, the Queen of England passed three weeks as its guest. We visited a church which claims to have been founded A. D. LXVIII., and the adjoining chapel of John the Baptist. On the outer wall is a picture of the baptism of Christ. The cloister is decorated with crucifixion scenes. There is also a "sepulchre," in which is an image of the Saviour. This is about four feet long and lies in a glass case, with an angel at the head and at the feet holding candles. It is hideous, of course. It may be that there are persons who are affected for good by such attempts at realism. It seems almost necessary to suppose so. What looked like a monastery is connected with the church, and near by is an asylum for children.

Between Baveno and Pallanza lie the Borromean islands. On Isola Bella Count Borromeo, two hundred years ago, built a château, and covered the rocks on which he placed it with terraced gardens, richly furnished with trees and flowers, and adorned with fountains and statues. A part of the showy house has fallen, but most of it remains, with doors which can be opened with a silver key. We contented ourselves with a distant view, and the story. There are also on the island hotels, which seem to be chiefly restaurants. The Isola dei Pescatori belongs to fishermen, as its name leads one to infer. The islands are a pleasant feature in the lake. They would be worth exploring if there were leisure.

The mellow bells were ringing early in the morning. But we could not stay. We waited as long as we could, and then took the steamer up and across the lake and landed at Luino. It is a favorite place for summer visitors, but we were tourists. Not Garibaldi's statue, nor the silk-factories, nor the ruins of the Borromean Castle could detain us. We took a carriage immediately and drove to Lugano, on the lake of the same name. The lake is smaller than Maggiore, but its banks are pleasant and well adorned. The groves are delightful to look into, and the buildings among them have an enchanting look. Lugano is a large town, with six thousand people. We found comfortable quarters amid a variety of associations. The hotel was once a government building. There is a monument to the architect, Canonico di Tesserete, and a marble bust of General Dufour. These adorned the stairway. Finally, the house is named "The Washington." In these distinguished surroundings we took up our temporary abode. The town has a busy look, with its arcades, and workshops, and paved streets. But something of its renown disappeared with its monasteries, nearly all of which have been suppressed many years since. We visited the Church of S. Maria degli Angioli, which has survived the departure of the house to which it was attached. The chief attraction of the church is in the works of Luini. He was the follower, if not the pupil, of Da Vinci, and his works are deserving of admiration. They may be found at Milan, Como, Florence, and elsewhere. This church at Lugano has a fine fresco by him of the Crucifixion. The figures are numerous, and represent different scenes, making an impressive picture. There is one fresco of The Last Supper, and another of the Madonna. When we had spent the allotted portion of time, we took ship once more and went up to Porlezza, at the head of the lake. The attractions at this place, according to the best authority at our command, were a custom-house and a harbor. The latter we had entered, the former we had no desire to enter. It is also mentioned that Porlezza can be left. We acted on this hint and availed ourselves of an omnibus, which took us safely, if not comfortably, to Menaggio on Lake Como. The Romans called it Lacus Larius, and Virgil was pleased to write: —

"Our spacious lakes, thee, Larius, first."

Many agree with the line from the Georgics, as they glide on the pleasant waters, past vineyards and gardens, mountains and forests, and the showy villas along the banks. The lake is thirty miles long, but very narrow. It was refreshing to sail upon it. For the roads of Italy are not free from trouble. The dust of Italy is as the dust of other lands. No classic memories can make it agreeable. It may blow from plains where emperors have walked, along roads which imperial armies have trodden; but it is still dust, insinuating, persistent, disagreeable. Italian suns may look down upon the orange groves and chestnuts of to-day, on the ruins of temples and tombs, but its beams in midsummer are as hot as if they fell on the vulgar fields or paths of western lands. It was good to escape to the cool breezes of the lakes which for centuries have been giving rest and life to weary men from many climes.

Menaggio has its Grand Hotel Victoria. It is not especially grand, but it has a fine outlook across the lake and out upon the banks beyond. The house boasts a steamboat pier, at which the passing boats stop when they please. When they do not elect to do so, the numerous boatmen improve their opportunity and carry the traveller to the regular stopping and starting place, which is not very far away. Menaggio has its silk-factory, and little besides which is its own. We chartered the rowboat of a willing proprietor who carried us across to Bellagio, which is much more of a place. It stands superbly at the end of the promontory which stretches up into the lake, and divides the lower end into two portions. It luxuriates in hotels, which is an index to its character. Any one can see by the maps that it is a place to be sought. It has a thriving business in wares of different kinds, and each visitor bears away a cup, or box, or knife, with the name of the town upon it, that he may not forget where it came from. So tenacious are associations! Of course we strayed into an old church, but there is nothing more to be said of it.

We left Menaggio the next morning at one of the hours when the steamboat did not stop at our pier. We were loaded into a large boat which took us to the steamer, and we came to the southern end of the lake and stopped at Como. Como could be described, if there were space, even though we did not remain there. We read that the Plinys were born there; that there is a fine marble cathedral, with several hundred years upon it, and handsome windows within; that there are twenty-four thousand inhabitants, and more; and that the town is environed by mountains, save where the waters of the lake rest upon its shores. It has a railroad station, also, and with that we were just then more concerned. For some of our party this was not the first visit to the lakes, and those had enough influence to draw the others away. It was hard to turn from the fair, alluring, rewarding waters.

While we are on the way to Milan, let me insert a few disconnected remarks. We found the Italians whom we met very talkative, even noisy. In their intercourse among themselves they fairly blustered, and any one watching them would think they were angry, when really nothing was meant by the threatening manner. We had men with the air of brigands to wait on us at table, and to show the candy and gloves in the stores; but they were harmless and considerate. It was a rare thing to see a fine-looking man or a handsome woman. Some of the girls had fair faces. They seemed in general kind and light-hearted; slow, and not inclined to go out of their way to meet trouble. Women washing clothes on the shores of the lakes made a common sight. Now and then a man was seen in the same occupation, which might have been indefinitely pursued. They had a board at the water's edge, with an upright board which formed a sort of box near the upper end. Kneeling on this, within the box, the women scrub and pound. It must be good exercise, and more helpful to them than to the fabrics they manipulate. These are small matters. Yet there is an interest attaching to the people of any land, who should be seen at home to be truly seen. They blend with the pictures which the mind carries away and often looks upon.

It may be doing some one a good turn to say that while in Milan we stayed at the Hôtel de l'Europe. The picture of the house which we cut from the head of our bill presents the edifice in a brilliant red hue. The picture is misleading. There is nothing remarkable about the exterior. But we found it a very convenient and comfortable house. It is very near to the cathedral, which is an advantage. It has on the wall of the reading-room an immense painting of a carnival, which serves to amuse leisure moments. The souvenir presented to the parting guest is a photograph of this painting. I believe that the landlord figures as one of the participants in the national sport.

A proper caution was exercised in admitting our company of five persons into the Capital of Lombardy, where an archbishop has his seat, and an army corps its headquarters; where art had flourished and been rewarded; a city with suburbs and more than three hundred thousand residents; where the making and selling of silks and woollens and other things is upon a large scale, and prosperity has descended from generation to generation. The railway station is out of town, either for its own security, or for the safety of the city. Frescoes and sculptures and custom-house officers have combined to make it attractive. Even our luggage received attention in the excess of hospitality. It was duly examined and adorned with a label which seemed to give us the right of entrance into the city. It was not quite so. At the gate an alarmed officer looked into the omnibus in which we were making slow headway towards our hotel, that he might be certain that neither the nation nor its treasury would be defrauded if we were allowed to move on. On a later day, when we were returning from an excursion into the country, a cautious officer passed through the horse-car in which we were entering the city, but was able to find nothing which looked suspicious except a small basket which a child held in her hand. He gave his whole mind to that for a time, and after proper deliberation decided to take the responsibility of allowing the girl to go through the gate. Yet all his care might have failed to detect the tobacco or fire-arms which the basket might have contained. A dog has been made a smuggler before now; why not a young girl?

But we were always admitted to the guarded precincts. It was worth far more than it cost to be there. For some of us it was not the first visit; to all it was crowded with delight. Every one knows the treasures of Milan, and many have described them with pen and pencil. Their work need not be repeated here. Yet the pen refuses to pass on until it has told its own story in few and unadorned sentences. First, the Cathedral. The simple mention of it presents to the reader's eye the magnificent house of Mariae Nascenti, whose statue rises above it. The marble house has been tarnished by wind and weather, but its wealth of ornament remains. Over its broad roof we walked as on a floor, among the ninety-eight gothic turrets, and more than two thousand statues which look out from niches and off from pinnacles. These statues have been carefully made, and all the workmen in stone appear to have remembered that "the gods see everywhere." We found men replacing some of the carvings which had fallen under the burden of years and the assault of storms. It has been often and truly said that the front of the Cathedral is not high enough for its place. It should seem to be springing into the air instead of settling down to the ground. But it is only at the front that this impression is received. The interior, as a whole, is surpassingly fine. I mean that it was so to me, despite all which critics of architecture say. I know that architectural claims are not satisfied. I have no doubt that German taste affected Italian taste. I am sorry for the pitiful and deceptive paint and plaster ceiling, where honest and graceful stone should be. When all has been said, I modestly maintain the superior grandeur and beauty of the Milan Cathedral. Its fifty-two pillars, twelve feet in diameter with capitals of canopied niches tenanted by marble statues, above their lofty summits branch into the arches which form the majestic vault over the mosaic floor. It is hard for a layman in art to think of anything better than this. The vastness of the whole structure impresses him as he walks through the nave and its four aisles, and the transept with its naves and aisles while the light which longs to reveal the stately and delicate beauties of the house clothes itself in glory, and in an exuberance of color passes through the immense windows and illumines the radiant glass. I never saw golden light until I saw it there. "The poetic beauty of the interior," and the "magical brilliancy of the marble splendor of the exterior" are apparent to the trained eye and the untrained imagination.

Like all cathedrals, this needs to be seen many times and under varying conditions. In the broad sunlight it can be studied in detail. But its charms appear when the light of the full moon is upon it, silvering the pinnacles and arraying their saints in white, and setting the towers in bold relief upon the shadows. It is like a palace built by all the fairies. Within, it must be seen in the morning light and the evening shadow. A day might well be spent in watching the progress of the light from morning to evening, or catching the changing effects which it produces among the columns and arches. I cannot lose one picture. It was early, and the sunlight was entering by the upper windows and flooding the house with gold. At a side altar were a priest and a few worshippers. At that moment the light from a single window in the dome fell upon the group. It transfigured them, and framed them in, and the little company stood in the glory which was but wide enough to cover them, and separate them from the dimness which was about them. They did not know that the brightness was upon them, but we who were beyond could look in and admire.

On Sunday we attended the morning service in the Cathedral. It was less impressive and instructive than the house. The performances of men must needs be feeble in the presence of such majesty. Only the highest grandeur of simple worship, and the strength and beauty of loftiest truth, could stand where art has wrought her wonders, and the centuries have added their renown. I can readily conceive that those who were more familiar with the place, and better able to comprehend all which was done, may have enjoyed the service more than strangers could. A procession was moving through the Cathedral when we entered. We hired rush-bottom chairs, and secured good places for them. It was not favorable to the spirit of worship to be interrupted by guides, who sought to beguile us into the places of secret treasure. There was the usual High Mass. The music was poor. There was a sermon by an old man with a good voice, and it seemed to be a good sermon. The frequent repetition of "Christiana Carita" told us his theme. He preached for some time, then took his seat for a moment, after which he arose and proceeded with his discourse. He sat once more, and sitting said a few words, whereupon men began to go about with bags for money, while the preacher again stood up and talked. He was teaching charity by an object-lesson, which is the best way. There was a large attendance, and people were coming and going all the time. As a religious service it was far inferior in value to that which was found that day in many a humble meeting-house in the New England hills. The Cathedral has its sacred curiosities, some of which are to be seen in the treasury. It has a wonderful candelabrum of bronze, mediæval in age and style. It is sixteen feet high, and rises in the form of a tree, with branches and leaves. Dragons are at its feet, and clusters of figures adorn it, or make it instructive in sacred history. The whole is finely finished, and jewels enhance its beauty.

Out-of-doors there was little to remind any one of Sunday. Most of the stores were open, and the streets seemed as busy as on other days. The steps of the Cathedral were encumbered with persistent merchants who sought to exchange pictures which nobody wanted for silver which everybody wanted. Apparently their efforts were not remunerative.

Milan has many things to show to the stranger. The large arcade or gallery, with its imposing façade, its roof of glass, its fine frescoes, and its fine stores with windows all full of temptation and delight, is in itself an attraction. In the light of its two thousand gas-jets the place is very brilliant. But this is new. It is the old which the traveller seeks.

The Brera gallery has pictures, and books, and casts, and other ancient and modern works, which it opens to the stranger. Then there is the Ambrosian library, with its books, and manuscripts, and other literary treasures, with paintings and engravings.

The Church of St. Ambrogio is reputed to stand where once Bacchus had a temple which none too soon was destroyed. The church is very old and its gates claim to have been those which Ambrose closed against Theodosius. The emperor had sent an army of barbarians against Thessalonica to avenge the killing of some of the officers of his garrison. The people were invited to the circus, and there slain by thousands. Ambrose refused to admit the guilty emperor to the church until he had performed a fitting penance. The emperor yielded, endured the penance, and the doors were opened. It is to the credit of both that they were fast friends after this. But the church rejoiced that it had maintained its authority over the state. Why should not these be the gates which an emperor's crime closed and an emperor's penitence opened? It is not very long since A. D. 389. The iron crown which used to be put on the heads of kings and emperors in this church is now in a casket over the altar of the Cathedral of Monza. Should not Milan keep the gates of St. Ambrose? His church has one relic about which there is no doubt. It is the brazen serpent which Moses lifted up in the wilderness for the healing of his smitten people. The Scripture says that it was broken in pieces by King Hezekiah because the people did burn incense to it. But here it is, and the incense is still fragrant about it. It supports its curved length on the top of a lofty column, and there is no extra fee for believing in its antiquity.

The monastery of S. Maria delle Grazie was suppressed into barracks for cavalry. The refectory was saved from such sacrilege and remains a bare and deserted room. Upon the wall at one end is one of the chief glories of Milan, in the painting of the Last Supper by Leonardo da Vinci. No painting has become more familiar. It is well that it has been in some measure preserved by photographs and engravings. The monks cut a door through the table, and time has carried their inroads upon the picture still further. The paint was not adapted to the wall on which it was placed. But it is nearly four hundred years since the colors were laid in oils upon the plaster. The faces are marred and faded, but much of the beauty of the work remains. It was not without difficulty and delay that it was executed. The artist told the impatient prior that he had not been able to find a face which he could copy for Judas. The prisons and the haunts of vice had no model for the traitor. He silenced the prior by suggesting that he should sit for the likeness. So the story runs. The central face does not satisfy. No picture of Christ has contented his friends. Da Vinci waited long before he could create a conception of it. His conception is not on the wall. Others have touched what they have not adorned. To me it is not now a pleasing face to look upon. There is a constrained look about the mouth, a lack of the calmness, of the Divine consent to the Divine sorrow, by which the hour and the event were marked. The sketch for this face which is now in the Brera gallery seemed to me much finer. But there is a peculiar interest in looking at the wounded and bruised painting, and in letting it bring before the mind the scene which it represents. Never could it have equalled the simple narrative in the Gospels, while it may have stood in their stead for many a devoted heart who could not read what was written but could feel what was painted.

It would be better if this memorable picture were alone in the room it consecrates, but there are copies which men have fallen low enough to make, and which bear the names of the painters, who would be quite glad to dispose of their productions. It might be supposed that a man who had any appreciation of the grandeur and beauty of the work would be reluctant to attempt to transfer it to his own canvas. The supposition would be erroneous. There are few things in this direction to which men are not equal.

One afternoon we went out to the Certosa di Pavia, by the steam tramway and an omnibus. The Certosa was a Carthusian monastery. It was founded in 1396, suppressed, restored, and finally suppressed with the other Italian religious houses. It is now kept as a "national monument." The church surprises the visitor by the solitariness of its position.

It is a palace in a desert. It is literally alone in its glory. It is a deserted house. The façade is filled with statues and bas-reliefs. Many artists brought their skill to it. "The church may be reckoned among the noblest of those structures in which the Italian love for spacious effect finds in the Gothic system a perfectly unfettered and beautiful expression." This description seems just, though I could not have given it. The church is indeed spacious and beautiful. It has a nave and aisles, and fourteen chapels which are finely decorated. Ten slender columns sustain the dome. The high altar is rich in mosaic work. There is an air of luxuriance through the whole edifice. Marble is made to do its best. Neither cost nor pains has been spared. All this for a monument in a wilderness! We looked into the refectory and the library, and walked among the marble columns of the cloisters. The buildings are all in excellent condition, and are well kept by the few monks who remain in charge. There are many small houses where the monks lived in the days of their presence. The rooms are small, but pleasant, and well adapted to study and meditation. It looks as if they had a comfortable time, where their lines had fallen in pleasant places. They must have been sorry to be driven out. But for their ecclesiastical character we should be disposed to think that they grumbled, or did even worse. They left their quiet rooms which now wait for new occupants who do not come. I think that if I were to become a monk I should apply for one of these pretty houses, and for the privilege of carrying on my solitary career amid their congenial surroundings. The battle of Pavia was fought near by, but it is hard to bring the armies back to the peaceful plain. The world has moved on, soldiers and monks have vanished, but the splendor of marble preserves the memory of them.

The day came when we paid our last visit to the cathedral of Milan, and then turned our reluctant feet eastward. It was a pleasant ride to Padua, over the plains of Lombardy, with the Alps in the distance, past the Lago di Garda, —

"Benacus, with tempestuous billows vexed,"

then quiet and fair. The village looked down upon us from the hills as we hurried on. At the gate of Padua a solicitous officer stared into the omnibus, muttered something, and glanced at our hand luggage and allowed us to proceed. We selected as our abode the Hotel Fanti Stella d'Oro. It is not an elegant house, but it is reasonably comfortable. It was something to be in a town whose history reached into the myths. Antenor I. was a prince of Troy, and one of the wisest among the elders of his city. He was in some way a family connection of Priam the King. He seems to have used his position for his own advantage. At least he did that which would be so described in modern times. When Menelaus and Ulysses came to Troy to recover Helen, he received the Greek ambassadors kindly, which was not a thing likely to be popular.

Nothing came of the visit, but the people called him a traitor. They found fault also because when Ulysses

> "had given himself
> Unseemly stripes, and o'er his shoulders flung
> Vile garments like a slave's, and entered thus
> The enemy's town, and walked its spacious streets,"

Antenor knew "who it was that passed," but failed to make him known. When Troy was taken he was spared by the conquerors. But what became of him is not quite clear. Some say he started a new kingdom on the ruins of the old one. Some that he went to Africa. But in Padua the thing to believe is, that he came to the western shore of the Adriatic, and, venturing a little way back from the coast, founded Patavium, which became Padova and Padua. This is probably true, for the sarcophagus which holds what is left of his bones is now standing in front of the house of Dante. To make this doubly sure, the sword of Antenor was found, with the fleshless hand still grasping the hilt. His city became great and flourishing. It grew wealthy through its manufactures and commerce. Attila plundered it, as a matter of course, and it was afterwards destroyed by the king of the Longobards. It has come up again, and is the capital of its province, and has between forty and fifty thousand inhabitants. The river on which it is built traverses it in various directions and makes numerous bridges necessary. The streets are very narrow and winding. Many of them contain arcades on one or both sides, something after the manner of the Chester rows. These arcades are very pleasant when the sun is high. There are many squares for many kinds of trade. The square before our windows was filled early in the morning by a company of women and girls, with two or three men and boys. They had come in from the country with freshly cut grass, which they sold to hackmen and to other owners of horses. The sellers were bare-footed, but they were cheerful and patient as they sat by their wheelbarrows, occupying their long waiting moments with the gossip of the day. It is a fine thing that the people who have so little indoor to solace them have a climate which permits them to be abroad. Or should I say that it is a pity they have not a climate which would compel them to live at home, and to make home attractive? As it is, they use the larger house. They throng the streets, and sit at their tables on the sidewalks and in the squares and porticos. The men all smoke and seem to live by it. The women are so used to being smoked upon that they are not annoyed, and courtesy asks nothing of the men in this regard. Ices and wines are the perennial comfort. Street musicians add their melodies, and collect their centimes. Life flows on easily, but apparently to no great purpose. This is the outside. Padua has its earnest life. Its University has been famous for six hundred years. Was not the "young and learned doctor" Portia from Padua? The faculty of medicine is renowned in its own country, and law, theology, and the humanities all have a place. The latest report I have gives sixty-five professors and over eleven hundred students. There are museums and libraries, and a botanic garden and observatory, and all which belongs with the life of modern times. Here Livy was born, and here Dante found one of his many homes. What did we see in our brief visit? We saw the Church of St. Antonio, very old, with seven domes, and a statue of the saint over the door. There are fine monuments and paintings and bronzes, and cloisters with high and wide arches. Very near is the Scuola del Santo, the hall of the brotherhood, with the walls decorated fittingly with seventeen frescoes in which the life of the saint is depicted. Some of them were painted by Titian, who had come from Venice to Padua. The neighboring Chapel of St. George has many fine frescoes, upon sacred and legendary subjects. The Church of St. Justin has a plain front of brick, and a floor of variously colored marble. It is fortunate in possessing the sarcophagus of St. Luke, a box of iron, apparently in an iron cage, and of St. Matthew, with the tomb of St. Justin above the high altar. The choir stalls are beautifully carved with representations of scenes from the Old and New Testaments. But I will say no more of churches. I might tell of the beggars at their gates; of boys who start up before every carriage when it stops, eager to open the door, of the custodians who live on the curiosity and credulity of strangers. But these are not peculiar to Padua.

An hour's ride brought us to Venice. The gondola took us and our belongings to the Pension Suisse, or Hotel Roma, — not a large house, but a pleasant one, well situated and well conducted. The palaces and canals were found as we had left them years before. There are some things which are too old to change. Yet many of the palaces have fallen to hostleries and warehouses, and a steamer is on the Grand Canal, much to the disgust of the gondoliers, who not only lose custom but have their waiting boats dashed against one another by the tides which the unhandsome rival creates. Every right-minded person sympathizes with the boatmen who belong to the canal in history and romance, and to everything which is good, unless hurry is good.

We saw one other novelty — a horse. He was not on land, to be sure, and never would be in the city. He was on a boat, and gliding quietly to his doom at the horse-railroad on the Lido. He had no idea that this fate was awaiting him. He had never heard the like from his ancestors, or in the legends of the stables. He gazed with curious eyes on the new scenes through which he was passing, and even seemed pleased with his solitary grandeur, and showed his pleasure by whisking his long tail towards the passing gondolas. Well might he greet them, for he had seen nothing more graceful in his travels by land or sea. What can exceed the grace of a gondola under the control of a skilful hand! The boat sits like a swan upon the water, and like a swan proudly lifts its head and silently winds its way over its native element, turning from the broad avenue into the narrow paths with a precision that adds a delicate amazement to the serenity in which one is borne along, hearing only the gentle plash of the oar and the quick cry of the gondolier, who seems to be a part of his gondola. If there is a poetry of motion, it is this. Surely it is this when the full moon lies on the still waters, and the boat moves through a stream of silver, with the stately fronts of palaces gleaming in the light, and the splendors of other and better days flitting from shore to shore in the brightness. It was a pretty sight at evening, when a gondola, adorned with colored lanterns, and bringing a company of minstrels, drew up at the steps of the veranda where we were sitting; and it was pleasant to hear the songs which were sung. The voices were not very sweet or smooth, but what the music lacked of melody was supplied by the boat, the lights, the water, and all the accompaniments. All this is the life of fairy-land.

Easily we pass to the Piazza. The Cathedral still turns its face down the broad square, and the four horses are in their place. The upraised feet remain raised up. The Campanile rises in majesty over all which surrounds it. The tall masts have been removed and now lie on the pavement beyond the Cathedral. The windows of the stores glitter with silver and gold, and jewels rare and not rare, and furnish a generous exhibition of beautiful things. The people are in their places, in the same chairs, at the same tables, busy with the same indolence, awakening to the same ices, listening to the same music, toying with the same flower-girls as when we were here before. The doves hear the stroke of two, and flock to the same window where they and their kindred have been welcomed and rewarded for six hundred years. They alight boldly at the feet of men, and take corn from the hands of children, upon whose arms they stand to be fed. We turn into the Piazzetta, and the two Syrian columns are in their place at the water's edge. St. Theodore is still upon his crocodile, and St. Mark, who supplanted him as the guardian of Venice, is represented by his winged lion. The gondoliers keep their headquarters where once criminals met their death, and importunity for patronage is heard where the words of the last farewell were spoken. On all this the Palace of the Doges looks calmly down.

Our house fronted on the Grand Canal. But at its side was a narrow alley, dark and not free from unpleasant smells, yet affording a convenient passage out among the shops. A little extension of our walk brought us to the Piazza. It was easy to enter the Cathedral door and stand on its uneven floor, under its domes and among its marble columns. A look of age is on everything; but it is of an old age beautiful in mosaics and gold and bronze. It is a building which grows upon one as he becomes familiar with its antique grandeur. Each visit discloses something more to be admired. There is a fellowship with the departed splendor, with the days when nobles came with their retinues, and power, ambition, wealth, and honor bowed at the altar. They have gone; but the signs of their presence are on the walls where they lavished their riches.

We saw the bronze Vulcan strike the hours with the heavy hammer on the resounding bell. We climbed up within the Campanile, and looked over the city of islands. We visited the Palace of the Doges, walked through its long porticos, stood in its spacious halls, studied its great paintings, and in the dreariness tried to bring back the vanished life. We stood in the hall of the feared and fearful Council of Ten, and thought upon the tyranny which was gone. We went into the prison and down into the submarine cells. Among others we saw that in which Faliero was confined. We went on the Bridge of Sighs, saw the stairs by which the prisoners ascended to their trial after crossing the bridge, and the stairs by which they descended to their doom, and the spot where men of rank were beheaded and humbler men were strangled, and the holes in the stones by which the blood escaped, and the closed window through which the body was lowered in its chains into the gondola, from which it was to be cast into the sea, where it could tell no tales. I give these particulars on the authority of our guide, but with an impression that things were not quite as he represented them. The place was gloomy enough for anything, and there were cruel days among those which are behind us. We tried to see the Arsenal. We did get into the Museum, and saw some relics of the palmy days of Venice, models of ships, the remains of the Bucentaur, banners from Lepanto, armor of old Doges, and of Henry IV. of France, old weapons of many patterns, and other curious things. We tried to gain admittance to the Navy Yard. Several persons tried to cut or break the red tape, but they kindly wasted our time without success. We did look upon the four lions from the Piræus, one of which is fabled to have come from Marathon.

It was a delight to visit the Academy once more and behold the Assumption, with its glorious face, and to see the Virgin as a girl of twelve going up the Temple steps for her presentation. Can it be she who attained the splendor of the Assumption? In the picture of the girl her light hair hangs in a braid. She wears a blue dress, which she holds with her right hand while she reaches out the left to the high-priest, who waits at the top of the steps to receive her. There is a bit of realistic relief in the old woman who sits at the foot of the steps with a basket of eggs. There is a charming simplicity about the child. She looks what she was. I can add nothing to this brief catalogue. Nor have I much to say of the churches, which deserve so much, but have been seen by so many. In St. Maria Formosa is the beautiful St. Barbara of Palma Vecchio. The Frari is one of the finest churches in the city, and has among its treasures the monuments of Titian and Canova. It is amusing to see the pains the sculptors have taken to rise to renown by cutting their names into these memorials which they had made for greater men. Titian's has Pietro Zandomeneghi F. and Luigi E. Pietro Zandomeneghi F.; and Canova's, Antonio Boso Scolpi, with others which I did not copy. St. Sebastian's Church has paintings by Paul Veronese, and his tomb. Tintoretto's pictures are in St. Rocco's care. How rich are the churches in these paintings, and how fortunate were the painters to find such places for their work! But the Church which gave the subjects for many of the best works deserves to have that which she had done so much to produce. We had a pleasant ride in a gondola to the Armenian Convent of St. Lazarus. The island is called by the same name. The buildings are large and pleasant. There had been a fire not long before our visit, and the work of restoration was not completed. The institution is really a theological seminary. It has twenty monks and thirty scholars. There is a good library, with mummies and other appendices, and a printing-office, where good work is done. Byron was at one time a student here, and his table, inkstand, and pens are exhibited, I suppose with admiration for the poet. It seemed a good place for study, if isolation is favorable to it. Perhaps men of more sense and broader sympathies would be produced nearer to the heart of things. A gentle monk, who spoke English well, took us over the place and told its story in a serious voice. He would take no fee, which was suspicious; but his attentions brought us to a small room where books, photographs, and embroidery could be bought at extravagant prices. To purchase was a way of giving a gratuity which could offend the feelings of neither party. Of the glass and lace factories of the city, the Ghetto for the Jews, the cemetery island with its brick walls, and many a place besides, I shall not speak. They are there when any would see them.

Venice must be seen. Descriptions are unusually feeble here. The times of greatness are gone, and the city lives in good part on its history. It is always pitiful when a place prolongs its existence by exhibiting its monuments. But the place is rare for situation. The traveller enters it with surprise and delight, and leaves with wonder and regret. Is there nothing there but pleasure? There might be some things set on the other side of the account. But to what purpose? There is the fragrance of the canals, under certain conditions: and mosquitoes which the smoky pastils subdue without destroying: there are guides who are worse than their winged associates: and men with pictures to sell at your own price, and men with boat-hooks studded with brass nails, who render a needless service and hold their battered hats for the fee which to them is evidently not needless; and there are beggars at the church doors, and beggars within who distract your meditations with the boxes of promises which they rattle before your face. These and like things are not agreeable. But why think upon them? The gondolas and canals, the churches and palaces, the pictures and the pigeons are there. The canals may be filled up, as some have proposed, and then the place will indeed be despoiled. But to-day Venice survives. Long as the city retains what it has not yet parted with will men from all lands flock thither as the doves to their window, and they will be rewarded for their coming with recollections which nothing can confuse or destroy.

# CHAPTER VI.

### TO AND THROUGH ATHENS.

WE have reached the dividing line in these movements. In the afternoon of the 28th of September we left Venice for the older world beyond. It was with rather heavy hearts that we glided in our gondola from the steps of the hotel, and left behind the dearest friends we had. But we had set our hearts on seeing the borders of the East. Our railway journey was not long and was relieved by our companions. We found in the compartment an Italian man and woman who appeared to be in some irrepressible period of love-making, if we might judge by their conduct. But we were more impressed by the behavior of another young man and woman who joined us. There was an excessive demonstration of affection on her part, to which he submitted in patience. This went so far that it became clear all was not right. This conviction gave a sad interest to the whole scene. Evidently, the mind of the woman had lost its balance, and her insanity, for the time, took on this gentle form. But nothing could exceed the gentleness of the man, who was taking her to some place of security, which should be also a place of healing.

At another point in the ride there came in an old

man and two women. After a season, with the usual German deliberation, the man fainted. The women had less of the national deliberation when they discovered his condition. There was a rapid mustering of bottles and handkerchiefs, and a quick succession of bathings and rubbings, with quite as much jabbering as could be helpful, till at length the old gentleman recovered his equanimity. Was he grateful for the attention which had restored him? Apparently not. He certainly resented the continued efforts of the women, and gave no heed to their anxious solicitations. One of the nurses carried her efforts so far as to sit on the man's hat. That seemed to mean nothing to him, and not much more to her, or even to the hat.

With these excitements the few hours passed by. We found at Gorizia, where the custom-house force assisted us, that we were crossing into Austria, and at ten o'clock we were at Trieste. We found pleasant quarters at the Hotel Delorme. From that moment we had little occasion to think for ourselves, so far as travelling was concerned. For we were in the care of an enterprising tourist company, and under the personal charge of Mr. Thomas G. Mill, of London. We were fortunate in being placed under his direction. He was a man who had seen not a little of the world, whose knowledge reached through a wide range of subjects, who was skilful in planning a journey and in carrying it through, who was courageous in difficulties and patient amid complaints, — a wise conductor, a genial companion, and a friend to be remembered.

If I ever travel again, I shall bespeak him for my guide. I want to insert here the address of Mr. Mill, at 49 Grove Lane, Camberwell, London.

If one is to go into the East, the first thing to do is to put himself into the hands of some one whose business it is to arrange the plans and details of the journey, and who has all that is necessary for its prosecution. For travelling, especially in unfrequented places, is now reduced to a science, and the prudent man will avail himself of the fact. The next thing is to connect himself with others who are of a like mind. Of course it is possible to travel alone, or with a single friend. But this is more expensive and has other disadvantages. As things are now managed, the party for a journey is commonly made up by the agent. Each person may have his one or two friends, but there must be the grouping of these into companies of convenient size, and this must be done by the wise man who is to have the control of the expedition. It becomes, therefore, a matter of great interest to discover who are to be the companions upon the journey in strange lands, where the association must needs be close. So many things go to make up a pleasant travelling companion, that there is always a large element of chance in this mode of journeying, and one feels this strongly when he first looks in the faces of those who are for several weeks to share his life. Concerning those who should be in our party we were in uncertainty for a long time. Indeed, the company was never made. The members of it simply drifted together, and half of them came when the journey was half over. There were rumors at Venice of three or four men who were to appear at Trieste, and the rumors remained in force all the way to Turkey. But those men have not yet been found, with one exception. Of that one I must now speak. I do it with pleasure, for he proved a good companion. When we went to breakfast at Trieste, we met at the table a gentleman with whom we were to move on. We looked hard at him for the sake of what was coming. A plain, honest, intelligent face answered our staring with its own. I suppose it would not be just to insert any more true names. It will answer my purpose to say that this was Mr. Garry, of Pennsylvania. In his calling he combined the merchant and the mechanic. He had risen by his own merit to a good position, and was disposed to use a portion of the leisure which he had earned by seeing more of the world than lay among his mountains. His chief thought in visiting Palestine was to see "where the Apostles and the Saviour lived." He cared little for cities, — "there are cities enough in America." In pictures and statues he had no interest. But he longed to look upon the places which are "mentioned in the Bible." I set him down for a sturdy, sensible deacon in the church, who had the Scriptures written in his mind, and whose pious designs were worthy of the indulgence which he purposed to give them. In this judgment I was not entirely correct. But I think that I did not over-estimate the man. He showed his character at once. For no sooner was breakfast over than he offered me his assistance in procuring anything I might need. In the few hours he had spent in the city before our arrival he had measured its capacity, and had found out what it had to offer in objects of utility and interest. His sight-seeing had already begun, though he had not come upon the footprints of apostles. He had been to the Château of Miramar, and had mourned over the fate of Maximilian, the beguiled and betrayed monarch of a land which had no use for him, and he had admired the splendors which the prince left for a throne and a grave.

There were a few purchases to be made, of things which pilgrims would be sure to need. There was one visit to be paid to an old and honored friend, Ex-Consul Thayer. We found him in his pleasant rooms, among his books and pictures; lingering in the land which had long been his home, yet hoping that his last days might be spent in the land of his birth. His hope is the desire of all who know him.

The half-day which we had in Trieste gave us no time to go about the city. It was a rainy forenoon, and all things wore a sombre look. We could see great buildings, clean streets, and the signs of a large traffic. For Trieste is the chief seaport of Austria, and has a fine position at the head of the Adriatic. It has its bishop and cathedral, its school of theology and naval academy, its museum and observatory. It is in effect an Italian city, though men of many nations meet in its markets. The steamers which are coming and going make the harbor a busy place. How long this will last, no one knows. Commerce changes its channels at its will, and the Suez Canal makes Trieste of less importance than in former years. The trade to India will naturally seek the shortest way, and this port seems likely to be left on one side. Such has been the fate of many places in the old world and the new. Whether the old city can adapt itself to new conditions remains for time to determine. Trieste is mentioned as a Roman town fifty years before the Christian era, when it was known as Tergeste. Roman has the sound of antiquity there. We shall soon be where Roman means modern, and the traveller hardly deigns to look on that which bears the name.

Early in the afternoon we drove to the steamer *Hungaria*, and were soon on our voyage towards Athens. We saw Miramar in the distance as we moved away. Mr. Garry reminded us that he had trodden its floor; and added that he could no more tell its beauties than he could tell how many pails of water we had passed since we left Trieste. The comparison was impressive, and calculated to make us dissatisfied with ourselves. But it was too late to fill up our deficiency.

The accommodations on the Mediterranean steamers are not entirely to the American mind. We found that our state-room was a small cabin with berths for five or six persons. We could get nothing better, and with protest settled down for the voyage. There was a variety in the passengers. Two young ladies were from Boston, and were on their way to Constantinople. There was a man with a tall hat, whose circumference increased with its height, and with long, brown robes. We judged him to be an Armenian patriarch. Then there were Greeks, and I know not what nationalities besides. Our first day at sea was Sunday. It was refreshing to open the port-hole over my berth and to catch a breath from the outer world. It was a fine day, with a mild but over-abundant air. Monday was cloudy and dreary, and few persons were to be seen on the upper deck. We passed down the hilly coast of Albania and in the early evening reached Corfu. It was too dark for us to see much of the town, but the lights along the coast made a very pleasing effect. Boats came off to the steamer, and we gave up some of our passengers and took on others. These were mostly of the third class, who found places where they could lie along the deck in poverty and unconcern. We wished that all who came were of the same grade, for one man of a slightly higher condition was thrust into our cabin. It was not his fault, but our misfortune. The next day was fair and bright. Our way lay between Ithaca and Cephalonia. The Kingdom of Ulysses was in appearance an immense rock, with green spots upon it. But it is some fifteen miles long and has some ten thousand people upon it. The ruins of the Castle of Ulysses can be seen on Mount Aëto, so the islanders tell, but the castle was not visible to us. Cephalonia is the largest of the Ionian islands. Its mountains are conspicuous and its currants abundant. The latter are the leading product of this and the neighboring islands. Ship-building and other industries have a place there. The island has its ancient fame and the necessary ruins to sustain it. Zante comes next and suggests raisins. The large vineyards are prolific, but the grapes are small, even as we see them in their dried estate. Zante has its place in classic history. Its capital, of the same name, boasts a Greek archbishop and a Roman bishop, with five churches, and other important buildings. Herodotus calls the island by its longer name and writes: "I have myself seen pitch drawn up out of a lake of pure water in Zacynthus; and there are several lakes there: the largest of them is seventy feet every way, and two orgyæ in depth; into this they let down a pole with a myrtle branch fastened to the end, and then draw up pitch adhering to the myrtle; it has the smell of asphalt, but is in other respects better than the pitch of Pieria. They pour it into a cistern dug near the lake, and when they have collected a sufficient quantity they pour it off from the cistern into jars." It seems that petroleum is not a novelty. But we saw no wells or lakes. Reading had to supplement vision.

We rounded the Peloponnesus and turned up the eastern coast of Greece. With what adjective shall I attempt to describe the sail along the classic shore? The Ægean was as quiet as Waban water. The islands rested peacefully upon its bosom. The sea, the land, the wind, the clouds seemed full of delightful memories which were wakened by the names we heard and the thoughts which came with them, as we drew near to Athens. We entered the Saronic gulf, and passed by Ægina, and then Salamis, into whose broad bay we could look over the waters no longer disturbed by contending navies. Themistocles and Xerxes were no longer with their fleets; but for us there was no other Salamis but theirs, and the Salamis of Solon and Euripides.

The hills are there still, and there are ruins, and imagination can do the rest to restore the vanished renown. Soon the masts of the Piræus appeared, and in the distance we saw Hymettus, and the heights of Athens. What a vision it was! Who can forget the moment when he first sees the columns of the Parthenon, the congregated wonders of the Acropolis! We passed into the ample harbor and stopped. An officer went on shore to secure permission for us to land. A long line of boats was in waiting till the permission should be given. At length the signal was given that it was granted, when there came a genuine boat race. Never were crews more eager. The men rowed with their might and shouted with their main. As they approached the steamer men in the rear boats leaped into those in front and thus made their way to the ship. We were assailed with a demonstrative hospitality. Hotels and boats were offered far beyond our capacity for acceptance. We had no part in the clamor. Mr. Mill knew the man whom he wanted, and we were soon in his boat and on our way to the shore, under a local guide. When we touched the pier our guide went off, and soon returned with two officials, who gazed at us for a moment and signified that they had no objection to our stepping upon the soil of Greece. We accordingly took the step. Indeed, we were there for that purpose. Our luggage was put on a carriage, a hack of familiar shape, and we were placed inside the same vehicle. Then we started for the city, which was one hour away. We were stopped once by an official of uncertain grade, to whom our new guide addressed himself in appropriate terms, and we were allowed to keep moving. Our only other pause was for the refreshment of man and beast, especially man, that is the driver and guide. There was little of interest on the road except that it led to Athens. We passed mills, or water-wheels, which looked like pictures we had seen, and men carrying in carts huge leathern bottles filled with wine. The way was dusty and without beauty. It was good to enter the city; to see Greek words on the signs; to look on Greek men and women in their homes; to know that we were in Athens. We found a delightful hotel near the royal palace, beneath Lycabettus and its lofty Church of St. George. The "Grande Bretagne" sounded well even in Greece.

The house deserved its name. It was spacious and attractive, and the table was excellent. So far as our experience went, this was the outer border of fine hotels. Beyond, only comfort could be secured. Athens threw in luxuries.

We were under the special care of Mr. Thomas Manessi while we were in Greece. It was very good care. He was intelligent and indulgent, as becomes a guide. Under his direction we saw the city pretty well, if the brevity of our stay is considered. We saw too much to warrant an attempt at description, and too little to make a description of any value to those who have the numerous books and pictures which have made Athens and its treasures and its history familiar. Athens is not so large that it cannot be known. The mind readily grasps its chief features and retains them. Nor are its records so indistinct that they cannot be read. The wonderful and imperishable interest which is attached to the city and to everything in it will make it more widely known as the years pass on.

Athens is now in three portions. In the newest part the buildings are good and the white walls give them a very bright, fresh look. The streets are wide and clean, and the whole appearance indicates thrift. I was not able to ascertain clearly upon what Athens depends for prosperity. But the amount of shipping in the Piræus shows that she is engaged in quite an extensive commerce. Wine was almost the only thing we saw which was likely to be exported. There must be grain, and perhaps other commodities, to be sent away, and the trade with the interior must be considerable. A town has grown up at the harbor, with the appliances of a large business.

On the other side of the city are the remains of ancient Athens, solitary and grand. Between the oldest and newest portions is the district which is neither old nor new: where the streets are narrow and not clean, and houses and shops are huddled together, after the fashion of most places in that part of the world. There was very little to remind us that we were in Athens. The ordinary European dress was worn by everybody, except one guide who hung around our hotel, waiting for employment. He wore the full white skirts reaching nearly to the knees, and the long white stockings reaching towards the same boundary line, with an elaborate jacket and cap. It seems a pity that the national dress has been laid aside. The copying of French costumes lessens the attractiveness of any people. The appointments of our hotel we should have found in Paris. We should have been better pleased with the fare of the country served in the national method. The carriages in the streets were such as one finds in Boston. The large, open barouche was the most common. We asked for something which we could carry away as characteristic of the place and people. Manessi said there was nothing. When we pressed him he suggested shoes. We saw the shoe-makers along the streets, and the large pointed foot-coverings, but they were not what we wanted. He also proposed silks, but he showed us nothing desirable. At length it dawned upon his mind that there was not far away an industrial school established by American missionaries. Our first attempt to visit this school failed. We tried again and gained entrance. We found children learning to sew and embroider and make lace, and women and girls weaving silk and making carpets. The implements were rude and clumsy for this day. But the work was well done, and we were glad to buy a few specimens of the silk goods as souvenirs of Athens. We did find, also, in an old market, a lot of national knives, with wooden handles and triangular blades. They are doubtless useful in the fish trade, but for general cutting purposes they are not of much value, as the price indicated. Our only mistake was in not buying more.

When Manessi entered upon his work of showing us Athens, he first chartered a carriage for four persons. We were to view antiquities, but with the modern appliances. But of ancient conveyances there were none, unless the human feet could be described under that term. The order of sight-seeing puts the carriage first. Walking comes in, but at a later stage.

Our first stopping-place was at the Stadium. This was an amphitheatre, in which the labor of men had improved the natural features of the hill of Agræ, which was in the form of a crescent, and had constructed a place for the games in which the people delighted. There gladiators contended, and wild beasts were matched against men. In its glory this was a magnificent theatre. It was nearly seven hundred feet long. It had marble seats for forty or fifty thousand people, and standing room for as many more. The games were on the same scale. At one spectacle, it is reported, a thousand beasts were killed. The Temple of Fortune, with an ivory statue of the goddess, was on one side. Little remains of the grand Stadium besides the hill, which keeps its ancient shape, and could easily be restored to its former uses if a degenerate age should demand it. In its present desolation it is difficult to think of the mad excitement, the fierce passion, the suffering and renown, which then made a part of the play of a great people. Yet the desolation is not deeper, is less oppressive, than that which broods among the ruins of structures which had a higher purpose.

We stopped next at the Temple of Zeus Olympius, if by that name it can now be called. Once it held high rank, as the largest and one of the finest of the temples of Athens. Pisistratus, the "genial tyrant," laid the foundations; but it was left for Hadrian to complete the work. The house was, therefore, nearly seven hundred years in being built. There were a hundred and twenty columns around it, but only sixteen of them remain. They have a very lonesome look as they tower sixty feet above the dreary plain. Even a hermit who once found a home on the architrave has disappearred. He has left the massive pillars to stand sentinels over their own past. Near by is the gate, or arch, of Hadrian. It does not appear to have been the gateway to anything in particular, but to have served as a boundary mark between the older and later Athens, the city of Theseus and the quarter which was the especial care of Hadrian. The gateway is some twenty feet wide and rises between two immense square piers. There were two Corinthian columns before each pier. The arch is in two stories, having a sort of attic over the gateway. Upon the frieze of the architrave, on each face of the arch, is an inscription. One of these declares that the city which it faces was the Athens of Theseus, and the other that the place which it confronts was the city of Hadrian. It is probable that the arch had a triumphal character, but there is nothing imposing about it now, and it has lost the special meaning which would have given it interest and dignity.

Before another building we were thrown into confusion. The book called it the Lantern of Demosthenes. Manessi insisted that this was a mistake — that it should be the Lantern of Diogenes. Probability leaned heavily on the side of the interpreter. We knew that the Cynic had a lantern, and had good use for it. Whether the greatest of orators had need of such illumination we were not so sure. But a better authority than guide-books or guides would have relieved us from the necessity of deciding between the two claimants. It is really the monument of Lysicrates. It commemorates a victory obtained at a public contest in music. Hence its title, choragic. It is on the Street of the Tripods, and is among the finest of the smaller monuments which have been preserved. It is a circular building, with half-Corinthian columns about it, and a square foundation beneath. Above are a beautiful frieze and cornice, while the top of the structure is elaborately decorated. Its shape is not very unlike a lantern, which may have suggested that name. The court of a French Capuchin monastery was once about it. We were told that Byron passed a night within the monument or lantern. It is of pure Pentelic marble, is thirty-four feet high, and dates from B. C. 335. There seems to have been another building similiar to this, which was called the Lantern of Diogenes. But there are no traces of it now. On the southeast side of the Acropolis we passed into the enclosure of Dionysus, or Bacchus, the wine god of Attica. Two temples were there, near the great theatre of Athens. The upper part of the theatre was cut out of the cliff, and the rest was constructed of wood and stone. It was a fine structure when at its best estate. The stage and auditorium remain, and the front seats of marble, which bear the names of the priests who occupied them. There are other seats above these. The place of the orchestra is clearly marked, and the open space where there was dancing around an altar. It is conjectured that the women had the upper seats, where they sat apart from the men. The centuries have been working out a deeper tragedy than was ever performed by the actors who have gone into the great realities.

We entered the sanctuary of Æsculapius, which was afterwards a Christian church. "The blameless physician" was very widely worshipped. All Greece paid him homage. His temples were numerous and were often built on hills and near wells whose waters were thought to possess healing properties. Care was taken to secure a healthy place for the worship of one upon whom so many depended for immediate benefit. This temple at Athens had a good situation. We found in a cave a well whose water is disagreeable enough to be salutary, and we could easily believe that the medicine concocted and compounded with it had the desirable qualities.

Herodes Atticus was one of the greatest of the benefactors of Greece. He had wealth, learning, and eloquence, and he used all for the advantage of his country. He almost despoiled Pentelicus of marble when he would adorn the Stadium, — so it was said, but not without exaggeration. He certainly ventured on a magnificent scale. He was of an old family of Marathon, and his father enriched himself by finding a hidden treasure. The father bequeathed the greater part of this wealth to the Athenians, but the son made a compromise with them, by which he kept most of the money. He inherited more from his mother, and more came to him by his wife. He was therefore able to be a public benefactor. A theatre, aqueduct, race-course, and hospital were among his gifts. Of his literary productions nothing has survived, but his material benefits have left their traces through the land. At the southwest corner of the Acropolis he built the Odeum or Odeon, to which he affixed the name of Regilla, his wife. It was a theatre which would hold from six to ten thousand spectators. Something of the walls and seats can now be seen. It had a roof of cedar, finely carved, and this was a distinguishing feature of the structure. The Odeum was devoted to the contests of poets and musicians. There the rhapsodist could display his skill, and the player on the lyre solicit the admiration of his listeners, and prizes could be gained which were held of great account. We found nothing of the kind going on. An old woman and a headless statue seemed to be the guardians of the place, from which music and poetry had fled.

Thus we wound our way up the Acropolis, tarrying among these annexed ruins in this subordinate desolation. There was some little life, but it was of the modern and vulgar sort. Coins of a professed antiquity were offered for sale, and shells from Marathon sought purchasers. Whatever may have been the intrinsic value of these wares, it was something that we could buy them there.

Now that we are fairly on the Acropolis, what can I say of it? I shall attempt little. The plans and pictures which are so readily found will give a far better idea of the place than any words could create. The name has a description and a history in itself. The higher or upper city is an instructive term. Sometimes it has been called "*the* city" to mark its pre-eminence. It is a hill or rock rising five hundred feet or more above the sea. There Athens had its beginning. The houses were small upon the hill itself, but as they were built beyond it, out upon other hills, they increased in size, and their arrangement became orderly as the settlement took on the form of a city. The Acropolis proper became a citadel, with the town around it, and walls enclosing the whole, with other walls reaching to the towns on the sea. Upon the summit were erected buildings which have given to the height its chief interest. The Propylæa was the gateway. It was built by Pericles, who died in B. C. 429. It was more than an entrance. Those who saw it in its glory thought it more wonderful than the Parthenon. Immense stones were built into it, and their strength was made beautiful. Sixty marble steps, seventy feet from side to side, led up to it, and through the centre of these steps was a road running to the entrance above. A portico with six columns was at the head of the steps, and beyond this was a large and magnificent hall, with five gates at its east end, through which entrance into the Acropolis was gained. The Propylæa, from its position and construction, was a substantial defence to the hill upon whose front it stood. On each side was a wing with Doric columns. In that on the north was the Pinacotheca, where the works of the great masters were displayed. At the right of the south wing was a small temple, twenty feet wide, devoted to the Unwinged Victory, and expressing the hope and confidence of the Athenians that the Goddess of Victory would never fly away from them. Passing through the Propylæa, there is seen upon the left the Erectheum. As the story goes, this was built by Erectheus I., or Erichthonius, an Attic hero, who drove out Amphictyon and became King of Athens. He set up the worship of Athena, instituted a grand festival in her honor, and built her this temple. His fame as the original driver of a chariot with four horses is now commemorated among the stars, where Auriga, or the Wagoner, or Charioteer, holds his place among divinities. The temple was conspicuous in

> "the well built town of Athens,
> Town of Erectheus with the noble heart,
> Earth-born, but fostered by Athena's care,
> Jove's child, and in her own rich temple set."

There were three parts to the temple, or three temples together. One for Athena, the protectress of the State; then the sanctuary of Erectheus, and finally the sanctuary of Pandrosos, "the all-bedewing" daughter of Cecrops. The building was oblong, with a portico at the north-west corner, and a smaller one at the south-west. This smaller portico, the Cecropium, is remarkable for the six Caryatides, who stand there in patience holding up the mass of stone which presses on their heads. These marble pillars are Attic maidens of rank and of beauty, and in their calm faces and flowing drapery, and their vigor and repose, they are good representatives of the glory which has passed from the temple which they adorn, and of the spirit which can be burdened but cannot be destroyed. One or two of the little company have been removed out of their place, and the substitutes of baser material and formation are in unpleasant contrast to their older but nobler sisters. The Persians destroyed the temple, but it was rebuilt. Little now remains of it — so little that it is impossible to determine the arrangement and uses of its many apartments.

The special glory of the Acropolis is, of course, the Parthenon. This too the Persians destroyed, and this too was restored. Ictinus and Callicrates were the architects, while Phidias and his pupils gave to it its wealth of sculpture. Indeed, Phidias superintended the whole work. It is of Pentelic marble. Three steps lead up to the base on which the temple stands. The temple itself is one hundred and ninety-three feet long and seventy-one broad. It is surrounded by a colonnade of forty-six columns, with an inner row of eight at each end, and others within the walls. The temple was in two unequal parts: the temple proper, where stood the "colossal chryselephantine image of the goddess," "a core of wood covered with plates of gold and ivory," the heroic work of Phidias; and the smaller apartment, which was the public treasury. There are signs that there were paintings on the exterior of the temple. Tints of blue and red are still to be seen, with traces of the patterns in which they were set. The sculptures presented historical and mythological subjects. Many of these were taken to England in the early part of this century. It is said that Lord Elgin exaggerated the permission which was given him to remove some of the marbles, and fairly despoiled the Parthenon of its treasures. However glad we may be to see them in England, when in Athens it can only seem a refined vandalism which has torn them from the structure of which they were a part. The Parthenon survived the special purpose for which it was erected. After a time the Virgin supplanted Athena, and the temple became a Christian church. But war has small regard for art or religion. In the conflict between the Turks and Venetians, in 1687, the Parthenon was destroyed. Destroyed is too strong a word. Its columns were chipped, and broken, and cast down; the interior was ruined; but enough of the columns and walls remained to be a witness to the skill and devotion which built the house; to testify to its magnificence, and represent its grandeur. Still stand the lofty pillars upon the lofty heights, visible from afar, upon the land and upon the sea, the proudest monument of the proud city which has been the teacher of the world.

Athens has a rightful claim to her illustrious position. She was the city of wisdom from the first. The story may be told again, and it comes in well at this point. Athena, Pallas Athena, who was called Minerva at Rome, and her uncle, Poseidon, whom the Romans called Neptunus, contended for the possession or ownership of Attica. Athena was the goddess of wisdom, and she had in her charge a variety of arts which were useful and ornamental. The plough and the needle were in her keeping; the ship and the loom. Poseidon was the god of the sea. He had a submarine palace off the coast of Eubœa, and there he kept his horses with manes of gold and hoofs of brass. He liked to come up for a drive, and the waves over which his chariot rolled became level for his convenience, and he had a famous retinue of his neighbors and subjects who frolicked about him as his steeds leaped over the waters. One would think that this might have contented him. He was too much like a man to be contented. He wanted a position on the land. So he applied for the protectorate of Attica, and the other candidate was his niece. That was in the reign of Cecrops, the first king of the country, and a monarch who made himself a father to his people, though he was only half human in form, if the legends are to be trusted — and if we do not believe them what can we learn of those distant times? In those days the Civil Service rules were in force, and there was a competitive examination. The candidate who should produce that which would be most useful was to have the place. It was a case in which taste and habit would have a large influence. Quite naturally, Poseidon offered a horse, and Athena an olive-tree. The commissioners, who were divinities, decided in favor of the woman. Thus wisdom was enthroned where Athena set her imperishable name. The accounts do not entirely agree, but the substantial points are quite clear.

Poseidon was not satisfied. What defeated candidate was ever content? But he left his mark on the place over which he could not rule. For at some time in this contest he struck his trident, the three-pronged sceptre, on the Acropolis, whereupon the salt water sprang from the rock. Some of these statements can now be verified. We saw the place where the spring was. But Pausanias, who made an extensive tour through this country in the second century, found the sea-water in the cave of Poseidon, and was not so much surprised as could have been expected. He was surprised to find that when the wind was from the south, there was a sound in the well as of the waves of the sea. He saw also in the rock the form of the trident. The marks may be seen now. There are but two of them, which is unfortunate. But it is a long time since Neptune smote the stone with his sceptre, and more important things than a hole have been lost. The story should not be allowed to suffer for such a trifling defect as that. Pausanias saw also the sacred olive-tree, the crooked "citizen" of the height. We also saw the olive-tree, a mere shrub, without impressiveness save that which its romantic history lends it. The tree was burned in the wars, but on the same day it sent up sprouts two cubits long. Herodotus says they were but one cubit long; but he is not altogether trustworthy. In either case its long life is accounted for.

Whatever may be the exact truth regarding details, there can be no doubt that Athena was the divinity of the city which has so long been called after her. We saw where her statue was, where she heard the prayers of the people, and the place underneath where the priest was hidden who responded in her name. There was the aperture, too, through which the suppliants dropped the money which rewarded the goddess and supported the priest.

We came down from the Acropolis and made the ascent of a hill which is much less imposing but which holds a prominent place in a history which is broader and larger than that of Athens. Mars' Hill, as we know it, the Areopagus, as it was called in the days of its power, is a mass of rocks, not large or high, and having no treasures of antiquity separate from itself. On the north side the ground rises gradually till it terminates in the broken ridge. The south side is a rough precipice, whose highest part is, perhaps, fifty feet above the valley, from which the hill looks like an immense boulder which a classic glacier has left in its advance. There is a feeling of disappointment in finding that there is no more of a place whose name suggests grandeur and importance. Its history is in several parts which are quite distinct. It gets its name from Ares, that is Mars, who killed the son of Poseidon, and was tried before the gods upon this hill. Euripides embodied the fact in his lines: —

> "There is a Hill of Mars, where first the gods
> In council sat and voted about blood,
> When cruel Mars slew Halirrhothius."

There is a different account given of the name, but this seems to be the most authentic. The hill was the seat of the famous court or council to which from ancient times were committed the gravest Athenian causes, both civil and religious. The court was held in the night, so it is said, that the judges might hear the voices of those who spoke to them, without seeing their faces. The sessions were held in the open air, that the judges and prosecuting officers might not be shut in with the criminals, whose presence would be polluting. The court met on the highest part of the hill. Sixteen steps, cut in the rock, led up to the platform, which can still be traced, where were the seats of the judges. These also were cut in the rock where they can even now be seen. Pausanias, the traveller, saw two rude stones on the hill, on one of which, during a trial, the accuser stood, and on the other the accused.

It was a wonderful place for a court. The Acropolis and its temples towered above it. The city was spread around it, even reaching to the base of the rock. A temple of Mars was on the hill, while in a chasm under the seats of the judges was the entrance to the sanctuary of the Eumenides, or Erinyes, or Semnæ, or, more popularly, the Furies.

The first name signifies "well-meaning," and was used because the people were afraid to call these dread divinities by their true title. Gods and men were afraid of them, and not without reason if they are correctly described as having black bodies, with serpents twined in their hair, and with blood dropping from their eyes. It is but fair to say, however, that their images have nothing especially frightful about them. Perhaps discretion prevailed over truthfulness in this.

Above the whole scene rose the colossal form of Athena, with her spear and shield and helmet, defending and adorning the city which bore her name. Greek tragedy found a place upon Mars' Hill, where so many real tragedies found their end. Judges and actors have disappeared. The plays are still read by scholars, and now and then become the delight of the few who see them again in living form, that the pursuits of other years may be the pastime of the present.

But for the most of those who know the Areopagus, and who have an intelligent concern with the course of the world's thought and life, the great interest in Mars' Hill is in the fact that there once stood upon it a man whose influence was to exceed that of his predecessors, and to stamp itself deeply and permanently into the lives of men. Nothing in the history of the place is more impressive or instructive than this single line, — "Then Paul stood in the midst of Mars' Hill." He addressed the world and the centuries when he said, "Ye men of Athens."

It was no man who that day was on trial for his life. The thought, belief, action, the civilization and religion, of the days when the Parthenon was in its splendor, were on trial. No: the trial was over. The verdict and sentence are in the ruins of the Acropolis, and the desolation it looks down upon. We stood where St. Paul stood. It was in the midst, or middle, of the narrow top of the rock. We must have been upon the very spot. There was no audience. But we could imagine the time when there was life among these temples, and the places of men's homes, and we could see the multitudes standing beneath the preacher as from his high pulpit he uttered his bold words. We could mark their surprise, and could see their faces as they turned away leaving him still in his place. "Some mocked: and others said, We will hear thee again of this matter." The place where the altar was on which he read the inscription which gave him a text is still pointed out. Upon it stands a Christian church. Paul has been heard again.

Nothing seems great after leaving the Acropolis and Areopagus. I can do little more than name some of the places which we visited. Close at hand is the Agora, the market-place of Athens. It was — I was about to speak of its ancient magnificence. But it is as well to stop with the was. There are ruins, and little besides. The most unsightly part of the city is now on the ground where trade and worship met in the best days of Athens. The market-place of the present is full of business and confusion. Manessi said that the buildings were to be removed that excavations might be made. It would be well to clear the ground and begin again, even if none of the ancient improvements were recovered. The Stoa of Hadrian is near, sometimes called his Gymnasium, a structure of great elegance in its day. Some of the fine columns which enclosed it are yet standing. The Tower of the Winds, or Horologium, is of marble, octagonal in form, having on each side, at the top, sculptures in relief which represent the different winds. On each wind is its name, upon the cornice. On each side was a sun-dial. The floor was arranged for a water-clock, for which the water was brought from the Acropolis. There was once a Titan on the summit, who served as a weather-vane. West of the Acropolis is the hill of the Pynx, out of whose rock was cut the place in which the Athenians held their political meetings. There was room for many thousands of people to be seated. Projecting beyond the solid wall, a part of the rock, was a cubic block, eleven feet long and broad, and five feet in height, resting upon a platform which was reached by wide steps. Other steps led to the top of the block. This was the Bema, on which the orators stood. It may have been that Demosthenes and Pericles stood there when they roused the people by their eloquence. We tried to reproduce the eloquence, but there was no response, and our audience was very small. The throngs no longer assemble on that spot. On the Museum Hill rises the monument of Philopappus, a Syrian. It was an elaborate structure, but much of it has fallen. One forgets that, when he sees the extensive view which the height affords him, over the city, the country, the sea. On the side of the hill of the Museum is the prison of Socrates. Three chambers have been cut into the rock. In one of these, twelve feet by seven, the philosopher was confined, and there he died. Such is the tale, which, I believe, no wise man credits. This is a pity, as the rooms of stone have a prison-like appearance, and seem to fit into the story very well. Some part of the prison is now occupied by cattle. In the front of the hill are holes in which beams were placed for the roof of a projection of wood.

The best preserved of the buildings of ancient Athens is the Theseum, commonly called the temple of Theseus, for the legendary hero who came to the aid of the Athenians at Marathon. The name of Theseus is denied to it, but there is no other to put in its place. So it stands with its walls and columns for general admiration because of its own merit. At one time it was dedicated to Christian worship and devoted to St. George, the dragonkiller. The interior is surprisingly small and very dreary. It is now used as a museum, but its curiosities are not extensive.

We went to the Burial Ground of Agia Triada, where excavations have brought to light many ancient tombs and statues. The treasures found in the tombs have been taken to the Polytechnic, a building for paintings and sculptures, with fine collections of antiquities from Mycenæ and Egypt. At the entrance to the burial ground is a small, rude Greek church, which we entered. The bell had been doing its best to summon a congregation, but we found no one except the two priests. As soon as we appeared, and as if they had been waiting for us, they began to recite something with great rapidity. Then a man came in and began to trim the lamps. Failing to find edification in the scene we withdrew, and the priests were relieved from the burden of ministering to us. Manessi said there was formerly a temple connected with this ground, which is very likely. We did not see that, but we saw a wall which had the marks of advanced age, and which he said was Pelasgic.

We examined the vegetable garden which holds the place of the Academy of Plato. A few pieces of broken marbles have been dug up and ranged in a row as witnesses to what may be still uncovered. That was all we saw which had an academic look. There is a very small church in the garden. These minute edifices are found almost always where a temple has been. They do their best to keep up the character of the places. We wondered why there was not a persistent effort to find whatever may be hidden in this garden with so promising a name. Perhaps Plato did walk there with his scholars, though no footprints are to be discovered. We tried the pomegranates of the place, but there was not much refreshment in their seeds.

There are two metropolitan churches in the city. The newer one is showy and large, and was built of material from seventy small churches and chapels which were destroyed in 1840. The smaller church is of more interest, because it was built of fragments of ancient buildings, whose old stones are well set together.

But I must not prolong this catalogue. It can be hardly more than that. It may be a hint of some of the notable things in this wonderful city. In the days we were there we were able to get quite a clear idea of the position of the points of special interest, which we visited as often as we could. Mr. Garry added to our common explorations his private tours of discovery. He seemed never to be weary, and no other place interested him so much as Athens. It was pleasant and amusing for many a day to hear him boast of his knowledge. With great animation and not a little pride he would declare, "I can tell you where everything is. Say we're standing on the Acropolis. There's Mars' Hill. There's the temple of Theseus. There's the prison of Socrates. There's the monument of — " " Philopappus ? " " Yes, Philopappus. There's the Stadium." And so again and again would he make himself the willing guide for any one who wished for information of this character. I have no doubt that many a company among the mountains of Pennsylvania has followed his outstretched finger over the hills and houses of Athens.

We had seen so much Pentelic marble that we naturally desired to see the place from which it had been taken. In the morning we started early in a carriage which took us to a monastery, which the guide-book told us was the wealthiest in Attica. If appearances could be trusted, the other monasteries of Attica must be poor. The buildings were old and their rooms were small, and had the bare look which has been thought becoming in places for meditation. Two or three monks who had no signs of wealth about them, unless a general shabby condition could be so regarded, were apparently in possession. We were informed that there were seventeen connected with the establishment. They have a custom, when a monk dies, of locking the door of his room and leaving it unoccupied. We saw several of these closed doors. If the monastic spirit should revive, so that these apartments were needed, I presume that new-comers would enter into the places of those who had passed on. It should be so, out of respect to those who had approved that method of life. A stray soldier or two hovered about the grounds, and two cats found a quiet abode in the hallowed precincts. The place now belongs to the government, which seems to have no use for it. There is a grove of plane-trees near by and a spring of good water. We were established in a room from whose windows we had a fine view, and there we opened our baskets of provisions and had our lunch. Mules had been ordered to meet us at this place, and they made their appearance not far from the time when they were due. They had the saddle of the country, clumsy and hard enough for any purpose, too much so for our uses. I made my own tolerable by adopting General Taylor's method of riding, with both feet on one side of the beast. We soon found our ascending road paved with white marble, or, if not paved, it was covered with chips of marble, which made it attractive to the eye. Perhaps the mules would have preferred nature unadorned. Thus we came into the midst of the quarries out of which so much of old Athens had come. Temples and palaces had been broken from these white rocks. The stones had been cut into countless forms of grandeur and beauty. There seemed to be enough left for other cities. But all was as quiet as if the world had no more need of marble halls. We found a large grotto, and walked over its treacherous floor, with stalactites hanging above us and beside us. There was not much for us beyond. The clouds gathered sullenly, and the mists soon shut out from us the wide reach of country we had hoped to look upon. It was dark and cold. The drizzle was as dismal as drizzle can be on a mountain. We pressed dismally through the wet obscurity, till hope utterly disappeared, and it was clear that nothing would be gained by reaching the summit, or nothing but the summit. We turned the heads of our mules downward, and they slowly crept from rock to rock along the narrow path till their part of our excursion was over, and we could resume our carriage. But we had fine views in going up and when we had come below the rain, the plain of Marathon, Parnassus, and Hymettus, and far way Acrocorinthus, while the whole country over which the eye wandered, and the long ranges of mountains, were full of delight. It was a very good day, even if it might have been better.

A day was devoted to Eleusis. It is one of the fascinating names. It was hard to make it real that our feet could stand in the scene of the ancient mysteries: that a ride of two or three hours could carry us so much further beyond the world we had entered. But little is known of the religious rites which had their seat in Eleusis. They have remained mysteries. They were of a very venerable antiquity. It has been thought that they were older than the mythology of Greece, and had their origin in a time when men were more earnest in their thought and in more intelligent connection with nature. They concerned the world which lies outside of this, and the years which are beyond these, which so often pass for the whole of life. They kept their influence as they came down through generations of men to whom, under the holiest sanction, they were imparted. In the early autumn, Demeter, or Ceres, the goddess of the earth, in whose care were the fields, and their harvests, in the great festival at Eleusis was honored with the splendid and impressive worship. Visitors came from all lands. From Athens to Eleusis twenty, thirty thousand people moved in procession along the sacred way. For nine days the festivities were maintained. Every Athenian who was freeborn was required to receive initiation into the mysteries. At night, those who were to be instructed and admitted to the brotherhood were led through the darkness into the lighted temple, where they saw and heard what they could never reveal. The secret has been kept. But that the mysteries were of high value is evident. One writer has left the remark that "those who are initiated entertain sweet hopes of eternal life." In times of great peril a man would turn to his friend with the question on whose answer hope seemed to hang, "Are you initiated?" It is said that the only secret of Eleusis which has come from the temple of Ceres consists in the mysterious words, Konx, Ompax.

We were very near the proper time for visiting Eleusis, but our solitary carriage would hardly pass for a procession. We took the proper course, over the sacred road, and ascended to the Pass of Daphni, where we stopped at the Daphni monastery. There was a temple there which is thought to have belonged to Apollo. Some columns are still standing, and pieces of others grace the British Museum. The monastery is six hundred years old and looks as old as it is. There is a dome adorned with mosaics: and there are two empty tombs, and a few empty rooms, and the appliances of a common Greek church. A little beyond we passed a wall in which were small, irregular niches. This is what remains of a temple of Aphrodite. There were also large stones which belonged in the fortification with which the pass was formerly defended. The drive along the Bay of Eleusis was very pleasant. We had a fine chance to see Salamis again, and the Bay of Salamis, and to think upon the battle which Xerxes watched from his seat upon the Attic shore. Probably he enjoyed the reality less than we were pleased with the memory.

The city of Eleusis in importance once stood next to Athens. It was the most sacred place in the pagan world. Its temple was the largest in Greece. It had the same architect as the Parthenon, and was designed in the time of Pericles. Pentelicus furnished the marble for the house which was to do it honor. Of all this little is now to be seen. An insignificant village, whose name is of so little consequence that it is spelled in various ways, occupies the site of the grand edifice. Ruins there are, but even the ruins are mostly out of sight. The modern village was built upon the buried temple. The houses have now been removed, that the former house may be unearthed. A new village, or collection of small buildings inhabited by a few men and women who seem to have been left over, represents the proud city. Eleusis was. The temple was so placed as to be conspicuous to the procession from Athens. Its white walls must have made a fine appearance. The ruins which have been brought to light give hints of the magnificence, and promise a fuller revelation. We saw what was to be seen, and imagined the rest. The ruins of the old gates, a few bases of columns, broken stones with something of their true character now upon them, make up essentially the architectural remains. The old church of Saint Zacharias was built entirely of stones which had served a grander purpose. With some delay, while the key and keeper could be found, we gained admittance to a sort of shed in which some fragments of stone are preserved, with their inscriptions and carvings. There was a paper plan of the place, which the venerable custodian offered to sell. Mr. Garry offered to buy it, and the price was agreed upon. It was one franc. The coin which was produced was pronounced by the

Eleusinian too much worn, and as our friend's patience was in the same condition the bargain fell through. In our rambles we came upon a man treading grapes. The grapes were on a stone floor having channels through which the juice ran into a small well, out of which it was to be dipped that it might be made into wine. It was a good object-lesson in temperance. No one would thirst for the wine who saw the process of manufacture. The wine-maker took us into his house, which was, for substance, one room. There was a table about a foot in height. In the corner were rolled-up beds. Two women and various children composed the family. One of the women took from the fire a mess of maccaroni over which she sprinkled cheese. This was the dinner of the household. Possibly it was also an exhibition for the benefit of the strangers. We saw, too, a very primitive loom. There was little besides. We found a rude sort of hostlery, where we brought out our provisions, and had a comfortable dinner. Then we took our way towards home.

We were in Athens at the time of the ingathering of grapes. In the vineyard women and girls were picking the dusty clusters and dropping them into baskets to be taken to the presses. A few men superintended the work. The grapes were commonly growing on what appeared like low bushes rather than vines. The pickers had the hard, bronzed look which comes from living out-of-doors, and, unless it was seen from afar, there was no beauty in the work. It was not much like the pretty pictures which make one wish he could rest under the vines and refresh himself with the tempting clusters. We saw goats in abundance in city and country. They are most useful animals, furnishing milk while they live, then giving their flesh for meat for the poor, and their skins for bottles. We saw some sheep and a few cows. In one field we noticed a herdsman with his flock, the sheep on one hand and the goats on the other. There were huts in which the shepherds and their families and flocks live in the winter, when they cannot be out upon the hills. The donkey is the beast of burden for the poor. He makes a comical appearance when loaded with immense baskets, with a man or woman at the top of the load; or bearing masses of hay, or fuel, far beyond his own dimensions, till he looks like a shrunken mastodon with wings. In it all he is patient, and as obedient and docile as animals of his class are apt to be.

We visited the University of Athens, if walking through groups of students, and then through the library and museum, and looking over a few manuscripts, can be called a visit. We were courteously treated, and at less cost than if it had been an English university. There are four departments — Theology, Law, Medicine, and Philosophy, and an observatory. There are about fifteen hundred students, and sixty or more professors and teachers. On the same street is the Arsakion, a school for girls, and the largest in Greece. The American Classical School is on the other side of the city, where it has made a beginning in its important work. This is hardly the place for an appeal, yet I cannot resist the desire to say a word in behalf of scholarship and patriotism, as these are related to this school. It is now in hired rooms, where the director and his family have their residence. The government of Greece presented to the British school a piece of ground on the southern slope of Lycabettus, where a suitable building has been erected. The government has offered to the American school a similar lot of land near that given to the English school, or in some other part of the city, if a different site is preferred. The money for the building has been provided. Surely there are persons enough who have an interest in such investigations and studies as can best be pursued in Greece to make it a simple matter, and one not long to be delayed, to provide the few thousands of dollars which will raise this promising American institution to a becoming place among the schools of Athens. It will be a prominent witness to American learning, and will give us a share in a work in which it should be our delight to engage.

# CHAPTER VII.

IN AND ABOUT CONSTANTINOPLE.

How little I have said of Athens! How small a part of all which we saw and thought can be transferred to paper! Our days were packed with interest. To be there was an unbroken delight. Whether we looked upon the old or the new, there was enough to keep the mind busy and to keep memory and imagination on the stretch. I find that I have written nothing of our visits at the house of the American minister, where, surrounded with orange-trees and flowers, he served his country and enriched the literature of the world. Nothing of Mr. Kalopothakes and his chapel, and the good work he is doing for his people. Nothing of the royal palace, with its tarnished glories, and its neglected park where we strolled in forbidden and unforbidden places, and came upon a sleepy lioness in whose cage courageous or initiated rats nibbled at a piece of raw meat, which they proposed to draw through the bars for consumption at their leisure. I have indulged in no moralizing, nor have I attempted to picture the future of Greece, when her energy and bravery shall have given her among the nations the place to which she is entitled. The past will not return, but better days than these may come. They will not spring from the vineyards, or be exhumed from the ruins. They will come from the works of justice and liberty, of education and religion, which have made younger nations great. To one who spends a few days in Greece there seems to be a lack of enterprise and of an earnest spirit. They seem not to be keeping step with the swift movement of the years. Her currency and her postage stamps in their insufficiency are small signs of large deficiencies. But from all this she will rise. Beside her ruins and over them will grow up the new Greece which will be worthy of the name.

It was nine o'clock in the evening when we turned reluctantly from Athens. At the Piræus we parted from Manessi, embarked in a sailboat, and were soon on board the steamer. We were most fortunate in our ship. The *Titania* was destined for the India trade and was then making an experimental voyage. Everything was new and neat. The state-rooms were large and convenient, and all the appointments were excellent, even to electric lights. Neither before nor after did we see so fine a steamer in those waters. It was at midnight that we were to sail out of the harbor, but in the morning we were still there and still taking in freight. It was a good place to linger in. Our last look at the Parthenon, Hymettus, Lycabettus, and all which could be made out from the sea was impressive. Tenedos, Lemnos, Mt. Ida, and the site of Troy all appealed to us as we made our pleasant way across the Ægean. We entered the Dardanelles, passing between the two forts on the opposite points between which Leander used to swim at night, for a worthier purpose than marked the similar feat which has been performed there in our time by Mr. Webb. We stopped for a few moments and the waiting boats came off to us. From a row of buildings on the Asiatic shore floated the flags of the nations which had their consulates there. On the last and most imposing of the series was the banner which is always so beautiful in a strange land. Then we passed through the Hellespont and across the Sea of Marmora and at midnight on the 12th of October came to anchor before Constantinople. The next morning the city was somewhat obscured by fog, which gave to the whole scene a spectral look. We moved farther on and again the boats gathered about us. It seemed a pity to leave a finer ship than we were to have again. But we took to the boats. Presently we were stopped beside another boat, which belonged to the government of Turkey, and the passport of one of our company was held up before the proper official. I believe that it was an English document, but it was just as well, and we were allowed to land. At the quay other officers lay in waiting. Some satisfactory arrangement was made with them by the man who had us in charge, and our luggage was seized by porters who had a peculiar cushion on their backs upon which heavy loads could rest as the men carried them. Carriage or dray there was none. We formed in procession, guides, travellers, porters, and moved up the street, if street it could be called. It was very narrow, very steep, very dirty and rough, and thronged with men and dogs. I suppose the boats could have taken us to a better place, but that was not their way. The porters were to be provided for. We toiled on and at length reached our hotel, the Byzance. We were in Pera, the part of the city in which the English have their homes. On the other side of the Golden Horn is Stamboul, the old city, while Scutari is on the opposite side of the Bosphorus. The view of the city from the water is wonderfully fine. The illusion vanishes when one is on the land. We had, as usual, our local guide who bespoke our favor by presenting the book of the Hon. S. S. Cox, in which his name appears. He was Dionysius of Ithaca, and in his directions we had entire confidence.

It has been very well said that there are four cities which belong to the whole world. One of them we had just left. Of course Rome is another, and Jerusalem, while Constantinople must be the fourth. If the reader is not perfectly familiar with the position of the city, let him turn to his map and see what an unrivalled place was chosen for it. It is on the highway between the Mediterranean and the Black Sea, between the continents, while it is defended by two narrow straits which can be readily fortified and easily held, with hills and lakes protecting it beyond its seas. It is the natural seaport for the vast extent of country which lies in every direction around its fine harbor. Chalcedon was said to have been founded by blind men, who could not see how much better was the other side of the Bosphorus. The city has had rich natural advantages. But when it is asked what it has done for the world, what great gifts it has conferred, we cannot answer as when the question relates to either of the three cities which are named with it. Greeks from Megara laid the foundation of Byzantium in 667 B. C. The Persians held the city for a time, till it entered the Athenian Confederacy and came with Athens under the Macedonians, and then under Rome. Constantine enlarged the place and called it New Rome. But the people called it for the Emperor. Till 1453 it was the eastern capital of the empire. Then the Turks became its possessors. Mohammed II. assaulted the city, and with his army forced his way into it over its defences, and drove the Greeks to St. Sophia, where women and children, old men and priests, had taken refuge. They trod down the fugitives, and the conqueror riding upon their fallen bodies entered the church, and struck his bloody hand high up against a column. The mark remains. That heavy red hand has crushed out the life of the people. The mad cry of the conqueror, with its eternal truth and eternal lie, has been darkness on the land, and the inspiration of cruel centuries. It is impossible to tell the population of the city. Estimates vary from five hundred thousand to nine hundred thousand. They are of many nationalities. Turks, Bulgarians, Armenians, Circassians, Greeks, Africans, Franks form the motley throng which moves through the streets. Perhaps one-half of the people are Mohammedans. These are united by their religious faith, and united in their hostility to all others. The other half have a variety of beliefs, but a common hatred of the Turks. The Turks fear the Christians, whom they associate with Russia and its intentions. The Christians feel that the Turks would be as willing as in other days to destroy them, if the word was given. The Turk knows the power of the Christian States to whose influence he is obliged to submit. The Christian as he walks by St. Sophia sees this sanctuary profaned by the infidel and recalls the slaughter of his brethren. With all these causes of division, there is nothing in the government to inspire respect, or in the national life to encourage public confidence. Meanwhile the position of the city gives it importance, and at once endangers and protects it. What the end will be, there is no prophet to declare. A change there must be, and a thorough one. It was with pride and thankfulness we saw that the best, most helpful, most promising institutions in Constantinople were American : — Robert College, the school at Scutari, and the Bible house with its printing-presses. The star in the west is rising with healing in its wings.

There is a modern look about Pera. The stamp of France is on it; on press, money, language, and manners. What is not Turkish, in the large sense, is French. We found some good streets and good shops. There were a few horses and carriages, but most persons trudged along in the middle of the street. We were looking for the native and his ways. Dionysius took us to the upper end of a tunnel through which cars ascend and descend. The force used is invisible. The trip lasts about three minutes, and is a great convenience. We were landed in Galata, below the high tower of the Gauls. This is the commercial part of the city, and is at the point where the Golden Horn and the Bosphorus meet. We made our way through the crowd to the bridge which is the chief thoroughfare between Pera and Stamboul. The bridge is said to rest on boats. It is a free use of the name. The boats are huge iron boxes which are anchored in their places. Upon these are planks, worn and broken with much travel till they make a very uneven road. A dense stream of men and women is constantly passing to and fro. Stretched in a line across the way, at each end of the bridge, are men in long white frocks who are kept very busy collecting the toll. They have to jump briskly from one person to another, but they miss nobody. There are beggars, too, who haunt the bridge, and with even more persistence, though with less reason and less success, seek tribute from the traveller. They whine, and smile, and pluck at your sleeve, and will not be denied, and are denied after all. They know the strangers, and devote their attention wholly to them.

After crossing the bridge we soon came to the bazaars. It is not easy to describe them. Let one think of a large market with its stalls, and extend it indefinitely, taking as many streets as he pleases into the enclosure, and he may have some idea of the general plan. Fill these countless stalls with goods of many descriptions, and the passages between them with an equal variety of people, and let the place be the scene of incessant bargaining, and he may get a faint picture of the bazaars. The ways are rough and dirty. There is nothing attractive besides the goods, but a lively interest is maintained as one moves from street to street, studying customs and costumes, and setting his money and wit against the wit and wares of the dealers. There is a system of classification which is convenient. Thus you have the druggists' bazaar, the goldsmiths', the silk-merchants', devoted to their special sorts of merchandise. The whole scene is novel and spirited, but there is seldom any rudeness, and no one seems surprised whether his goods are taken or refused. It is literally a place of trade. No one thinks of getting or giving the price which is asked for anything. The dealer names a price and negotiation begins. It is proper to offer anything, but not safe unless you are willing to be taken up. It needs a little hardening to make a good buyer. I was equal to considerable in the way of trade, but there was a line I could not cross. When I wished to make an extreme offer, from which my sense of propriety shrank, I resorted to Mr. Garry, who was fearless. The price would be five francs. "What do you want to give?" "I'll give one franc." "Let me have your money." Then taking the goods in one hand and the franc in the other he would push his hands alternately towards the astonished merchant, appealing to him all the while, "Which will you take?" It ended in his taking the franc, when the obliging broker would hand over the goods to me and the money to the merchant. I do not know what theory of philology Mr. Garry held. But he had facility in making himself understood, and was always willing to exercise his talent. He had learned something of colloquial German from living with Germans in Pennsylvania, and this served him well on some occasions. But he did nearly as well in Turkish and Arabic, and made up in patience and good-nature and pantomime what was lacking in language.

The usual difficulties of trade are complicated in Turkey by the state of the currency, if currency it can be called. I doubt if any but old residents are masters of even practical finance in Constantinople. I made several attempts to get a working knowledge of it, but never succeeded. I committed to memory tables of currency, but they always failed me when anything was to be paid for. I found out that forty paras made one piastre, which is about equal to twopence English. I find in my guide-book a pencil note in which I had calculated that twenty paras equal one-half a piastre; or a penny English. I know I was in a tight place when I made the reckoning. A pound sterling is one hundred and ten piastres; a Napoleon, eighty-seven and a half; a twenty-mark piece, one hundred eight and a half. Then we continually heard of bechliks, which are five piastres. Altogether confusion was confounded. I have not stated all the difficulties, nor can I. The names bewildered us. The Turkish franc was worth three-fourths of a piastre more than the French. The money of Roumania was at a discount, because the Roumanians had offended the Turks. The value of the piastre itself was uncertain. Thus a postage stamp was marked one piastre; but if you offered that coin more was demanded, on the ground that the stamp meant a gold piastre. There is no gold piastre, so that it was necessary to add the difference between gold and silver to the actual coin to make it equal to the imaginary one. There was only one solution of the difficulty, and that lay in an appeal to Dionysius. Either he was requested to pay for me and put it in my account, or I offered him such money as I had on hand and let him select what was necessary. In this unsatisfactory state we wandered about the streets, and roamed through the bazaars where everything could be bought, from a string of perfumed beads to a diamond necklace; from a pair of wooden shoes to a last year's dress from the Sultan's harem, rich in velvet and heavy with gold. There was variety in the methods of the merchants. Some were in their stalls, busy with their goods; some sat cross-legged waiting for the customers whom destiny might bring in their way; while others, more enterprising, came outside and with politeness and persistence invited the strangers to enter and examine their goods. But everybody was good-natured. Money-changers abound along the streets, but they keep a dear school in currency. There was a scarcity of change when we were in the city. I fancy it is a chronic trouble. It is a serious one. Not unlikely the ticket-seller at the railroad or steamer, who has you at his mercy, will refuse the money you offer, because he cannot give you change, or will enforce a discount which will make you careful the next time.

The mixed condition of things is somewhat increased by the two kinds of time which are kept. Civilized time is in common use, but you also find the Turkish, in which the day begins at sunset. They say that their style is the simpler, because no one can tell just when it is noon, but anybody can see when the sun sets. The daily paper publishes the time for the day, but I did not hear in what way the clocks are adjusted. It is well that the equanimity of the people is not easily disturbed.

I must name some of the things which are to be seen in Constantinople. It can be little beyond naming. Dionysius took us to the cistern of a thousand columns. I think that he overstated the number. But there were hundreds of them. It was a reservoir in its day. The Turks filled it up to the depth of nearly two-thirds of the length of the columns, and the place is dismal in its disused condition. We went to the tomb of the Sultans, or to the building which has that high-sounding designation. There is the tomb of Mahmoud II., the reformer, and of his sisters and daughters, and of his son Sultan Abdul Aziz. The tombs are handsomely decorated after the Turkish manner and are faithfully cared for. Mahmoud deserves the title of reformer, if he is judged in his own place. He improved roads, sent out ambassadors, enlarged the liberty of women, administered justice on an improved plan, but at the same time carried things with a high hand, and by his treatment of the officers of the realm, both in their person and their property, encouraged a perpetual revolt. It was a stormy time, full of perils. But it ended in 1839, and then followed the calm repose in which we found him, where marble and gold enshrine his dust. We passed into an older time when we entered the Hippodrome. The place is dreary enough. We saw no running horses. I believe there were two or three horses moving around over the sandy plain, but there was nothing exciting or alluring. The interest of the place is in its three columns. One of them is an obelisk from Egypt which is in good order and is like Egpytian obelisks in general. There is also the column of Constantine VII. with which time has dealt less kindly. But far the most important of the three is the serpentine column. It came from Delphi, and is a lonesome remnant of the pagan days. Three brazen serpents twisted together, without their heads, and carrying an old and weary look, and the mutilation which must come in twenty-three centuries of a naughty world, make up what has been called "probably the most remarkable relic that the world possesses." It may be so; but standing there, despoiled of its fair proportions, and separated from the environment of time and place which gave it meaning, it is not impressive. Not even its age can make up for that which it has lost. We saw another column in the city which has the merit of great antiquity. But it bears marks of time and violence and fire, and wears a pitiable aspect in the life of to-day.

The first days which we spent in Constantinople

belonged in one of the festivals, and many of the shops were closed. But enough were open, and the city was full of stir. We made our way into a large court-yard before a mosque, and found it nearly full of people engaged in holiday pursuits. Children were riding and swinging, and men were strolling about trying to be contented and to look at ease, and women were sitting on the steps and watching the crowd through their veils. The only disorder we saw was where a woman had removed her veil. The police appeared and commanded her to cover her face. They used the language of the police, which is the same in all countries. The woman refused. A crowd gathered and clamor began. Matters grew serious, and we waited to see what would come of it. There could be but one result. Threats prevailed, and the woman drew her veil over her unattractive beauty. Why call this absurd? It is the land of the absurd. Very little in Turkish usages does not suggest that idea to a traveller from the West. But shall not a country have its own customs? The veil but partially conceals the face of the wearer. Between the upper and lower folds may be seen the black eyes, which turn in curiosity towards the passing stranger. Nature will have her way. The women do not seem disturbed when a stranger looks at them, but the men regard it as a grave offence which they are quick to resent. Many of the dresses of the women are very showy. The contrast between the wearer and the garb are often very striking. It is amusing to see through the thin veil the face of a negress who gains by concealing her personality in the general attire of womankind.

It is a pity that the Turkish dress has been so much cast aside. French fashions have too far supplanted among the men what in the Orient at least is superior. If it had ended there, it would have been bad enough. But the young Turk has borrowed the vices of a nation whose virtues he has overlooked, and grafted them upon his own stock of weakness and wickedness. A company of persons of this sort is not a pleasant sight, or a hopeful one. The richer people, although claiming what rank there is, have less character and worse habits than the poor whom they despise and oppress. There is not much of the real Turk blood in the people, and the mongrel race which holds the ground now has little to commend it. If there is a future for Turkey it must come from without. There is no power of reform under the Crescent and the bloody hand. The years as they pass will bring in something for a land which has cast away its opportunities; for a people which has deserved a respectable government and a decent religion, and has had neither.

Constantinople is a walled city, that is the old part, Stamboul. The walls enclose all but that which lies along the Golden Horn. It had walls in Constantine's time. Theodosius built outside of these, and his walls were kept up till the Turks came into possession. The wall on the land side is stronger than that by the sea, being double, with a deep moat and large towers. Portions of the walls have fallen, and the marks of sieges and attacks are yet upon the stones.

IN AND ABOUT CONSTANTINOPLE. 245

As a defence they would be of small use. The government values them so little that it needed the interposition of the British Ambassador to save them from destruction. The Turks have taken the precaution to wall up a small gate in deference to a tradition that at some time a Christian army will come through, and they will be sent back to the places which they should never have left. There is a similar gate with a similar tradition at Jerusalem.

It is not easy to give any idea in words of the chief religious edifice of the city, the Church of St. Sophia. It was a Christian church before it sunk to a mosque. The building has kept its original character better than any other Christian church of the very early days. Constantine founded it, Justinian rebuilt it, Mohammed II. degraded it. The fourth, sixth, and fifteenth centuries have thus worked upon it. It has received some renovation in our own day. It was built of light bricks and lined with marble. Justinian brought eight porphyry columns from the ruins of Aurelius' Temple of the Sun, at Rome, for the adornment of this church and the support of its roof. Other columns were brought from the Temple of Diana at Ephesus, and from the Temple of the Sun at Baalbec, and from other famous eastern shrines. The church was of the highest type of oriental architecture. It is rectangular in shape, with a massive dome, one hundred and six feet in diameter, and very flat, so that it is hard to see what keeps it in its place. The walls and roof were resplendent with mosaics. The marble glittered with gold. Nothing of skill or cost was spared in the decoration. Prophets, bishops, and cherubim looked down into the sanctuary and added to its sacredness. Against all this the Turk protested, and when the church passed into his hands, some mosaics disappeared and others were covered with whitewash or plaster. They feared that the image might lead to idolatry. Through the thin covering the outlines of the figures can now be seen. Some of the mosaics have been copied. Much of the splendor has been lost. We read of the choir whose screens had silver columns and rails; and of the golden altar adorned with precious stones, and the high tabernacle of silver which was over it; and of the hangings embroidered with gold; and the pearls and gems which encircled the precious stones. This has passed away. But the house is there. The Mohammedans hung up texts from the Koran, and wrote others in massive letters about the dome; and below the dome they painted four archangels, or four groups of six wings as symbols of the beings whom no man has seen.

The whole effect of the sacred edifice is most impressive. Space, grandeur, unity appeal to the mind and heart. The history of the church enhances the impression. Here the Byzantine Emperors were crowned, and the Greek and Latin Churches were joined in a bond easily severed: and the last scene in the death of the empire was enacted, when the red hand and the red scimitar made the mark upon the pillar of stone. The false prophet has long held the house. But the old occupants are looking through the veil which was thrown over them, and we noticed that when the large cross was torn from the door the mark of it remained. It could be replaced in precisely its old position, even to the nails which kept it in its place. Some day it will go back, and the house will revert to the people from whom it was taken away, and be once more a Christian church.

When we came to St. Sophia we thrust our feet into commodious slippers, and then shuffled our way over the straw matting which covered the floor. Very few persons were in sight and we saw none of the worship. But we did mark the wonderful beauty which surrounded us and gazed with rare interest upon the roof, walls, pillars, the sacred texts and half-seen mosaics; the thrones of the preachers and the dignitaries of church and state, and the recess where the Koran is laid, and the places for the men who come to worship. We saw the square raised platforms where a family can gather for devotions, as we enter our pews and shut ourselves in. One column has the name of Helena. There is a small hole in it, and into this men put their hand and touch their eyes, that healing may come to them. We saw the process many times repeated, but perceived no benefit. Women, of course, do not attend the public services in the mosque, but sometimes they may be seen seated on the floor when there is no service, and sometimes a priest may be seen giving them appropriate counsel. All this will be improved when the cross is again on the door.

The interior of St. Sophia is very much finer than

that of any other mosque. They are usually very bare and dreary buildings. That which bears the name of Suleiman, or Solyman, the Magnificent, has a very fine exterior, much superior to that of St. Sophia, but within it is far below it, and it has much less historic interest. Its name is grand, as that of the great sultan who enlarged the power of the Ottoman Empire and advanced its literature and art. He was born about the time that Columbus discovered America. We admired his mosque, but were more interested in the mosque of Bajazet. Its court-yard was a busy place. There were letter-writers ready to put on paper the thoughts which others had but could not express. They were not doing much work just then. We were more pleased with the pigeons which resort to this yard to be fed. They came in large numbers, and flocked about those who had grain for them. They were regarded as sacred and were without fear. The service which they had rendered in a former generation was remembered to their advantage.

Dionysius took us through the Greek quarter. It was a long and tiresome walk over the rough streets. But he was patriotically bent on our seeing what related to his country and religion. There are twenty-one Greek churches reported in the old city, and the Greek patriarch has his seat there. We visited the Church or Cathedral of St. George. I suppose this is the St. George who has been honored as the patron of chivalry and held in special veneration in both the east and the west. It is impossible to trace his history. It ended in martyrdom, after an active and useful career. The dragon which he conquered was the symbol of pagan power which persecuted him. Soldiers have asserted a personal claim to him because the legends show him as a soldier. The Hellespont was once called St. George's Arm. I trust I am not giving the church to the wrong George. In the church are valuable treasures. The hand of St. Andrew is among them. There are the bodies of other saints. The throne and pulpit and book-chest of St. Chrysostom are there. Above the gate are the nails on which one of the patriarchs was hanged. I think he was a patriarch. The nails and the story are still there, if any one wishes to investigate the matter. One is less curious and critical in such affairs when he is on the ground, somewhat hurried and with a crowd of things to be seen and remembered. We saw the hole in the ground in which was laid the body of Constantine, the last of the Greek emperors. The grave is walled around, but has a neglected look. The Turk does not allow any care to be given to it, we were told. An old lantern hangs over it. Constantine deserved a better fate. He stoutly defended the city against the Turks in 1453, refusing all compromise, and when the walls were stormed he was killed. His body was found among a heap of his slain soldiers, and was recognized by the golden eagles which were embroidered on his shoes. Mohammed was generous enough to give the body an honorable burial, but the head had been cut off before this was done. There is a story that the head was sent as a trophy through Persia and

Arabia. It would not have been out of keeping with much that was done, but it is doubtful if this particular thing ever took place. Not far from the grave of the fallen emperor is a sort of iron cage in which is the grave of the man who killed him. He thought he was doing good service, but when the deed was done and confessed and proved, the conqueror had the man beheaded. There are some people whom it is very hard to please. It is a good old church, and has good right to the honorable place it holds in a city which the Greeks founded and lost, but may regain.

The Armenians and the Jews have their districts, but of these I will not speak. I must say a word of the Seraglio Palace, which is on the point where Stamboul pushes into the sea. This point is cut off from the rest of the peninsula by a wall. It was here, it is thought, that the earliest settlement was made. As you look at this point on the map, you think at once of the end of Cape Cod. But on the plan of the city, instead of Provincetown you see the summer harem. There the emperors lived in the early days, and the sultans after them, in a large fortress and palace, where cruelty could be concealed and crimes of every character be committed in safety. It was easy to sew in a sack any living obstacle, any officer who resisted, any favorite whose charms had fled, and to drop the bag from the walls into the sea which is long in giving up its dead. Fire has always had a large opportuuity in the city, and it has strewn the point with ruins. Something of the palace remains. A museum preserves in disorder monuments of art which have been brought from Asia Minor and the Isles of Greece. Utterly neglected, they form heaps of treasure. There is, also, the Church of St. Irene, the Holy Peace, which is a fine specimen of Byzantine architecture, though it has lost its true character, and is now a temple of war, with its walls adorned with swords and lances and rifles, while cannon with their balls rest idly on the consecrated floor. The beauty and honor of the place have departed, the shame has become inactive, the weapons are harmless; but the tall cypresses mark the spot, and draw to it the attention of the stranger, who asks what is there, and hears the tale of the changes which have been wrought for better and for worse.

I can say so little of all which should be said of this confused city that it matters little where I stop. There are hospitals, baths, schools, libraries, papers, but it does not seem worth while to write much about them. Some of the hospitals have provisions for Christians. The baths are for anybody who likes them. That there are many such persons is evident from the two thousand public places which are provided. We tried the Turkish bath in the home of it. We had the wetting, drenching, drowning, rubbing, warming, with a bed and a cup of coffee as a finale. I cannot call it agreeable. The attire of the boy who inflicted himself and the water upon us was extremely scant. But he did his work thoroughly. The effect was good. To have the process end was as good as any part of it. We could not then have left Turkey without this personal experience, but at another time we could do so.

Education is not in a flourishing condition in this city. It would be too perilous to all the institutions to have the people know anything. Reading and prayers are taught in the lower schools, and there are schools for adults. But the grade is low and will be kept so. The military schools are better, and there are other professional schools. The libraries belong to the mosques, and are of small service, though old manuscripts may be buried in them. What would be found in a small Western city, and would abound in a capital, cannot be seen in this metropolis. The government has no interest in such things, and the people make no demand for them. Hence there is a noticeable absence of museums, art-galleries, libraries, High Schools, and other marks and products of civilization. The reason is plain. Go back to St. Sophia and see again the mark of the red hand. Civilization is impossible under its palm, beneath its knuckles. It has no fondness for learning. Thought it dreads; life it crushes. It veils its women and blinds its men.

No one mentions Constantinople without speaking of its dogs. They are there. It would be an exaggeration to say that the streets are paved with them, but one keeps his eyes down as he walks. The dogs lie quietly and heavily where he would tread. He steps over them and they do not stir. He would not dare to kick them. The dogs might not care, but there are men who would resent such an innovation. It is hard to rouse the animals from their repose by any moderate suggestion with the foot. They are not handsome — far from it. They have all one look. They are useful as scavengers. Their fondness for bones is the relief of their owners. You cannot say that the streets are kept clean by them; but you do not see in the dirt anything that a dog could eat to advantage. I said owners. But private ownership does not prevail to any extent. The dogs are a public institution. They have their districts, like their betters. The dogs of any quarter are its defenders against all comers. A dog who ventures on the precincts of others is the common enemy. For the time being sleep is over, and the canine host advances on the intruder, who pulls down his flag and retreats.

The most evident sign of the life of the world which the city affords is the Tramway. Horse-cars in Constantinople have a modern look. I think the cars were taken from America. They run on a plan of their own. The intervals between their startings vary. They are fond of keeping together, so that you may see many when you want but one, and wait a long time before another group comes your way. They pass around the outside of the city and wander into the country. There are steam railroads also, which connect with Adrianopole and various other places. Steamboats are running to and from the city all the time. But the boats are old and poor, and we found too many passengers for our comfort. The Golden Horn is a great thoroughfare. The name is said to have been taken from the vast shoals of fish which came down from the Black Sea and were captured in these waters. The trade was so brisk and lucrative that the name "Golden" was set upon the horn of plenty. We found a motley collection of fellow-passengers whenever we journeyed where the fish used to come: Turks of many grades, and men of other nationalities; women in a place curtained off for their seclusion; beggars, of course; and once a ragged hermit, who was seeking alms. There was no conceivable reason for showing this last beggar any favor. Nothing in his person or his trade commended him, and he seemed aware of this. Superstition must have fallen lower than usual before it could encourage his peculiar style of rags and laziness. There are many objects of interest in a sail through the Golden Horn. We saw in the distance the place of the Sweet Waters; saw the ruined palace of Belisarius, whose victorious life had so disappointing an end. It is denied that in his last days he wandered a blind beggar through the streets of the city which had honored him aforetime. But he was impoverished, and he did spend in prison the most of his last year, because he had conspired, it was charged, against the life of Justinian. Nowhere are the vicissitudes of fortune more seen than in these eastern lands, where home and life are held by so slight a tenure. We passed, also, in the Golden Horn a showy building of brick and stone in which a Greek school is established. The building had an encouraging appearance, and gave signs of life. There are many wooden houses in the city and on the shores of the sea. The villages come to the very shores of the Bosphorus, as on the Swiss and Italian lakes. The street cries are very harsh and loud. But the people in general seem to be good-natured, either content with their lot, or in despair of improvement. Time and fate roll on together, and the people go with them.

But there are better things in this great city than these of which I have been speaking. The outer and truer world has begun to flow into the gates which have been reluctantly opened. Life and light are to be found where domes and minarets rise over darkness and death, striving to shut them in. We may well be grateful that American enterprise has found a place within and without the walls where it is working for the sake of the Name.

One morning we went on board a steamer at the old bridge, which is the common pier for the steamboats, and turned up the Bosphorus. We sailed past the Sultan's palace, whose long white front makes a fine appearance. It looks very pure without. We could not see what was within. We saw on the hill a smaller palace in which the Sultan was at that time residing. There were palaces for the Pashas, also, and an attractive building at the "sweet waters of Asia," which we were told was a summer resort for bathing and other recreation. It was a fine ride which we had over the winding course of the Bosphorus, among its rocky hills and quiet villages. We went up far enough to look through the entrance into the Black Sea and then turned back. On the return trip we left the steamer at Roumeli Hissar, the station from which Robert

College is reached. But we were far enough from the college itself, which we could see above us. We admired the sagacity of the founder who had built upon the hill. We knew that the view from the college must be fine, for the large stone edifice had a very commanding site. We soon began to doubt the sagacity of the founder, as we toiled wearily up the steep and rough path to the classic grounds. When we were in the college grounds, there was still an ascent to be made before we reached the building. We thought that the hill of learning must yield excellent and abundant fruit to attract students. But the climb brought its usual reward. The view was, — but my adjectives were long ago exhausted. Say it was extensive, superb, magnificent, not to be excelled by any school in the world. We looked down on the Bosphorus and far away beyond it. We looked back upon the city and the waters which enclose it. The eye wandered from height to height, finding everywhere something to admire. Below the hill were the old towers of Mohammed II. with others on the opposite shore. This is the narrowest part of the Bosphorus, and from this point boats were carried by Mohammed over the land and launched in the Golden Horn. If the towers could but have followed the builders! Below the hill, again, on the city side, could be seen the modest building of the Bebek Seminary, where good work was formerly done by American missionaries. The building of Robert College is large and substantial. It seems strong enough for a fortress, and its massive stone walls could stand a siege.

This appearance was enhanced by the iron gratings at the windows, which are very strong in the lower story. There have been times when the need of these bars was felt, and no one can tell when Mohammed may come up the hill, and discarding his old towers, assault the citadel which imperils the tyranny and cruelty and ignorance which are dear to his heart. He was very unwilling to have the college built. First, land was promised. Then came weary years of waiting. Negotiation yielded nothing. Permission to build could not be obtained. Lay this book aside, and read the story of the college told by the only man who knows it. Cyrus Hamlin, the learned scholar, the ingenious mechanic, the man of inventions, the devoted missionary; wise to teach, skilful to devise, patient in waiting; who could give to the people whom he had sought the bread of life, and at the same time feed them and the English army of the Crimea with bread; whose genius and courage stood guard around the impoverished Christians, while he planned the deliverance of the land; whom no duplicity could deceive, and no obstacles discourage;—his name and deeds deserve the renown which attends them wherever they are known. A boatload of bread for the army brought the missionary into connection with Christopher Robert, and out of that meeting sprang the college which bears the name of the New York merchant. The timely arrival of Admiral Farragut and his fleet, and a question quietly asked at the Sultan's table by the American sailor, secured the permission which had been waited for in vain, and at length the walls of stone towered over the Bosphorus. There are times when the American flag floats from its lofty staff. The Turk does not like to see it there. But the late American minister said that if any serious objection was made he would have an office in the building, which would keep the flag of his country over the American college of Turkey.

The building is constructed around a square court, and on the sides of this are the rooms for the students and for the officers who live in the college. At the time of our visit there were two hundred and seventeen students. There were twenty-five or thirty Protestants among the students. The students are of various nationalities, but the Turk rarely is found among them. The language of the college is English, but instruction is given in fourteen other languages. Latin is required, and Greek taught without being required. The students were reported as very ready in learning from text-books and lectures, but lacking in those qualities of mind and character which come from constant intercourse with thinking people. They have not been trained to observe and discuss; to read the papers, and to have an active interest in public affairs. They come to college without this sort of discipline which the youth of America have from their childhood. Time will change this in some measure. The college is doing excellent work, and in many directions. The results are very encouraging. A broad Christian training is given; and this lasts, and repeats itself when the students have gone out to their work. The appointments of the college are good, but should be much better. It was fairly pitiful to look at the lean library shelves and the starved cases of apparatus for scientific study. There is a fine chance to invest money, if any one wishes to give for Christian manhood, for civilization and liberty. President Hamlin is now in America, where he has just closed a useful college presidency. But President Washburn will carry forward the grand work which has been so finely begun, and widen its proportions, and in this will have the devoted service of his associates. Let me ask the reader again to lay aside this book long enough to draw a check in favor of Robert College, Constantinople. Thus I put my small boat-load of bread where some large-hearted man may come.

Another day we crossed the Bosphorus and landed at Scutari. Some of the party wished to see the ground where the English soldiers who died in the Crimean war were laid. I preferred to see life, and, under the guidance of an American young lady whose delight it is to teach in Turkey what she learned in New England, I went to the Girls' School, which is more commonly known as the Constantinople Home. The school is in fine buildings which belong to the Woman's Board of Missions, and they are finely situated where they look over the Bosphorus and the Sea of Marmora and up the Golden Horn. A hundred and thirty girls, or about that number, were found to be connected with the school. The teachers are young ladies, Americans, who have a little help from non-resident masters. The scholars are Bulgarian, Armenian, a few Turkish, and a few are from English and American families. After graduation many become teachers, thus extending the influence of the school. The appointments are modern and homelike, such as might be found in the schools of our own country. The girls assist in the domestic work, which is of especial advantage to them, and will be felt in their homes. The dormitories are arranged for four, six, eight, twelve scholars. A girl would be lonely and homesick if she were put in a room by herself or with only one companion. But each girl has a closet, three or four feet square, in which she can keep her personal treasures, and secure retirement when she desires it. The customs of the country are regarded so far as it is expedient. The girls would hardly know what to do with the pitcher and bowl which are found in our chambers. But as a substitute for water poured over the hands they hold their hands under a long pipe which has numerous faucets, and thus combine ancient usage and modern conveniences. The scholars are fond of music and carefully instructed in it. The whole aim is to make them intelligent, refined, Christian women, who shall brighten the homes in which woman has been allowed to do so little, and shall thus enlighten the land.

The ladies in charge of the school spread their table for us, and we had the great pleasure of breaking bread with them in their own house — an American home in a strange land. I have brought no more pleasing picture from the East than that which is clear in my mind as I write — that cheerful room with its wonderful outlook: the fair table and its hospitality; the simple elegance, the sweet serenity, the earnest temper, the ministering spirit, the inspired hope, and, best of all, the American women themselves, who in their youth, the days of their gladness, when the years were lying at their feet, have carried their life where it will become life for other women, and make the name and the grace of Him who was born of woman familiar to the ear and precious to the heart. The young lady of whom I first spoke had been a teacher in the school at Scutari, but had left it that she might engage in missionary work at Stamboul. We saw her in her new home, the house of Mrs. Schneider, so long and so well known in connection with the missions in Turkey. She was engaged when we were there in what we should call city missionary work. With her assistants she was holding a Sabbath-school in her own home, which was attended by two hundred scholars, of various ages, who were interested in the effort which was made for them. The teaching was in several languages and was followed with good results. Besides this was the work for individuals and families, so far as these could be reached. So long as it is with extreme peril that a Mohammedan becomes a Christian, the direct and open influence of the mission must be restricted. But the work is well planned and must continue to prosper. It was a real pleasure to come so near to so good an enterprise. I cannot refrain from expressing the delight we had in seeing in Constantinople that Yankee institution, the Doughnut. It was refreshing to partake of this missionary bounty and the cup of tea which was given with it. The room we sat in has a very cheery look as I recall it — a bit of home in a very unhomelike place.

At the front of mission work in Turkey is the Bible House in Constantinople. It is a large building, substantial and plain, with a look of permanence and enterprise upon it. We found it the scene of an earnest life. Its printing-presses were busy, and the work of publication going forward with great zeal. It is furnishing a Christian literature for Turkey. School-books and religious books and papers in different languages are constantly sent out. Its book-room is like an armory, furnished with many kinds of weapons for the overthrow of iniquity — weapons which will work surely and steadily, if they make little noise. The men who administer the affairs of this institution are diligent and alert, well qualified for the difficult work intrusted to them, and patiently carrying it forward. When we were there they had received some encouragement through opposition. A Turkish newspaper had been printing a series of violent articles against Christianity, and these had been collected in a book. I saw the book, but had not time to read it. I must not say much of its contents, lest the erudition should be revamped here and put upon the market. But, among other things, the learned writer said that Saul of Tarsus wished to marry Gamaliel's daughter, and, when the course of true love did not run smoothly, became vexed and turned Christian; and that Paul and Peter quarrelled so much that the emperor was pained in his heart and put them both to death; that Luther sold indulgences until Tetzel undersold him, when he became a Protestant. I need not multiply these fragments of history. They interested the people. The sale of Bibles increased for a short time. One of the missionaries seized the occasion to prepare an account of Christianity, which the same paper published, adding comments by way of counteraction. Perhaps not much came of this movement; but it is suspicious on the one side, and hopeful on the other, when a man begins to read. If a Turk should really begin to think, who can say what might not come to pass? The fear of the Turks is both amusing and suggestive. De Amicis' book on Constantinople was not only seized at the Custom House, but burned. There is a natural and wholesome fear of hymns. People might learn to sing if they did not learn to read. Hymns with "king" and "kingdom" in them are condemned. "Hold the Fort" aroused the fears of one magistrate. "The children are gathering from near and from far" has been condemned. But not hymns alone are watched. There was an innocent Sabbath-school book on conquering giants, and, though the giants were of a moral or immoral character, the word had to be changed to "spiritual enemies." A man published a series of fables, one of which brought in the *ignis fatuus*, which he called the "star bug." The sultan's palace is known as the "star palace," and this story was regarded as a reflection upon him and his residence. They told me a story of a safe which remained in a part of the wall of an old building which had been destroyed. It had not been used for a long time, and the key could not be found. The police were alarmed. They demanded the lost key, but it was in vain. In vain was the assurance that there was nothing in the safe. Who knew that? They would see. Police and soldiers and workmen gathered, and an admiring group of spectators, to uncover the treason. It was a long job; but at last the door was forced open, and something was found in the safe — an old umbrella and a pair of overshoes. Then the laugh went round, and the chaffing. These are small things, but they manifest the constant fear of the government. No one can be trusted. A perpetual watchfulness is the price of tyranny. From the sultan to the beggar no man can count upon life or liberty, to say nothing of the pursuit of happiness. Uneasy lies the head which is under the red hand.

We attended one service at the Crimean Memorial Church. It is a fine house. A hundred persons were present. The service was restful and pleasing, though for the most part its words could not be distinctly heard. Fortunately, we knew the most of them by heart. The American flag was there, and that is always a good thing to look upon. Here, then, I close these rambling notes on Constantinople — with an English church, with memories of the Crimea, and under the American flag. They all mean life. It will come. The crescent is very thin. By and by it must change and grow wider and then wider, till the full, round moon looks down upon the Bosphorus and silvers the waters of the Golden Horn.

# CHAPTER VIII.

#### FROM CONSTANTINOPLE TO DAMASCUS.

ON Thursday the 18th of October we were taken to the steamer *Oreste*. Some of the ships of the Austrian Lloyds had been detained by the quarantine, so that one of the smaller steamers was put on this route for this voyage. It was an unfortunate time for the substitution. Many of the people of these regions, who had been driven northward through fear of cholera, chose to return in this steamer. The result is evident. The ship was crowded to the last degree. When we went on board, the upper deck was in possession of the natives. They were settling into their places, and seemed likely to leave no place for any one besides. We gained a foothold in one corner and waited. Strange faces and costumes crowded about us, and strange voices added to the confusion. After a time the Moslems were huddled together on one side of the deck, and the other side was given up to us, while a fence separated the two parties. Our neighbors were only women and children. For the most part they spent their days and nights in the same place. The men were quartered on the deck below, and some women and children were with them. It was always an interesting episode to watch the arrival of the families of the country, as we had frequent opportunities of doing. They came with huge bundles of bedding, and with provisions for the passage. They found as good situations as they could, using as much care as more favored voyagers employed in securing state-rooms. A pile of boxes or a row of barrels offered a desirable site for a home; or the elevated hatchway, which had the disadvantage of instability, as the family had to move whenever the hold was opened; or a more or less protected place under the lee of the high rail or the friendly house. In some selected if not sequestered spot housekeeping was carried on. In fine weather there was a reasonable amount of comfort. When showers came up, an awning was spread for protection, but the quarters lost the attractiveness they had in the warm sunshine. The scene was novel and picturesque, and we enjoyed watching the separate families as they prepared their coffee at their little fires, and at night as they made ready to encamp, or as the dim lantern cast its feeble light on the slumbering groups. The men passed their time in smoking, playing cards, and eating, as the slow hours moved on. Now and then those who were separated from their households would come up to our deck bringing water, and offering to the women such attentions as circumstances required and permitted. The women sat in stolid silence all the day, smoking cigarettes, and staring out over the sea, while their vacant faces gave no sign of life or thought. There was one little family of a better appearance than the rest.

The mother had a fairly intelligent face, and the daughter was actually pretty and spoke French. They had a cabin by night, and camped out by day with their less favored sisters, in their regard for their national customs and the religious principles which kept them apart from the people over the fence. We were told that this was the family of some official at Jerusalem. We should have been more than glad to have some intercourse with our neighbors, but barriers of language and still more insurmountable barriers of race and religion made this impossible. We could only look on, so far as propriety and timidity allowed, and do such thinking as was appropriate. There was sufficient stillness save when the children cried in the notes and tones of the common humanity. We had a good opportunity for studying the looks and manners and customs of the people, and in this we were more than repaid for any inconvenience caused by their presence on the ship.

We were less fortunate in another part of our freight. At Constantinople we received thirty-two oxen, who had been brought from Odessa in another steamer. They were afflicted with the cattle disease, and had suffered on their previous voyage, so that to all appearance they were dead when they were hoisted aboard our ship, by a rope fastened around the roots of their horns. It was a painful and disgraceful sight, but not an unfitting souvenir of the country and its government. Most of the poor creatures completed their dying in a day or two, and the rest were killed, and all were thrown into the sea. The process, often repeated, broke the monotony of the long days.

At the Dardanelles we were visited by the usual fleet of boats. The scene was less imposing than in the days when Xerxes joined the continents with his bridge of boats, perhaps less exciting than when the bold swain swam from Abydos on his visits to Hero. Ours was a less romantic spectacle. If a confusion of voices makes a Babel, this site would have answered for the tower. Words rose perilously near to fights, without quite reaching them. There was a humble traffic in fish, fruit, bread, and pitchers, carried on by men and boys on the one part, and by our housekeeping passengers on the other part.

On Saturday we entered the magnificent harbor of Smyrna, and came to a stop near the fine quay. The large city is mostly on the plain between Mount Pagus and the sea, with a portion of its houses stretching up the slope of the hill. The history of the place is interesting, but it need not be recited here. It was probably settled by Greeks, and it was one of the cities of the Ionian league. It has had its full measure of vicissitudes. It has been destroyed by war, thrown down by earthquakes, and ravaged by fire. But it has risen again and again, and is now a very large city. The books do not seem to know how many inhabitants it has, but we were told there are two hundred and twenty thousand. Its situation is quite sure to keep the place large and flourishing. The Christians have so large a preponderance of the population that the Turks call the place the Giaour-city, or Dog-town in our vernacular. Here was one of the seven churches named in the Revelation, and the message sent to it then announced the tribulation which was to come. In that letter are the words which have given so much of fortitude to suffering souls in many generations: "Be thou faithful unto death, and I will give thee the crown of life." Polycarp, the disciple of St. John, was bishop here, the man who answered the pro-consul who would have him curse the Christ whom he served, — "Six and eighty years have I served Him, and He has done me nothing but good; and how could I curse Him, my Lord and Saviour! If you would know what I am, I tell you frankly, I am a Christian." He would not let them fasten him to the stake, but amid the fires calmly witnessed to his faith.

I have spoken of the large number of Christians. It is not to be inferred that they are a vigorous religious force. There are, however, vigorous Christians here, who are quite worthy of the place into which they have entered. Again it is the West casting its life into the East, and holding up its light. There is a fine stone church, built by our American Board, where services are held every Sunday in Turkish and Greek. There is a flourishing girls' school connected with the church. Smyrna is fortunate in having the enterprise and devotion of George Constantine. He is a Greek, as his name suggests. He was born in Athens, but he graduated at Amherst in 1859 and at Andover in 1862. After preaching in his native city for eighteen years, he went to Smyrna in 1881. He was still to work for his own people. In a conspicuous place on the quay is the Smyrna Rest, a place where the stranger can rest, can find books and papers, and wholesome food, and, better than all these, a friend. Over this house Mr. Constantine presides, with his active assistants. There are times when the business is so good that the resources of the establishment are taxed to their utmost. I heard an amusing account of the arrival of an English man-of-war with troops from Egypt. The strangers made an inroad on this house and demanded eggs and other edibles with such extravagance that they seemed likely to create a famine in the land, certainly in the city by the sea. The minister and all became waiters and sent away their good-natured guests satisfied with their entertainment. On the walls of the pleasant "Rest" are Scripture verses, which are the more impressive because they are in Greek. Among them is the sentence already quoted, first written for Smyrna, — "Be thou faithful unto death." Near the "Rest" is a commodious chapel where Mr. Constantine preaches and teaches. He has also the Greek service in the stone church. No mention of this man would be complete which did not pay its tribute of respect to the noble American woman who bears his name and shares his abundant labors.

Smyrna in some ways resembles Constantinople, though on a small scale. The streets are narrow and dirty, though less so than in the larger capital. There are bazaars on the same general plan as those which have been described. They are, of course, much less rich and interesting, but the prices are more stable. Not much is taken off from the sum first named. Trade is, therefore, far less exciting. The narrow streets were encumbered with strings of camels tied one to another; often the driver, or master, preceded the line upon a donkey. This last useful animal presented himself for our patronage, or, more accurately, his owner presented him. The donkey is a serviceable though tantalizing beast. He seems always to have a grudge against somebody. Discontent lies in the curve of his humble back and clings to his bristling mane. He seems bent on a persistent revenge. His favorite device is to grind his rider up against a wall of stone or plaster, as if he would rub him into it. I understand now the verse in Numbers which tells us that the "ass thrust himself unto the wall, and crushed Balaam's foot against the wall." I know how Balaam felt when "he smote him."

For occasional variety the donkey is pleased if he can find a shutter of the lower story of a house hanging out over the street. He will insist on going under it that he may strike his rider's head against the blind. I once had a donkey try the same experiment under the low branch of a tree. I saw my approaching fate, but no persuasion or force could change his purpose. Under the limb he went, and the helmet I chanced to be wearing took the blow he meant for my head. The donkey is larger in the East than with us, and his saddle is needlessly high. The rider is perched on an insecure place. I have known the saddle to slip because the girth was not tight, and the helpless rider, with nothing to which he could cling for support, could only roll ignominiously to the ground. It was not very far, but it is humiliating to fall from a donkey.

Our one ride in Smyrna was to the summit of Mount Pagus, where are the remains of a Macedonian and Crusaders' castle. Little is left except the walls. The ruins were more interesting than they would have been a few weeks later, when we had learned to think of the crusades as of modern times. The view from the hill was remarkably fine. We looked down on the new city and on the plain where the old city was, — for here, as at Athens, the new is not in the place of the old. We saw the bay and its winding shore, and the ships in the harbor of this important seaport. We looked on the old aqueduct, and the railroad to Ephesus. Then we came down, passing in our descent the tomb of Polycarp. From his lofty grave, if tradition can be relied on, he still watches the city which he loved and for which he lived.

Our stay was too brief. In the middle of the afternoon we were moving out from among the ships of the harbor. It was Saturday. As the week ends, let me pause long enough to mention a few of those who were sailing with us. One was Mr. Karey, or El Karey, an Arab, and a Christian missionary at Nablus. He had been in England and was returning with his wife and her sister to his home. Another was Mr. Greenlee, a young man who had devoted his life to the missionary service, and was on his way to Zahleh, where he was to begin his work. He was a man of fine spirit and manly bearing; one sure to have the success that crowns intelligent endeavor. Of three others I must speak, because we were companions in the journey to Jerusalem. There is no reason why I should not give their names, except that they might not like the public mention. I will call one Mr. Browning. He was an Episcopal clergyman from our West. He was always dignified, courteous, well informed, and most appreciative of all we saw. Mr. Logan was a Congregational clergyman, a bold rider, a strong swimmer, a good singer; making the best of everything and helping others to do the same. Mr. Keil was a German who had made his home in America; a decorative artist; a man of good taste and a generous temper; a genial comrade, who did more to make us merry than any one besides. These three men had drifted together. A common purpose to see Jerusalem was keeping them in company. They had not proposed to ride through the country. But they found that this was our plan, and that they could join us, so they cast in their lot with us and we were thenceforth one party. Add Mr. Mill, Mr. Garry, and the boy, and you have the whole of us. But we were not formally organized till we reached Beirut.

Sunday, October 21. In the night we stopped at Scio, or Chios. This morning we passed Samos. There is rare beauty in these Grecian islands and rare interest in their story. But it was of far more worth to us to pass near to Patmos. We had the island in sight for a long time, and were able to see it from many points. I had thought of it as rugged and desolate. More than once have I spoken of it as a rock in the Ægean. We saw a long, low island, quite green, but showing no trees. This was certainly its appearance. But I have seen it described as "an irregular mass of barren rock twenty-eight miles in circumference." We could see the houses of a village, with one large building, an old monastery, which shelters some fifty monks. In the days of the Roman emperors this was a place of banishment, and thither St. John was sent by Domitian. It was there he received the Revelation whose record closes our New Testament. The cave is now pointed out in which the vision of things to come was given to him. It was with an absorbing interest that we looked upon this quiet island in the light of the Lord's Day. We looked into the sky which was over him, and out on the waters where rested his weary eyes, — the waters which parted him from all which he held dear. It was in the vision of the world to come that "there was no more sea." Weariness and loneliness would be forever in the past. It was good thus to enter a little way into his life and to think his thoughts after him. I was glad to read his words, "I John your brother, . . . was in the isle that is called Patmos . . . I was in the spirit on the Lord's Day . . . I heard behind me a great voice, saying, What thou seest write in a book, and send it . . . unto Smyrna." The hours when we were near Patmos were among the best which are written in this book. It was a quiet Sabbath at sea. We communed with our own thoughts, and one with another. We sang our hymns, in which the English ladies held a prominent part. I shall never hear "Beulah land: sweet Beulah land," without recalling those hours among the Greek islands. It seemed fitting that we should have a religious service, as we had so many ministers. We consulted the captain, who readily gave us the use of the saloon. The steward added his consent. All seemed to be going on well, when the captain appeared and said that we could have the service, but must have no singing. The reader thinks that he did not like our style of singing. But that was not the trouble, for he said that we might sing on deck. We sent a committee to assure him that we were not the Salvation Army, but very quiet and well behaved people, and to ask the poor privilege of lifting up our voices in song. The captain was firm. He said he had already granted a large favor. We might pray all we pleased, and sing on deck; but sing in the saloon we should not. Why? Some persons might wish to converse; praying would not disturb them, but singing would. We should oblige him by having no singing, as he had already done what he had no right to do in giving the room to us. There was no appeal. We had found the one point on which official authority would assert itself for the comfort of passengers. We went below, read from the first chapter of Revelation, had our prayers and a brief address, and thus wound up the day. About nine in the evening we anchored off the island of Rhodes. It was too late to land, but we saw the lights of the city, and the place was pointed out on which the Colossus stood. Boats came off to the steamer and there was the usual clamor. Then all was still and we sailed on into the night.

We came to anchor before Cyprus, at Limasol, and again at Larnarka, where the European consuls and merchants reside. These are the chief commercial cities. We expected to go on shore. But the captain was in an unamiable state of mind and would not promise us even an hour. He could not say how long he should remain. He waited about five hours, but we had only the satisfaction of looking at the island which has held so good a place in history. The island is very long, and we could see the mountains towering in their long ranges back of one another. The houses appeared to lie along the shore, but really reached back for some distance. Two minarets were in sight and some trees. There was nothing to remind one of St. Paul, but it was natural to recall the incident described in the thirteenth chapter of the Acts, and to think of the blinded sorcerer and the astonished and believing pro-consul.

On Wednesday morning, October 24, Mt. Lebanon was in sight. But the light was dazzling and the mist was lying heavily on the hills, so that we could not see the snow or the cedars. We sailed into the majestic and beautiful harbor of Beirut, and could then see the high mountains and the snow which adorns their summit. Few places are so fine to look upon as the harbor of Beirut, with its background of mountains. The boats came off, and in one of them we saw a gentleman who was pointed out to us as Howard. The name we knew. We had grown familiar with it, as we had looked forward to a journey through Syria. Alexander Howard is the grand dragoman of this country. He is an Arab, was educated in England, has visited America, and is in a large way a man of the world. He has hotels at Latrûn and Jaffa, and all the equipments for camp life. We had fairly touched the East when we took his hand. We were soon in a boat and on our way to the shore. There was an older and smaller man than Howard in the boat. He was dark, with a shrewd but pleasant face, and bright eyes behind his spectacles. This was Ibrahim Mordecai, who was to be our special dragoman. He was a Jew born in India, long a resident of Jerusalem, at one time an apothecary, and now one of Howard's lieutenants. We landed on the rocks and were escorted to the Hôtel d'Orient, close upon the sea. We were hardly established in our rooms before the American consul sent for us. We answered his summons and were told that a complaint had been made to him that a company of Americans had landed without passports. It was a critical hour for the Turkish Empire, or at least for some of its officials. The consul did not hesitate to assure us that the sole object of the complaint was to extort money from us. We easily satisfied him and were dismissed. The next day our passports were called for. They gave satisfaction, and as there was no hope that anything else would be given, no more obstacles were put in our way.

Beirut has a long and eventful history. Like every place of consequence in this part of the world, it has passed through many and violent changes. The Phœnicians have the credit of building it. The Romans captured it. The Moslems took it from their hands and twice gave it over to the Crusaders. The Druses held it for a time, and were succeeded by the Egyptians, who were driven out by the English, who gave the city over to the Turks. It was here that St. George killed the dragon, and his name has been given to the bay which is the best place for anchorage on this coast. The city has, perhaps, eighty thousand people, about one-third of whom are Mohammedans. Christians, Druses, Jews make up the rest. After the massacre at Damascus many Christians found a new home at Beirut. The place has become the commercial centre of northern Syria. The Christians, especially, are industrious and enterprising. The climate is fine. The heat, which is seldom oppressive, is tempered by the sea breezes. Many of the Europeans pass the months of summer upon the mountains. The old town has not much which is attractive. The streets are narrow and rough, and the houses are closely huddled together. But a little out of the old district the streets are wider, and in the suburbs fine modern buildings are found on sites of remarkable beauty. There is nothing of special interest in the bazaar, which has lost much of its oriental character. Nothing which we found among the shops solaced and refreshed us so much as the stands for lemonade. I recall one booth in an open square, with its inviting array of many-colored syrups. In the centre rose a long spike of iron and on this was a block of ice.

When we called for lemonade, the man poured syrup into a glass and then with a knife scraped ice into it, and gave a delicious drink which was most refreshing. It does not seem much in the telling; but as recollection carries me to the warm days of Beirut and to the weary streets, the cool flavor of that eastern beverage comes back to me, a reviving memory of the Orient.

The most encouraging and creditable things in Beirut are the Christian schools. This is the centre of the missionary work of our Presbyterian Church. The mission was established fifty years ago. On the hill at the south of the city is the college, with its preparatory schools and its schools of medicine and theology. The buildings are large and substantial. That which is devoted to theology is very imposing with its white walls and marble floors. No seminary in the world can be more beautiful for situation. From these seminaries men go out to help and save their land, carrying what they have learned to those who have sore need to receive it.

In the town is the large mission church, and near it the Bible house with its printing-office and bookstore. Very near is the large girls' school, the Beirut female seminary. We had a very pleasant visit at the school. The accomplished lady who is at its head was very kind to us, showing us all which we wished to see and answering our numerous questions. We saw the girls together and heard them sing "Hold the Fort," in Syriac words. On the chapel wall was a characteristic picture, of the maid who came to the wife of Naaman the

Syrian with her report of the prophet who was in Samaria. The picture was well chosen. The girl and the girls' school are to enlighten Syria with the good news first heard in Israel. It has the deepest significance, the educating of girls in the East. It means a noble womanhood, the home and the home-life, the coming of the day when they that sit in darkness shall see the great light.

I should enlarge this account of Christian work in Beirut by the British Syrian schools, and the schools and orphanages of the French and Germans. The massing of Christian institutions at this point shows the importance of the place in its relation to the whole land on whose coast it stands, facing the West. One is impressed with the grandeur and stability of missionary work when he finds it thus established in permanence and strength. The whole endeavor long ago passed from the period of experiment and is now wisely and stoutly bent upon enlargement until its work is accomplished.

Our stay in Beirut could not be prolonged. In this brief sketch I have brought together two visits which we made. Our eyes were on the interior. But before we started on our long ride it was said to be expedient that we should try our horses. I am by no means sure that this was the design of an excursion which we made to Dog River, called by the Greeks Wolf River. There is a legend that once a dog cut in stone stood by the river and barked when an enemy approached. A portion of the statue is pointed out, where it has fallen into the sea.

On Thursday morning the horses were brought in

front of the hotel that we might make our personal selection. That was not difficult, though there were elements of uncertainty in the choosing. The matter of saddles entered into the experiment, as some of the horses had the ordinary English saddle, and others that of the army pattern. To the horse which fell to my lot I gave the name of Prince, from his resemblance to a horse at home who bore that title. When we were mounted trouble began. The horses were restless and frisky, and careered wildly in the narrow street. The more we pulled and shouted, the more they dashed about. The confusion was increased by the comments of bystanders and by the counsel of the grooms who were in charge. They knew but little English, but they knew their horses and they saw our difficulty. Madly screaming "Slack bridle! slack bridle!" they at last persuaded us to give the steeds their liberty, when they were as quiet as well behaved horses ought to be. We had no serious results, save that Mr. Browning pulled his horse to his hind legs and then gracefully or ungracefully slid into the street, to the amusement of the crowd. The poor man lost off his glasses, which were promptly appropriated by somebody to whom they did not belong. Another horse was provided for the unlucky rider, who would not be persuaded to mount to his former place. He was a loser by the exchange, as his second horse was much inferior to the first. The amount of protest which the good man lavished on the new beast before we reached Jerusalem cannot here be stated. At length we were ready, and with slackened bridles we rode slowly in a long line through the streets of Beirut into the open country. I shall not linger on the ride, which had nothing of marked interest about it, except that it was the beginning. We went over part of an old Roman road, and lunched at a khan. This we were to do many times afterwards. There was some riding which then seemed rough. It was nothing in comparison with that which we were to find. There are in the face of the cliff at whose side we rode and walked nine old sculptures, of which three are Egyptian and six Assyrian. Not much is known of these curious works, which represent gods and kings. They stand in the desolation, a reminder of days which have gone. It is strange that so little remains of the times which were crowded with great events.

We were all tired when we reached our hotel. No one seemed to think that we had gained much by our long ride to Nahr el-Kelb. But it gave us one day's trial of the life into which we were entering. Friday morning, October 26, we made our real start. It was rather an imposing affair. We had about twenty-one beasts in our caravan, horses and mules with a donkey or two. There were nine or ten men besides the tourists proper. We had five tents, with the appointments for a three weeks' ride. Howard rode with us the first day, to see that everything was properly arranged. The first stage of the journey was to end at Baalbec. We rode about sixteen miles, and then rested and lunched at a khan. Nine miles more finished the day. Our ride up the slopes of Lebanon was extremely fine. The views were magnificent as we looked down into the valley and far out over the blue waters of the Mediterranean. We had a good view of the mountains of Anti-Lebanon and the rich plains of Cœle-syria, with Hermon in the distance. It was a delightful ride, and gave us much encouragement for our long pilgrimage. As we came down the hill above Mexy we saw our tents for the first time. It was a charming sight, especially after a day of so great pleasure. Our camp equipage had preceded us, and the tents were awaiting us. Three of these were to be our houses, one was the dining tent, and another the kitchen. They made a pretty group. From the three in which we were to live floated the stars and stripes. The flag never looked better to us than when we saw it in a strange land, floating in the evening light under a clear sky. A camel-camp was near us, but everything was still. We took possession of our tents very quickly, enjoying the novelty and excitement. An excellent dinner was soon ready for us. We had a good talk with Howard, who told us many things of interest, and marked out the daily life we were to lead. Thus ended our first day's ride in Syria.

This way of journeying, travelling on horseback and living in tents, has been reduced to a science, and Alexander Howard is a master in it. In this part of the world, as I have before said, it is necessary to travel in parties, and under the charge of some one who knows the country and the people, their language and customs, and is provided with all the needful appliances. To travel in any other way would be difficult, and at times would be perilous. Very much depends on the character and disposition of those with whom one is thus thrown into close relations. But in a journey of this kind through Palestine, it is more than likely that the members of a party will be reasonably intelligent and considerate. It was certainly so with those who were set in our company. Our diversities increased the interest and advantage of our journey. We were all amiable, and each one contributed his portion to the common stock of comfort and happiness. Our arrangements were very much the same for our days of riding. We were called very early, even while it was dark, and were no sooner out of our tents than they lay upon the ground, to be at once put on the backs of mules, with our luggage. Of luggage we had as little as would serve our purpose. Mr. Garry was the most encumbered, as he had a leather trunk. But this was a public convenience. If anything was to be carried which was in danger of being broken, there was room for it in the trunk. I had a distinct bargain, by which Mr. Garry should carry a bottle of ink which I had bought at Dr. Lorange's in Beirut, and in return should have the free use of the same in his correspondence. The breaking-up process in the dim morning light, the loading up, the unloading and resettling at night, were the daily events in which we were all concerned.

Soon after we were out-of-doors, breakfast was served, and as soon as possible after that we were on our horses. This gave us the cool hours of the morning for the greater part of our ride. About noon we stopped, sometimes at a khan and sometimes in a field or by the roadside. In either case we had our own provisions. Joseph, the Arab steward, would spread a rug on the ground, set out our tin plates and mugs, much battered by long use, and then produce a cold chicken, which he dexterously pulled apart and distributed. To this he would make variable additions of such things as he had in stock. When lunch was over, Mordecai, who always had a special care for my comfort, would bring me his saddle-bags, which made a good seat. The rest of the party chose the softest places they could find. We had a very little conversation, a little reading, a little writing, and some sleeping. Thus the noon passed, when we resumed our horses, and rode two or three hours to our camp. The theory was that our tents should be in readiness when we reached the camping-ground. The fact was commonly the other way. Our mules did not always take the same road which we followed, as their purposes and wishes were more restricted. They reached the place for the encampment about the same time with ourselves. This was well enough when the weather was good. We enjoyed the liberating of the poor mules, — or pure mools, as Keil used to call them, and truly, for they were cruelly overloaded, — and the raising of the tents and the settling down for the night, perhaps for a longer time. But when it rained all was changed. We stood around in the wet, and watched the unloading of our tents and other furniture, which were wet in spite of their coverings, and saw the wet canvas rise into shape over the wet ground. It was dismal, and gave us unpleasant suggestions of colds and malaria. It was not often that we were afflicted and endangered in this way. But one who has not come in a wet state into wet tents on wet ground can hardly realize the danger and discomfort. We had changes of raiment, when we could get to them. But what was to be done with the discarded garments, and how could they be dried? There was no fire, except the feeble coals in the kitchen, and the cook naturally objected to have us around his camp-range, holding our soggy boots. Mordecai would strain a point, and surreptitiously get the boy and myself dried out in the course of the night, but the whole business was attended with embarrassment. One who rides all day on horseback in a driving rain-storm is helpless. He can only sit still, and take the drenching as it comes. A rubber coat is some protection, but not enough. The rider should be completely encased in rubber, in a single garment which should leave nothing uncovered except his face. This he can provide for himself. The baggage should have a similar covering; this others should be required to provide. There remains the wet ground, over which boards should be laid to make the flooring of the tents. The tents usually shed the water very well, but between the side wall and the upper canvas a storm of any spirit will get in. Whatever lack of energy may be detected in the East it does not appertain to the storms. Nature has all her energy well in hand and makes it felt.

But if there is discomfort for the dwellers in tents, those who are without even this protection are in a much worse condition. The habit of life may have hardened them to exposure, but it cannot be otherwise than distressing to spend both day and night out-of-doors, as our patient muleteers were accustomed to do. Whether they found any shelter in the night when it rained, I cannot tell. Possibly they covered themselves by some means. I believe they crawled into the dining-room and kitchen. Even then their lot might well make us content with our own. We had all the necessaries of life. Our tents were furnished with iron cots, and the beds were fairly comfortable. They were more than comfortable after a tiresome ride; and the other arrangements made for us were quite sufficient for our few wants.

When we were established in our tents the signal for dinner was sounded. Each man picked up a camp-stool and found his way to the dining-room. The dinner was elaborate for the place. We had several courses, from soup to dessert, and all were well prepared. Joseph and Mordecai officiated as waiters, and we dined in style. The dinner of the first day was beyond the common run of such repasts; but our ordinary fare was very good. We had to live on the country to a large extent, and the products of the country had a sameness. Still, there was enough, and there was small reason to complain. It was a cardinal point in making our camp to be near water. This was easily managed by those who knew the country. The water was over-warm for our taste; but our authorities were easily satisfied and the rest of us were fain to be content. But I have written enough, for the present, of the conditions of travel in Syria. As I look back upon the journey it does not seem a hard one. The discomforts are forgotten in the thronging recollections of the things which were enjoyed.

We were called at six o'clock on our first morning in camp, and were on our horses at seven. We had a general order of march. Mordecai led our line. He wore a faded olive suit. On his head was a covering of white cloth, and over this a purple shawl, kept in place by black cords. His costume was appropriate, being a combination of the Orient and Occident, as he was in person and in office. Behind him came our string of horses who were arranged by chance, save as Browning very much preferred to be near the leader. The black horse which he had secured after his disaster in the street of Beirut was too small for his length of limb, and, what was more serious, was devoid of that activity which had characterized his predecessor and had caused his own promotion. In fact he was slow. His rider was kept in constant exercise by his effort to keep the steed in exercise. Even then his success was only partial. He thought he secured a more tolerable rate of progress by keeping near to Mordecai and having a diligent beast in his rear. The case was so good that no one disputed Browning's right to the second place.

Keil's trouble was somewhat different in its nature. His horse was active enough, but the physical conformation of the animal was such that it was hard for the girth of the saddle to get a firm hold upon him. Consequently when we rode down hill our German friend was compelled to rest on the horse's neck, and when we went uphill only continued vigilance could keep him from receding over the opposite extremity. Here was an occasion for frequent remonstrances and readjustments. But, from the nature of the case, the evil could never be remedied. Yet Keil was very patient. I hope that it was some compensation for his difficulties that they were amusing to the rest, despite all our sympathy. It was hard to keep back the smile and retort at his frequent cry, "Antoine! Joseph! My saddle's slipping off!" On the whole, we were well mounted. The horses were strong and were sure-footed. The latter quality was indispensable. After the first days we seldom saw a road. Indeed, roads are a rarity in Palestine. Our way often led where there was not even a path. Sometimes we rode in the dry bed of a brook; sometimes up and down hills and across fields. Frequently the way was very steep, needing the greatest care on the part of the sagacious horses. Yet they seldom slipped. Now and then we dismounted and let the horses find their own way over the rugged places, while we made our way from rock to rock as we could. Several times Mordecai found that he was out of his true course, where there were no landmarks, and Joseph's additional knowledge would be called into requisition.

Travelling on horseback seems attractive and romantic. Under easy conditions it is most agreeable. But as we found it, it is a wearisome method of journeying. The ways were so rough that our horses could rarely do more than walk. They were so narrow that we commonly rode in single file. Where the country was interesting, in itself or its history, all was very well. But there were most tiresome days. To move slowly up and down the hills, day after day, and yet be reasonably patient, needed all our resources. One should be on good terms with himself if he attempts it. I tried all the devices which I could think of to wear away the hours. I played games with myself, repeated poetry, capped verses, called up scenes which were past and friends who were far away, anticipated the getting back to my work, and what would be done when home was reached, guessed what time it would be when we reached a point before us; — did all I could think of to break the monotony. It was always so good to stop; to stand on one's feet; to exchange comments on the day.

There were times and places when we rode side by side, and chatted as we went. I received some choice bits of personal history in this way. Or we could dash out over the plain, and refresh our horses and ourselves. It seems now as if there was nothing very hard in those days of riding. But I cannot forget that some of the hours were very long and very lonely. I thought then that nothing would induce me to repeat the journey. I am less confident now.

From Beirut to Damascus there is a fine diligence

road. It was made in connection with the French expedition of 1860. It is seventy miles in length. There is no road like it in Syria. We enjoyed this for the first day and so long as our course would permit. Our second morning was less interesting than the first. Before noon Howard bade us adieu and went back to Beirut. Thenceforth Mordecai was in sole command of our troop.

In the autumn Syria has a barren look. We saw few flowers in all our long ride. In many places the ground was so thickly covered with stones that it seemed well nigh impossible to find a place for seed. The stones serve a useful purpose in holding the soil in place in the heavy rains. Hermon was in sight as we rode on and the Anti-Lebanon mountains. We passed through Zahleh, where our friend Greenlee was to have his home. The town had an uninviting appearance. There is no beauty in the low, square, dull houses, with their flat roofs. Yet this is a place of considerable importance, having a population of some fifteen thousand, the most of whom are nominally Christians. The people are described as of a turbulent character. The treatment which they have received may account for this in a measure.

We turned aside for a little while to visit the tomb of Noah. We found it in a stone building connected with the ruins of a church. The tomb is apparently built of stone, and covered with plaster. It is very long. Its length is given as forty-four yards, but I think that this is an over-measurement. We remarked upon the length of the structure.

The guardian assented to our view of the case, but said that Noah was a very tall man. The tomb was covered with cloths of different sorts; a common custom in Mohammedan countries. I suppose that this is thought to be a benefit to the owner of the handkerchief or veil rather than to the occupant of the mausoleum. The keeper seemed to have small confidence in the efficacy of these adornments, or else small care for those who sought to appropriate it. For he readily consented to sell to Keil and myself a couple of the veils at a moderate price. I trust that no one became the poorer by this transaction.

We passed large herds of cattle as we journeyed, and sheep and goats who were kept together. In one place we saw two men and a boy running one shovel in the construction of a ditch. Two were in the trench, which was about two feet deep, and the other was on the ground above. One had the handle of the shovel and the others worked ropes which drove it into the ground, and then hoisted it to the surface. The boy seemed amused at our amusement as we watched this laborious process.

We had our usual nooning. I remember nothing of it, except Keil's appearance. He wore a tall, black hat, which was quite unsuited to a tour like ours. For greater comfort he had put Noah's handkerchief over his head, and his hat over that. When he removed his double covering, it was found that his forehead was gaudily frescoed with the colors and shapes which adorned his mortuary veil. As he was a decorator by profession, there was an appropriateness in this display, upon which we did not fail to comment.

In the afternoon we passed what is known as the Temple of Doris, or Tomb of Doris. It is octagonal, and constructed of pillars and other stones from Baalbec. An antique sarcophagus, standing on one end, made a small but convenient place for prayer. We rode into a quarry from which stone had been taken for the temples, and saw one immense stone which had not been wholly cut from the rock of which it was a part. We walked on the top of this block, which is seventy-one feet in length, fourteen feet in height, and thirteen in breadth. We got some idea of the labor of those builders of the olden time when we looked upon the stones which they piled, and wondered by what means they were able to set them in their places.

Thus we came to Baalbec. We entered the precincts of the temple by a long passage, which was so dark through much of the way that we could see nothing clearly, and could only let our horses take their own course through the gloom. We came into the great entrance court of the temple, and pitched our tents against the north wall. It was a superb place for our little camp, and we were in a state of rare delight as we looked on the massive walls and tall columns, and remembered where we were. It was Saturday night after an eventful week. Where could its days have a better end?

But what shall I write of the place? I could fill pages with descriptions and reflections. But the pictures which any one can see are more satisfactory than words, and reflections are not of much account unless one makes them for himself. No one can tell when the temples were built whose stupendous ruins are solitary and deserted. Baal is found in the old Hebrew scriptures; but whether Baalbec is referred to in those ancient writings is uncertain. In the early Christian times we find the place under the Greek name of Heliopolis. The City of the Sun was a Roman colony, and as early as the second century, it would seem, two temples were built by imperial authority. It may be that one of the two found on the coins of Septimius Severus was never finished. When Christianity became the religion of the empire, one of the temples was changed into a church, and the other was destroyed. Moslems and Crusaders appear in its later history. Earthquake has completed the work of war, until only fragments of grandeur remain to excite the wonder and admiration of travellers.

The temples were higher than the town, on a platform which was reached by broad steps. The tall columns which adorned the portico have gone. Beyond was a hexagonal court which opened into the Greek court, a quadrangle four hundred and forty feet long and three hundred and seventy wide. The bare walls, despoiled of their beauties, enclose a desolation. It was in this court that our five tents were set up, while a little beyond them our horses and mules rested in the sacred domain. Beyond this court was another which was yet higher, in which was the Temple of Baal. Six massive columns of the peristyle remain in their place, but of the Temple walls, if they were ever erected, no trace can be found. The columns were of a yellowish limestone. The base was in one block, and the shaft in three, which were held together by clamps of iron. The iron has proved more attractive than the architecture to the Turks and Arabs, who have broken the stones that they might appropriate it. These assaults and the more steady wearing of time seem likely to throw down these tall sentinels, and leave the ruins unguarded.

In the west wall are the immense stones which are often referred to. In some respects they are as wonderful as anything which is seen. They are the largest stones, so it is said, which were ever taken from a quarry, or ever set in a wall. I must give figures, which will have some meaning if the distances which they denote is paced on the ground or measured off on the side of a church. The three famous stones are respectively sixty-four feet in length, sixty-three feet and two-thirds, and sixty-three feet. They are about thirteen feet high and thick, and are placed twenty feet above the ground. We may well wonder how they were ever taken from their place, brought to the height where the temple was to stand, raised to the place they were to fill. They were so nicely fitted one to another that the blade of a knife could not be inserted between them. There are nine other stones of about half the length of these. As we look upon them in amazement, we gain a crude idea of the skill and force which entered into the masonry in the times of the lost arts. Now they are curiosities and memorials.

Outside of the courts, parallel to the temple of Baal, is the Temple of the Sun, which the Romans consecrated to Jupiter. This is smaller than the other, but it is now the largest temple in Syria and the most beautiful, while it has additional interest as the one which is best preserved. It had a magnificent entrance, of which very much remains. It was forty-two feet high, and the width is half the height. The ornamentation of the stones is most elaborate. Vines, grapes, acanthus leaves, figures of men and animals, adorn the gateway in the greatest profusion. The portal was nearly shattered by the earthquake of 1759, when the huge keystone dropped some three feet, where it hung in the centre of the lintel for over a hundred years. Then the English consul built under it a pier of stones on which it may rest for a long time. There are stairways within the stones which form the side of this gateway. One entrance is closed, but if you are willing to creep through a low opening on the other side you can climb to the top of the wall and get a broad view of the courts and temples, the expanse of ruins. The boy of the party naturally made the experiment. Many of the columns of this temple are standing, with portions of others, while one has fallen against the wall, where two portions of its shaft still lean.

At the east of the Acropolis, in the modern village, enclosed by garden walls, and standing among mulberry and poplar trees, is a small semi-circular temple, whose exterior is very attractive with its columns and carvings. The building was once a Greek chapel, but it is now becoming ruins. We get so accustomed to that word, ruins! Yet how much it means of thought and toil which have left no mark; of human passions and desires which have burned to ashes; of centuries which have gone over to the rapacious past! The golden capitals have fallen, and the proud pillars which they surmounted. Statues have fled from the niches which they graced. Altars have disappeared and oracles become dumb. Temples and men have passed into the realm from which there is no return. " Ruins," we say, and gaze at the lofty piles which are waiting for the word. I did not mean to moralize. But who could spend a quiet Sunday among the fallen splendors of Baalbec and not be set a-thinking? The walls would rise again. The priests would stand at the altars. The people would bring their offerings and their prayers. The old Psalm would sing its way into the silence and the long procession move through the imposing gates. What did it all mean? Who shall say? Who can doubt that sincere hearts were here, with honest thanksgiving and fervent petitions? For the multitudes, the blind led by the blind, and not unwillingly, I have now no word. But surely there were some here who under strange names and with strange rites paid a true homage to the God whom they dimly saw, for whom their hearts longed, in whose hands they knew that their life was. Some went down these steps and back into the world with a clearer vision of unseen things, and with a firmer purpose to follow the inner light and to hearken to the inner voice. It is easy to believe this, waiting in the temple, keeping the Sabbath Day, sure that God is in this place.

The priests have gone. I will not take their office. It was a restful, impressive day: a good pause between the new world we had left and the old world into which we were advancing.

There are remains of the old town in heaps of stones, some of which retain signs of their former use and beauty, and from the ruins statues are sometimes brought to light. There is a modern village at the east of the temples, partly upon the site of the town. There are two hundred and fifty houses, more or less, occupied chiefly by Greek Catholics. A school for Syrian girls marks the presence of Christian teachers, and is another bright spot in a dark land.

The laugh and talk of our German companion roused us earlier than was necessary on Monday morning. But we secured an early start and a long ride in the cool of the day. There was nothing of special consequence in the forenoon. The red fields looked finely in the sun, but the paths were narrow and rough. We had our lunch in a dreary place by the roadside, near the village of Surghâya. The village is among corn-fields and orchards. Rock tombs are to be seen on the hill. In a small stream near our halting-place women were washing clothes, in the Italian manner substantially, with much rubbing and pounding. One woman was washing a reluctant black sheep. We wanted to inspect these processes, but were warned that it would not be safe. We ventured near the washing-place and saw all we could, and returned in safety.

The afternoon was more eventful. We had hardly started before the rain began to fall. It rained. It rained hard and long. The drops pelted us like hailstones as the wind hurled them in our faces. Our rubber coats proved an incomplete protection, and nothing remained but to take the drenching provided for us. After a long time the rain ceased, and we expected to get on better. We had begun to cherish this hope when Mordecai leaped from his horse, which was the signal for us all to do the same. We were to descend a hill which was too bad for riding. It was too bad for anything. If I should say we walked in mud, the expression would give no idea of the reality. We ploughed our way through deep, sticky, heavy, red mud. We stumbled, slipped, struggled down the muddy hill, leading our dripping horses, and wondering what and where the end would be. We went through, or this record would not have been written. At the same time the rain seemed to be through. The scene had been brightened by lightning and enlivened by thunder, but these were over. The sun came out and made fair proposals, but he could stay so little time that he did us little good. We did hope to be sun-dried, but the hills were too high and the light went down behind them. At the end of the ride we found a comfortable house, with good fires, hot drinks, dry clothes, and all which wet men needed? Far from it. We stopped in a dreary open field. Not a tent was up. But at length the wet canvas covered spaces of wet ground. Rugs were spread over the damp earth, and such changes of raiment were made as were found practicable. The iron bedsteads were put up and the wet corners of our mattresses covered as carefully as was possible. Our situation had little to alleviate its dreariness and discomfort. We seemed, also, to have a reasonable chance of malaria. The conditions were favorable. We had quinine, the standard specific, but it did not dispel our fear. Such a dinner as could be served was given to us, and we seasoned it with suitable grumbling against our preparations for rainy weather and wet ground. We knew that Arabs were not far away. Mordecai had the camp pistols fired, that the natives might know we were strongly fortified and keep away from us. So the day ended, and early sleep came with its forgetfulness.

The morning was clear, but we were not in condition for an early start. We did very well, however, in the uncertainties touching the issue of our adventure. We took quinine, and moved on. Our camp had been near the town of Zebedani, famous for its apples and grapes. The place is finely situated among the mountains of Anti-Lebanon, nearly thirty-six hundred feet above the sea. It is in the midst of gardens and vineyards, and has a flourishing fruit trade with Beirut and other large cities. There are three thousand inhabitants, one-half of whom are Christians. The traveller can find tolerable entertainment in the town, as he can also at Baalbec. But it is more convenient to carry your own house and furnish your own table.

On our ride we soon came to the river Barada, one of the "rivers of Damascus," and better known as the Abana. The river has its rise high above Zebedani, and rushes swiftly down a deep gorge. We had to pass the tombs which are in the cliffs above the river. The stone doors are gone, and the sepulchres are untenanted. We could not even linger to visit the place where Abel was laid, if we may trust the Mohammedan tradition. But we had a long noon at El-Fijeh, the great spring which pours it waters into the Barada, and may almost be called the source of the river. The copious spring bursts from beneath the mountain, and rushes violently over the rocks, soon to become a broad stream. Above the place at which the spring issues from the ground, there was a small temple, standing on a platform of rocks, and below are seen the walls of another edifice standing in a beautiful grove. This was, very likely, the shrine of the deity of streams and springs. The rivers are not impressive, but the place is charming in its solitude, with the living stream which still goes on, while men come and go, and, for the most part, leave it to its memories. Some of our company could not resist the temptation to swim in the clear waters, while the rest were content with inferior ablutions. There are a few houses near the spring, and some of the natives, chiefly in the juvenile period, made their appearance. We had no intercourse with them, beyond an exchange of staring.

Our afternoon ride was unusually pleasant, as we rode down the bank of the Abana. As we watched the clear, sparkling water, and saw it break over the stones into countless waterfalls, we were not surprised that Naaman the Syrian preferred it above all the rivers of Israel. When we had seen the Jordan, we were still less surprised at his hesitation to leave his own noble river that he might bathe in the turbid waters of a strange land. The river we judged to be some twenty or twenty-five feet wide through most of its course. The trees upon its banks added much to the beauty of the scene. The green was in so great variety that the appearance was like that of our own woods in autumn, even though the reds were wanting. But we saw red leaves the night before as we rode in the dry bed of a brook with bushes on both sides of us. Through all this beauty and life, we made our pilgrimage towards Damascus. We took a circuitous route that we might have the best view of the city before we entered it. Late in the afternoon we reached the hill of Kâsiûn, barren and sacred. We rode as far as we could upon its rough slope, and then, dismounting, clambered over the rocks to the summit. Legend has dealt generously with the mountain, for it makes it one of the homes of Adam, and there it has Abraham receive the sublime doctrine of the one God. The red stones were stained with the blood of Abel who was laid in the cavern in the hill. From this height Mohammed, the young camel-driver from Mecca, looked down upon the ancient city, and, though allured by its beauty, turned away because "there is but one paradise, and mine is fixed elsewhere." On the summit is a small, open building which is called the Dome of Victory, and also the Dome of the Camel-drivers.

It is a wonderful sight upon which one looks down. The barren country through which he has passed gives place to the broad plain, with its forests and streams, and resting among them, silent and beautiful, is the great city of the East, lifting among the trees the domes and minarets of its hundred and one mosques. Nothing could be more fascinating. To believe that paradise was here requires but slight effort. Whoever is here, let him linger and prolong his rapture. He will never see the quiet beauty again. Once in the city the charm will be broken. He may come again to the mount of vision, but the "tender grace" of his first vision will not come back.

The path of the Barada is marked by the luxuriance of the grass and trees which it nourishes and beautifies. The river rejoices in the liberty of the valley, and, breaking into small streams, carries its life and beauty over all the wide plain, and finally disappears in the marshes and lakes of the desert.

Upon the calm and wondrous scene we looked as long as we were permitted, then reluctantly made our way down the mountain, and entered the city. We were very quiet as we rode along the streets, and drew up our horses at the gate of the Hotel Dimitri. We were in Damascus.

## CHAPTER IX.

#### IN DAMASCUS.

WE were in Damascus. The golden dream of years had come true. We were in the city of the eastern world, among the treasures and mysteries and traditions and legends of the Orient. All this we felt as we passed through Dimitri's narrow portal, and it was surpassed as we stood in the large court of this eastern dwelling. In the centre of the court was a garden, with orange and lemon trees, vines and shrubs, and a fountain casting up its cool waters. Around the court were rooms for many uses, and there the traveller might lie at his ease on a broad divan, like a man in a story, and dream of Araby the blest, while, if that were his fancy, he smoked his fragrant nargîleh, or sipped the dark coffee in its tiny cups. The mysteries of the rambling house never lessened. We enjoyed our large rooms, and liked to wander in all open places, yet there was the consciousness all the time that we were on the border of our dwelling-place, and that the Arabian days and nights were beyond us. There were no splendors, and few luxuries. The ease of the East was everywhere apparent, a carelessness which was almost negligence, but which was soothing to strangers from a far land.

The house was quite shut in from the city and the street. It would stand a considerable siege. The large gate was closed and stoutly fastened. Through it was cut a small, low door by which all who had a right went in and out. This is for security against a mob which at any time might renew the bloody work of 1860, when six thousand Christians were slain in Damascus. It is thought that fourteen thousand perished in that outbreak of fanaticism, when the red hand sought to crush out the life which it could not control. We saw in one of the streets a stone column which still bore the stains of that time of carnage.

The little door was fastened by a curious wooden lock or bolt which it is impossible to describe. I brought away one similar to it. It is ingenious, and effective under ordinary conditions, though it would not be hard to break it. These locks are sometimes very large and heavy.

It is common to say that Damascus is the oldest city in the world. If that is claiming too much, it is not too much to say that no other city has for so long a time maintained its greatness and importance. It is the centre of Syrian life, and the metropolis of the East. It is mentioned in the annals of Abram, whose steward was Eliezer of Damascus, but of the origin of the city nothing is certainly known. Its history is associated with that of the Jews, but it held much wider relations, which extended wherever civilization and commerce flourished. The West sought its market-places, and from its gates the caravans ventured into the farther East. I shall not attempt to trace its eventful story. It became, of course, a part of the empire, and Christianity was early established among its people. It had its bishop, and its ancient temple was changed into a church. The name and the place must always be conspicuous, if for nothing else, because it was near the city, and while he was hastening to enter it, that there came the change in the life of a man who beyond all other men has impressed his character and his faith upon the world. It was in Damascus that St. Paul "proclaimed Jesus, that he is the Son of God."

It was in the seventh century that the Arabs half seized and half received the city which they had besieged. The Christians then had fifteen churches there. The city was made the capital of the vast Moslem empire, and though it has felt the curse of Moslem rule, and has lost much of its importance, still, with its fortunate situation and its high renown, it has in a good degree preserved its strength, while it offers to the traveller an unequalled opportunity for seeing the people and ways and means of times which are past. To the Arab Damascus is like paradise. The conception of paradise which he gains as he reads the description which is written in the Koran takes its form from this city of his delight, from the fair fields and ripe fruits and sparkling fountains of Esh-Shâm and Dimishk. To the stranger Damascus does not readily suggest paradise. It might be so if he was content to remain on the hill where the young camel-driver paused, and to gaze on the enchanting beauty beneath him. But the illusion vanishes when he walks through the narrow, rough, unclean streets, jostled by Jew and Bedouin, imperilled by horses, provoked by donkeys, annoyed by dogs, overshadowed by camels, with wild boys and untamed girls confusing the complexity. The cry for bakshish is surely mundane. We heard it frequently, and usually from the children, who seemed to have no need of the gift they asked, nor, it should be confessed, much desire for it. It may be added that they rarely received it. They had conformed to the custom which had been bequeathed to them, and with that their responsibility ended.

We had, as usual, a local guide in the city, though Mordecai looked after our general interests. Damascus has been compared, as regards its shape, to a spoon. It has different quarters for different classes, Christians, Jews, peasants, though the Moslems naturally occupy most of the ground. The quarters are divided into small sections having wooden doors which are closed at night. The streets are dark at night, and the stranger needs a guide who is familiar with all the turnings and windings of the ways, and is furnished with a lantern of his own. The sensation is very peculiar as you grope your way through the gloom, following a man you never saw before, knowing that treacherous characters are on every side of you, haunted by strange stories of mysterious things which have been done in these streets, and with an undefined fear which increases the romantic interest of the walk. But we were rich in confidence, though the domain of knowledge was beyond the sea, in the office of

Jenkins, who intrusted us to Mill, who put us in the hands of Howard, who handed us over to Mordecai, who had us follow the Arab who knew Damascus.

Let me write of some things which we saw. We were taken to an immense plane-tree, which is said to have grown from a stick planted by Ali, the friend of Mohammed. They told us that the tree is forty-eight feet in circumference. One of its branches has ghastly associations, in that it is now and then made to serve as a gallows.

We went into the bazaar, which is saying little more than that we walked among the shops and stores, wondered at the endless variety of wares, watched the manners of the dealers, listened to the jargon of voices, bought such things as we were able to pay for and carry away. Near Dimitri's is the horse-market, where one may hire a donkey, if he feels the need of discipline, and where on certain days horses are collected and sold. Many of them are uncomely, but some boast a purer blood. The Arabian horse of story and song, beautiful, swift, intelligent, the friend of his master and the play-mate of his owner's children, we never met. He must belong further in the East. The horses we saw were far enough from this description. The connection is not a happy one, but this is a good place to say that the entrancing beauties of the East, the fair Arabian women whose charms a jealous manhood conceals behind the veil, whose presence is redolent of witchery and love, into whose fathomless eyes one gazes only to be lost, we never saw. Veiled women were in abundance, the thin covering but imperfectly concealing the face beneath, while the eyes turned boldly in the slit between the upper and the nether veil, and were not ungenerous in their glances at the passing Frank. But the women of ballad and romance did not come in our way. True, we did not cross the threshold of the harem, and saw only the daughters of the people. Yet peasant women have their full share of beauty and grace, from the fjords of Norway to the lakes of Italy.

We are lingering. The saddle-market is, very properly, near the horse-market, and stalls for the sale of grain are even nearer. Very brilliant are the horse equipments, with their gaudy tassels and cloths and spangled bridles. We watched the coppersmiths at work in their open shops, and a blind man working the rude bellows for the fire over which another was lining a kettle. In the Greek bazaar were all sorts of shawls, weapons, coins, gems, and curiosities. We went into the rooms of an old man who is called the " father of antiquities." His wares so nearly covered the floors of several rooms that it was not easy to move among them. There was a general sense of disorder and dust. The prices were not fixed in their amount, and we succeeded in bringing away some attractive things in brass. We also found in the cloth and silk bazaars many goods of great beauty. The prices were said to be absurdly low, as trade was extremely poor. We had a long process of bargaining, and our only error was in not buying more. I think that feeling is common when one reaches home. There is no need of extending this list to the fanatical booksellers, the bakers and confectioners, the pipe-dealers and fruit-dealers. No bazaar is more interesting than that of the goldsmiths, who are in a large building, very old and dilapidated, which is little more than a roofed space, with passages through it and among the numerous stalls where the cunning workmen in precious metals ply their trade. Much of their work was beautiful, and they were very eager to dispose of it. They brought forth hidden treasures as they caught sight of us and followed us with their eager solicitations.

The wholesale trade has its separate place, where the different trades are divided, and the business is on a large scale. It was instructive to examine the great collections of merchandise and to see the methods of traffic, the bringing in and the sending out of goods. In these walks through the city the people, their houses, dresses, manners, usages, are all seen together, and the complex impression is of great value.

"The street which is called Straight" still runs through the city, though it has lost much of its original grandeur. It was about a mile long, reaching from the east to the west gate, and was more than a hundred feet wide. It was divided into three avenues by Corinthian columns. The middle avenue was for foot passengers. Remains of the colonnades are now to be seen. The street is now essentially straight through the greater part of its length, but it is much narrower than it was. The buildings at its sides are very ordinary, and have the look of age without being very old. The street is the most interesting in the city because we know it by name from our childhood, and because it is connected with events which concern the common life. The house of Judas is pointed out, where Ananias found the praying Saul of Tarsus. The building is ancient, but not old enough for that, unless it is in some of its stones. It is now a tiny mosque, and by its side is the fountain from which the water was taken for Saul's baptism. One would like to believe this. We could not be far from the place where these things were done. We went into one of the buildings to see one of the old pillars and found ourselves in a small school. The teacher and the scholars were sitting with their books behind low benches, and did not seem disturbed by our curiosity. Not far away, on a side street in the Christian quarter, is the house of Ananias, or a house with that name. Now there is a small chapel there, which we wished to see. The key could not be found. We interested the neighbors, who gave us the benefit of all they knew and did not know. They were bent on furthering our desires, and finally succeeded in finding two ladders which they tied together and thrust through a window into a room below. The descent was difficult and not free from peril, but we went down and found a rude room with an altar and a few benches. If this was the place where the man lived who laid his hands on the man of whom he had been in dread, calling him "Brother Saul," — but who shall say that it was not the place of his dwelling? I suppose that tradition is willing to be truthful when it can be. It points out the place where Saul was smitten by the great light and fell to the earth. This is the Latin tradition. A low structure with an inscription marks the spot. In the Middle Ages a village six miles away was regarded as the place of the conversion. The house of Naaman the leper has disappeared, but its site is shown, and upon it stands a large building which is fittingly used as a hospital for lepers. We did not go into the house, but we saw, sitting on a donkey, a forlorn man who was said to be a victim of the frightful disease. Mr. Garry expressed his doubts regarding the man's malady, but I could not see that he had good reason for his suspicion. Is it not probable that those poor men, dying by slow degrees, think often of the prophet of Israel, and long to throw themselves into the Jordan, even with Abana and Pharpar before them? In the south wall of the city we saw the place down which St. Paul was lowered in a basket that he might escape from those who sought his life. The tomb of St. George is very near. This was not the saint whom we found at Beirut, but the man who helped St. Paul in his flight. There are many Christian graves in the burial-ground by the tomb, but the Moslems have dealt roughly with them. It gives additional interest to this neighborhood that Buckle, the English historian, was interred in this Christian cemetery in 1862. It will be remembered that he had spent the winter in Egypt and had crossed the desert to Syria, and was stricken down with fever, to die at Damascus. We passed a Moslem graveyard, where men and women were in a tent. They were mourning for one recently taken from them. They may have been friends whose grief was profound. The signs of grief are often boisterous. But on some occasions mourners are hired and then the exhibition of sorrow must be excessive. It is common for the mourning family to spend two or three days beside the grave, reading the Koran and offering prayers. The numerous methods of expressing sorrow of which we read in the Bible are still to be found in the land of the Book which in many ways gives so good a comment on the sacred narratives.

A caravan had come in from Bagdad as we were riding one day, and we were glad to see this ancient method of travel and transportation. Rugs and tobacco are brought from Persia, and other merchandise is carried back. The camels were shaggy and unattractive, but they had done good service in their long march, and were as grave as if they felt their importance in the work of the world. Perhaps they do. The camel is a serious animal. He sturdily maintains his dignity, and is ready to assert his rights. He will bear so much burden as he thinks suitable. If more is put on his back as he kneels, he quietly remonstrates. If his remonstrance is not heeded, he has a way of rolling off his load and compelling his driver to begin again and proceed with more discretion. I do not know that any other beast of burden thus asserts himself. I never saw anything to exceed the pack-mule of the East. Stubborn he may be by nature, but he is effectually subdued and made to carry a load which it would seem impossible for him to hold. For pathos and sorrow and despair, no sound can surpass the complaint of the eastern donkey when his heart is touched. He cries, murmurs, wails, as if in a hopeless misery, loudly combining all sounds which are dismal, hoarse, asthmatic, while all the time he has no burden or pain, and apparently no definite object in his objurgation. Something may be on his mind, yet he excites no compassion and finds no relief. Evidently he is discontented with his lot, and lacks the patience of the mule and the resistance of the camel.

We attended a dramatic exhibition one evening, and had a fine sample of this kind of work and play as it is pursued by the Arabs. We went in procession under experienced guides, and carrying paper lanterns. There was an air of mystery about the whole business, but this was probably due to the strangeness of the expedition. By a long and circuitous walk through the dark we reached a large hall which we found well filled with men. Not a woman was to be seen. There was an orchestra composed of five men, four of whom had musical instruments, and all of whom had voices. They sat cross-legged on a high platform, and interspersed their melodies where they were deemed appropriate. That they were anything more than appropriate can hardly be claimed. They had a mournfulness which seemed out of keeping with the occasion, but this appears to be characteristic of the music of the country, and so could not be deemed out of place. I noticed that the low singing or humming with which our guides and muleteers relieved their long marches was always plaintive. At this exhibition the performers were all men, some of whom wore the dress of the women whom they personated. The chief piece was a love story with tragic elements. For the most part, it was very dull, though there were striking incidents. There was much of the recitative, delivered in the most monotonous manner, with equally monotonous chanting. One performer followed another, almost as if it was an exercise in declamation. Then swords would be drawn, and waved with loud vociferation, and there were startling effects with colored lights. We were left to conjecture what it was all about, and this we were unable to do; nor could we get assistance. Mordecai said that they used the "deep Arabic," which he could not understand. I inferred that they used the classic forms rather than the dialect of the people. It is my conviction that Ibrahim's knowledge of Arabic did not extend far beyond the colloquial necessities of a dragoman. After the tragedy came a pantomine, which was cleverly done and readily understood. It was full of fun and was the more amusing for the rarity with which anything of the kind was seen. To see the people on and off the stage, to examine their costumes and to observe their ways, was of constant interest. We sat in large arm-chairs. The audience were much at their ease. They used a large liberty, relieved the tedium with eating, drinking, smoking, and chatting, and everybody seemed amiable and contented. But for the novelty of the whole scene, the evening would have been dull for the stranger. As it was, while we should not care to repeat it, our visit to the Oriental drama was entertaining and useful.

Damascus is a walled city. Romans, Arabians, Turks, at different periods have laid the stones which shut it in. Towers, round and square, have been erected for greater security, but these would not offer much resistance to an assault. They have grown weak and assaults have grown strong as the centuries have wrought upon them. The wall presents a feeble appearance. There were many gates in the old days, and some ten or twelve are now open. Of gates within the city mention has already been made. At the ends of the Straight street are gates in the wall. The east gate, Bab est Sherki, claims attention for its antiquity. The gateway was nearly a hundred feet long. It was divided into three ways, two of which were long since closed and made part of the wall. The small north gate is now open, and over it rises a tall, square minaret.

Damascus has its citadel, a heavy square structure, of the thirteenth century, surrounded by a moat, which is concealed by a dense growth of reeds. The general look of the fortress was sombre and solid, but not warlike. We ventured through the gate and were ordered out. At another time we invaded the martial precincts again, and passed through the open, desolate square with impunity. I have not said much of the buildings of Damascus, for there are few of which much can be said. The architecture and arrangements of eastern houses are familiar, and those of Damascus follow the general rule. The outer walls are of a dull gray. The windows are small, if indeed there are windows. The door is narrow and opens into a hall, which again opens on the interior court, paved with marble, and enclosed by parti-colored walls. In the centre of this space a fountain throws up its clear waters from among the stones which stand about it. Around the court are the rooms of the house, with their beauties of adornment according to Oriental taste, and the conveniences and comforts which life demands and enjoys. Such things, there as everywhere, must vary with the means and taste of the proprietor. I have an impression that the visitor misses the splendor and grace which he has been led to expect, the gorgeous beauty which belongs with every conception of the far Orient. Visions dissolve as one threads the streets of an eastern city with the "Arabian Nights" in his mind, or enters where time has drawn its hand over the pictures of luxury and repose.

We were admitted to the house of the late Shammai, a rich Jew, or to one room which is very richly decorated. There is a small synagogue with a library connected with the house. We also visited the house of Josef Ambar, a rich Jew. The rooms are arranged about three courts. The walls are of white marble and the floor is laid in mosaic. This is elegant, but cold and hard; good for exhibition, but chilly for a home. But home means different things in different lands.

By the latest figures I have there were in Damascus seventy-one large mosques with a large number of chapels and schools, in which study and devotion were united. Many of the schools have been closed. The fame of the schools and scholars of Damascus belongs in the past. The schools which have the patronage of the authorities are chiefly for theology. The Koran, of course, is studied and the sayings of the Prophet, with enough philosophy and grammar to help out the higher learning. There are schools of a lower grade, and a military school, but education is not the strong point of the Moslem faith. Naturally, there is more life and hope in the Christian schools. The Greek and French schools are doing a good work in promoting the idea of learning and elevating the standard. We were more interested in the English schools which we visited. In one, the scholars welcomed us with the salaam, touching heart, head, and lips, and greeting us with, "Good morning, ma'am." One class sung to us in Arabic of "the home over there." We found a very pretty chapel, which had just been renovated. The motto of these schools is well chosen, — Jehovah-Jireh. An English gentleman accosted us on the street, seeing that we were strangers, and told us that he was engaged in mission work in the city. He was doing it in an informal way, meeting the people as he could, hearing and answering their questions, and telling them the good word of God. We visited a school which is under his care. We found a few boys and one male teacher. One boy read a little simple English quite well. A poor rabbi was doing his best to teach Hebrew to a young boy. He read the text and the boy read with him and after him as well as he could. It was done in a chanting tone, and I could not easily follow the reading, even with a book. The task, which seemed unpromising for the pupil, must have been dismal for the teacher. Yet I dare say they were both used to the labor and accepted it as a part of life.

It is encouraging to remember the Christian schools which are doing faithful work against a mass of darkness and superstition, looking for the better day which they are bringing nearer.

Mosques are not interesting places. They are usually very bare, and so dreary that it seems scarcely necessary to make it difficult or impossible for the visitor to gain admittance. Few of them would be often invaded by those who are seeking the picturesque or the beautiful. There are some which have a history enhancing their attractions, as St. Sophia. The great mosque of Damascus stands in the place of a heathen temple. When Christianity was established in the empire, the building was changed into a church, and was called by the name of John the Baptist. When the Mohammedans came in, they shared for a time the use of the house with the Christians, whom they finally dispossessed. Then a magnificent mosque was erected, which retained a part of the old walls. Extravagant praise is poured upon the edifice which architects, artists, and genius created. Precious stones gleamed among the marbles, and gold glittered in the ceiling, under which hung six hundred golden lamps. Fire came and war came, and much of the glory vanished never to return. The house can no longer be called magnificent. But it is impressive by its size and the remains of its better days. Its length is a hundred and forty-three yards, and it is divided into three aisles by rows of columns. In the transept is the shrine in which is preserved the head of the saint for whom the church was named. This marble shrine is quadrangular, adorned with columns, and decorated with extracts from the Koran, and above is a gilded dome surmounted by a golden crescent. There are three minarets. On the loftiest Jesus is to descend in the great day and sit in judgment over the nations. We ascended the western minaret, and were repaid with an extensive view of the city and the country around it. Far in the distance Hermon lifted up his head on high, and beyond lay the land towards which our hearts were reaching. When we had left the mosque, we looked into the marble chamber where Bibars, the soldier, usurper, and ruler, who fought valiantly against the Crusaders, whose name and deeds are in high renown among the followers of the Prophet, after his eventful life was laid for his last repose. We saw the fine mausoleum which bears the name of Saladin, but we could not stand beside his tomb. We looked upon the graves of two of the Prophet's wives and of his daughter, Fatima, over which stands a dome of clay. The names revive the heroic days — the days which are fully of the past. The new already presses hard upon the old. The proud Moslem sees the star which is coming out of the West and feels that the crescent changes at its approach. New arts and industries are coming in, with new men before whom he must recede. It is the inevitable, and he does not bow to it with his wonted resignation. Against fate he cannot contend; but he can revenge himself upon those who bear the name he hates, who belong to the steadily advancing force of the new day. Surely it is coming. The Moslem who stands on the minaret is crying better than he knows. The hour of prayer draws on. We heard his cry from a grated window in "the street which is called Straight," hard by the house where Saul of Tarsus prayed. The voice will be heard, and here men will kneel beside the world's apostle. On the wall of the great mosque, over the central gate, is a sentence in Greek which has been strangely preserved where it waits for its fulfilment: "Thy kingdom, O Christ, is an everlasting kingdom, and thy dominion endureth throughout all generations."

# CHAPTER X.

## BÂNÎAS AND TIBERIAS INCLUSIVE.

WE left Damascus in the care of the Psalm which rules above the gate of the mosque; for we were compelled to move on. The great city, with its teeming memories and traditions, with its hope and promise, we left behind and turned our faces to the south. A crowd of bystanders watched our departure in the early morning. We rode by the Pharpar, which is narrower than the Abana, but whose swift waters are clearer than those of the Jordan. In itself our day's ride was not remarkable. There was one incident which was exciting and painful. We had not ridden far before Mr. Garry's horse, which was one of the best we had, showed by plain signs that he was not able to go on. Our men tried several methods to relieve his evident pain, that he might pursue his journey. They bled him. They burned him, I suppose on the same principle that we apply a blister to a man. They compelled him to run at the top of his speed. The result was that he pushed on till noon, when we reached our stopping-place, and then again fell to the ground. All the surgery of the camp was put in requisition but to no purpose. As the men were keeping up their vain efforts an old fellow came riding by, who cast a look at the horse, and, saying that he could cure him, rode on. Mordecai shouted to him to come back, and promised him a napoleon if he would save our horse. He seemed confident that he could earn the money. He dismounted, and ordered a fire made. Then he tried the burning process once more, and the horse sprang to his feet, only to fall again. The doctor sent away for charcoal, and a small quantity was brought. He heated an iron, and thrust it into the leg of the horse just above his hoof, but no impression was made. He cut the ears of the dumb patient, but could not bring him back to life. He saw that the case was hopeless, and went his way more quietly than before. In a short time the poor horse was dead. His work was done. We left him where he had dropped. Every one felt the pathos of the event. Our sympathies were touched by this death in a strange land. It was a horse who died, but death is always a serious thing, and we were not ashamed of our pity for the creature, who had been faithful to the last, and had died at his post.

We rode on into the afternoon. From the top of a hill we saw our tents in a field, near a lone tree. Soon it began to rain, and we began to be wet, getting more and more wet till we reached the camp. We did not seem to be very badly off, though it was bad enough. We were near the Moslem village of Kefr-Hawâr. The name is said to refer to the silver poplars which abound there. But Mordecai said that it means "the place of unbelievers." Both may be right. Whatever the word means, the situation was far from cheery. A brook ran before

the camp with its unwholesome suggestiveness.
We heard the half-human bark of the jackals, as
they made their way home. The natives around us
might prove troublesome neighbors. Mordecai had
the camp pistol fired. In each tent a chain was run
through the handles of bags and valises, and bells
were affixed to the chain, which was fastened to the
tent post. The theory was that if robbers came
they would attempt to reach under the tent and
draw out the luggage, when the bells would sound
the alarm. In addition to this precaution, three or
four men were brought from the town to serve as a
guard through the night. Then we settled down,
for everything seemed secure. Soon the rain, it
rained again, and in earnest. How it poured, and
how it assaulted our frail tent! It made its way
into the tent, and the beds on the windward side
were in a sad plight. I was aroused by the flood
without and the river within. It was a hard case
under our conditions. I found a rubber cloth, which
I spread over my bed, and, dressing myself, lay on
the edge of the cot, and waited for happier times.
The rain still rained. I could hear it, and occasionally a drop fell on my face. Slowly, how slowly!
the hours of that night wore away, while the boy
slept serenely on the dry side of the house, perhaps
dreaming of the fountains of Damascus. It was
about half-past five when I heard the inspiriting
voice of Mordecai, "Doctor, it's time to get up."
"How's the weather?" "Bad." He was right.
It was bad. When we mustered for breakfast there
was hope of a change. But the air was raw and

chilly, and we put on our winter coats. We fortified ourselves with quinine, and mounted our horses. Soon the rain, it rained again. Apparently it was the first shower after a protracted drought. We went up and up, down and down, over the rockiest hills. Hermon showed his white head when we started, and for a little time afterwards. Our way lay along the slope of the mountains. Soon nothing was to be seen. The mists and clouds gathered thickly about us, and it rained. The cold wind drove the heavy rain into our faces. For a few minutes the clouds would break, and we could see the sun glimmering through the mist. Then another cloud would come along the valley, silent but resistless, and the rain would fall as if we could be more wet than we were. There is said to be a limit to the capacity for absorption. A man on horseback is a long while reaching the limit. Our road changed. There were fewer rocks. There was more mud, — thick, heavy, sticky, beyond anything we had ever seen. It was pitiful to see the jaded horses sink into it, then pull out their weighted feet, and struggle on. There was an end to the mud, and we came upon rocks once more. We trusted that the worst was over, when Mordecai drew up his steed. He said that he did not know where he was, and could not see through the mist. Back we went into the mud, and forced our way on till another halt was called. Mordecai and Joseph Saab held a consultation, and we turned for another attempt. Another halt, and the wind and water were doing their worst. The glimpses of light made the returning gloom more intolerable. Mordecai and Joseph held another council of war, and separated to see what could be found. Some of us followed one, and some the other. We kept behind Mordecai, as the authorized guide. Presently some one behind Joseph shouted, "Come on, come on." We turned and followed the successful leader, and the rain, it rained. The intervals of sunshine continued, but they were brief and disheartening. We left our horses, and walked for a time to get some warmth into our chilled feet. At length we went down the mountain till we reached the little Druse village of Mejdel-esh-Shems, in "the place of sunshine." Mordecai waited till we all came up, and then made a concise address. He said, "I don't think I can lead you to Bânîas. I know the way, but there are several paths, and in this fog I cannot tell which one is right. If you say so, I will do as well as I can, or, if you think it best, I will try to get you lodging here." There was but one answer — "Here!" He went to the nearest house and soon returned, saying that he had engaged it for us. We made no delay in moving in. It was a neat stone house, of two rooms, with an entry between. Beneath were apartments for horses, donkeys, camels, etc. The best room was given up to us. Our men had the other. The family occupied the hall between. When we entered, the woman of the house was sweeping the floor with a small broom. There was no window, but a wooden shutter covered an opening in the wall, and there was a side door which could be opened for light. Furniture there

was none, if I except two wooden boxes, such as are carried on a donkey. There was a feeble fire in one corner of the room, and this was replenished for our benefit. When our luggage arrived, we were able to make a change of raiment, and there was fire enough to dry the garments which we removed. Our beds were laid on the hard floor. We had our table and dishes and food, with our usual attendants. Glad and grateful for the shelter into which we had been brought, we were ready to seek our couches in good season. The fleas of the country received us with open arms, and did their best to entertain us. They carried it too far, as we remembered long afterwards. It was Saturday night when we went to housekeeping. Sunday found us "prisoners of hope." But we were very comfortable. Our large room showed signs of skill and taste. The floor was of hard earth. The ceiling was of small trees or poles, on which brush had been laid, on which earth had been put, making the common hard, flat roof. Some of the space in the partitions was used as a granary, and from a hole in the wall the grain could be drawn. There had been a little attempt at decoration, and the plaster festooning had a pleasing effect. The weather was far from clear and settled, and we speculated much on the chances of our getting away. Logan sang two verses of
"Are your windows open towards Jerusalem,
Though as captives here a little while we stay."

The words seemed appropriate, and the song was enlivening in a moderate degree. We were to have had this Sunday at Bânîas, but we consented cheerfully to this shutting in. The morning passed quietly, with reading and thinking. It was a wholesome pause. In the afternoon the weather was much more promising, and we walked up into the village. It was a rough and weary walk, over a steep muddy path, strewn with pieces of rock, which were of help to us and served to keep the earth from sliding away. We heard a tiny bell and found our way to a small stone building of two rooms, one of which was a Protestant chapel, while the other was the residence of the young minister. We went into the chapel and were received with real courtesy. Seats were brought for us, though the congregation had dispensed with such comforts. Only a few persons were present. A small line of women stood and sat against the wall, and a little group of men held the floor in front of the desk. Civilization had so far penetrated into this region that persons dropped into the service from time to time after it began, in the American fashion. One man came who was plainly of superior distinction. We fancied that he was the head man of the village, or at least of the church. His dignity was made evident by his better dress and by the boots which he kept on his feet while the other men left theirs at the door. It was made apparent further by his sitting on a stool and on a cushion which a young woman brought for him. The preacher was a young man from the seminary on Mt. Lebanon. The service was in Arabic. There was singing, then prayer, and the reading of the Scriptures by the minister and people.

After that was a catechetical exercise, in which the minister asked questions and the people answered. The head man took part with the others, and all seemed interested in the exercise. We regretted that we could not understand the inquiries and replies. More singing followed, which was conducted chiefly by the minister and one girl with a shrill voice, and the service closed with a prayer and blessing. Then the minister gave us a friendly greeting, and the men and women clustered about us, the sheik or deacon with the rest, and shook our hands with great cordiality. Some extended both their hands to seize and hold ours. An American congregation would not have given strangers a more honest or generous reception. We had no common language but that of smiles and sympathy and hand-shaking, but each one knew what every one meant, and we had a good time together. There was a small box for offerings. We comprehended its language and intent, and were more than glad to make a contribution for some good work. There were about thirty persons present beside ourselves, including the dignitary and two babes in arms. The men were not attractive in appearance. On the road they might have passed for bandits, with their dark faces, heavy brows, and unkempt locks. But their faces were bright as they joined in the simple exercises of the church, and illumined at times as they felt the glow of spiritual thought. The truth which had been brought to them had transformed their character and bearing. We passed a few moments in the preacher's room, which was simply furnished for a good man's dwelling, and, wishing him well, found our way down to our residence. This visit was the sunshine of our Sunday in Mejdel-esh-Shems.

On Monday we resumed our journey. The head of the house which we had hired and occupied was absent at the time that we took possession. On Sunday afternoon a tall man stalked into our apartment and gazed about him with an air of mingled curiosity and authority. We made him comprehend that we regarded him as an intruder, but our statements to that effect probably lost some of their force in being transmitted through a language which he did not understand. But he withdrew without remonstrance, while we were somewhat shocked when we learned that it was the proprietor of the dwelling whom we were ordering out. The family, for the most part, kept to themselves, though the children visited us and stared in wonder at our watches and other appointments. Mordecai had more trouble with our landlord and his household, who wanted, as it was explained to us by our dragoman, that we should "make them rich." The altercation was protracted and spirited; but it ended at last, and we rode away. In two hours we came to Bânîas, where we were to have had the Sabbath. We saw nothing to make us regret that we had tarried at Mejdel.

Yet this was the Paneas of the Greeks, and here was a sanctuary of Pan, the divinity of flocks and shepherds. Long before, it had been called Balinas, after Baal, who was worshipped here. Indeed, the place has had many different names. Here is one of the chief sources of the Jordan, which flows from a cavern over which Herod the Great built a temple in honor of Augustus, who had appointed him ruler of the district. Philip made the city larger, and gave it the name of Cæsarea, to which his own name was afterward appended that the place might be distinguished from another Cæsarea. King Agrippa tried to have it called Neronius, but the ill-omened title passed away. It was a famous place. When Jerusalem was captured, Titus here celebrated the conquest with gladiatorial games, in which Jews were compelled to fight one with another and with wild beasts. The town was conquered again and again in the Crusades, and the remains of its strong fortifications bear witness to its importance. All that is of the past. The place is wretched enough now. The situation is very fine and could not easily be impaired. Nearly everything else is gone. There are some fifty houses, most of them within the wall of an old fortress. We saw something of the better days. The ruined castle looked down upon us from its height. We did not go up to it. I do not know when this hill was first fortified, but the greater part of the castle belongs in the Middle Ages. In this land structures of that period are of small account. Even older ones are little regarded. Mordecai rode by ruins which would be the fortune of Europe, and, when we asked what they were, answered carelessly, "They're only Roman." Antiquity is a relative term, and varies with the boundaries of nations.

We left our horses and walked a short distance to

see the cavern from which the river emerges. The cave has been much diminished as the limestone cliff has become worn and broken. The fallen rocks lie at the mouth of the cavern, and the full stream of clear water rushes over them. In the cliff are votive niches, and over one is the inscription, "Priest of Pan."

There is another cave, in which Elijah rested, if the Moslems are to be believed, and to which he will return. On the hill above is a small mosque. The Moslems have been careful to put a religious structure near a sacred place, and in this have shown more discretion than in most other things. The village of Bânîas is dismal enough, as I have intimated. It seemed to be market-day when we were there, though I fancy that market-day is a movable feast, depending on having something to sell. We found a gathering of inhabitants in an open square. Some member of the bovine family had been slaughtered, and was now to be disposed of. The head and blood were on the ground. The dissevered members were hung up where they could be examined by those who were in need of fresh meat. The trade did not appear to be brisk, and evidently time was of no account. In the midst of so much which was forlorn, it needed an effort to recall the years which were gone. To have a place named in the Bible, and especially in the New Testament, is to invest it with an importance which it retains when its strength and honor are taken away. The region around Cæsarea Philippi has a prominent place in the life of our Lord. When he had made

Judea unsafe for him, and the Jews sought to kill him, he sought the retirement of this part of Galilee. Here Peter made his grand confession: " Thou art the Christ." On one of the hills of Hermon overlooking the city the Lord was transfigured. These things bear the mind away from the desolation now resting on the city which was once renowned.

Our riding away was not at all like the march of the Crusaders, with their flashing armor and flying banners and martial music and martial steeds. We went quietly and in solitary reflection. I do not know how it happened, but I found myself left behind by all our company. In the windings of the path they were lost to sight among the trees and bushes. Nor did I know which path to take that I might catch up with them. I began to be alarmed. It was fearful to be left alone, and there. Would they miss me and come back? That was not likely, for I very often rode at the end of the line, and no one would notice that I was not with the troop. What could I do if they did not come back? Where should I come out if I took the wrong way, as I could easily do? I knew there was meat in the market, but I knew that I had no words in which to bargain for it; nor was meat the sole requirement of a man on a horse. But something had to be done. I was sure that Prince knew as much as I did, and possibly he knew more. His instincts were more trustworthy than my reason; so I slackened bridle once more, and let him choose his path. The confidence was well placed. Before long he brought me where I could see the advance guard, and at his superior pace he readily joined the line.

It is worth noting, as we lose sight of the Castle of Cæsarea, that in the crusading times this was the seat of "the old man of the mountains," the sheikh of the assassins, the clan of fanatics who were held together by a medley of beliefs, and who with their atrocities made themselves a terror in the land. Great princes paid tribute to the chief, that they might be secure against the marauding of the band. He used to stimulate his followers to their cruel work by giving them *hashish*, from which they were called *hashishmen*, which was corrupted into our word — assassin. That is one account of the origin of the name; but some say that they were named after their first chief, Hassan; and others that the stealthy method of their work gave them their title.

We came to Dan, which was Laish till the Danites took it and called it after their ancestor. It was the northern landmark of Palestine, and is best known from its connection with its co-ordinate term, Beersheba. Dan is now represented by a fine oak-tree, which stands, quite naturally, over a Moslem tomb. From the hill or mound on which the tree stands issues the Little Jordan, one of the upper streams of the great river. Thus we entered Palestine.

We passed two Bedouin villages. Their tents were long and low. Some were made of black goat's-hair, and others of what looked like our straw matting, except that it was coarser. In some only the lower part was made of this matting. There was nothing pleasant about these rude dwellings, but they were picturesque, and were of interest as belonging to the country. We saw what Mordecai called Bedouin buffaloes, which we should have called oxen. Life must be dull to these tribes when they are at home, and their nomadic habits do not carry them very widely. The men probably have their own excitement, especially when they are further away from civilization. Yet I think that their ordinary life must be unromantic and unprofitable.

The villages which we found, whether they belonged to the dwellers in houses or to the dwellers in tents, had a dreary, desolate look. Sometimes only broken walls and fallen stones showed where men had lived. But where there were still people, they seemed to be very poor, stupid, lazy, forlorn. The color of the houses — or the absence of color — increased the sense of dreariness. The women looked much like American Indians, and the men not much better. Those whom we saw at Mejdel-esh-Shems, where the Christian church is, were of a higher order. We saw signs of the native taste, in the black paint around the eyes of children and sometimes of older girls. Some of the women had their hands and the upper part of the breast tattooed, and we saw similar marks just over the feet. I think the color was not put in in all cases by the slow and painful process employed by Pacific savages and others, but that it was a superficial painting. The amount of ornaments of silver and other materials depended on the means of the wearer, though most persons seemed to be able to have a little of this kind of adornment.

Riding in these narrow paths is not without difficulty. It is not agreeable to meet any one. The not infrequent sight of an approaching string of camels loaded with household furniture, which seems to cover the whole path, if not more, with wardrobes and bureaus grazing the cliff on one side and hanging over the abyss on the other, cannot be considered a pleasing episode. We always managed to get by, in spite of the stolid faces of the camels, who have the habitual look of creatures who are outraged and are sensible of the outrage yet do submit for reasons best known to themselves. This day we met a string of donkeys carrying disproportionate loads of wood. The horse of the boy collided with one of the long-eared caravan; the stirrup caught in the wood, and, as the horse was the stronger, the donkey was suddenly wheeled around. I cannot say what might have happened, but the stirrup gave way, and the donkey was free to take up his march. We repaired our damages and passed on. I must remark again that an overloaded donkey is a queer sight. He seems concealed beneath his encumbrances. Often nothing can be seen but an immense moving mass, with four short legs under it, and a small head peering out in front. At times the load is less bulky, and a woman sits upon it in man-fashion. It is not always easy to tell a man from a woman, but we marked that on the road the women are more likely than the men to be barefooted. That is not a certain sign, however.

We had our lunch under an old bridge at the River Hasbâny, another of the streams of the Jordan. The way was very rough this day. Just as we were going into camp it began to rain, but this did us little harm. We made our camp about an hour from El-Mellâha, near a swamp and a brook. It was a poor place. But the moon and stars appeared, and looked in a friendly way down upon our little village of tents, and we ended the day in hope.

I do not mention all we saw. There were distant views which were of rare interest, especially mountains of historic character, towards which we turned eager eyes but could not set our faces. Not a day, not an hour, was devoid of scenes, memories, and impressions which we could have had nowhere else. There is but one Holy Land. The next day's ride was one of the best. We had on one side the mountains of Naphtali, while the mountains beyond the Jordan could be seen in the distance, and Hermon was still visible behind us in his majesty. It was pleasant to be making our way southward. The country had the bare look of autumn, but there was seldom a place so rocky that we did not find a few delicate flowers. Our road took us quite near the waters of Merom, or Lake Hûleh, which is supposed to be that which is known by the former name. Merom is once mentioned in the Scriptures as the place where the confederate kings of Northern Canaan came together, and where they were subdued by Joshua, who "houghed their horses, and burnt their chariots with fire." Other noted events took place in this neighborhood. Huleh is the later Arab name, and applies to the plain and marsh as well as to the lake. The region is a fine hunting-ground. Wild animals in great variety and profusion are found, while water-fowls haunt the lake. The wide plain is fertile and beautiful, but its insecurity repels inhabitants. It is the resort of robbers from beyond the river. The lake is triangular in shape, being some four miles wide at the upper part and ending in a marsh which is impenetrable from its thick growth of cane. There are places, however, at which the shore of the lake can be reached. One who has travelled extensively expresses his opinion of the region in these enthusiastic terms: "The Hûleh — lake, and marsh, and plain, and fruitful field — is unrivalled in beauty in this land, no matter when or from what point beheld, — from the heights of Hermon, the hills of Naphtali, the plain of Ion, or the groves of Bânîas, in midwinter or midsummer, in the evening or in the morning." It may be remembered that the Rob Roy canoe found its way to the waters of Merom.

We lunched at the Khân Jubb Yûsef, the inn of the pit of Joseph. The Khân is an extensive building, or series of buildings, affording shelter to soldiers, farmers, travellers, — to any one who may need its hospitality and carry his own provisions. We spent our noon-time in examining the large edifice, which in appearance is almost a castle, having even a rude chapel. In a yard at the side of the Khân is a well thirty feet deep into which Joseph was cast by his jealous brothers. We have both Christian and Mohammedan traditions as vouchers for the identity of the place. Unhappily, the pit at Dothan was two days distant from this field, and this well has an unfailing supply of water, while that into which the luckless youth was lowered had no water in it. We were sorry for these facts, as it would have given the place greatly enhanced value to our eyes if we could fairly have found the story confirmed by the truth lying at the bottom of the well. It seemed a pity that when we had this well and no other we should lose the story. All this was soon forgotten in the rare delight of our afternoon ride. The supreme moment in Palestine is when the first view of Jerusalem is gained. Next to that is the hour in which one first looks upon the Sea of Galilee. Long before we reached the sea, it was lying before us in its placid beauty. It could only be with deep feeling that we approached the lake which had beyond all others been sacred in our thoughts. The lake seemed almost a part of the Bible. It was there that words were spoken and works were done in which heaven and earth were together. It seemed almost as if on the shore of the sea we should meet the Christ himself. We had looked forward to this hour and talked of it. When it came, there was nothing to be said. We communed with our own hearts and were still.

We reached the Sea at Khân Minyeh, which, like Khân Yusêf, is on the old Damascus road. The Khân reckons its years from the time of Saladin, but is now in a dilapidated condition. It has been thought by some that this was the site of Capernaum. Mordecai declared himself of that opinion. But the weight of argument, I think, favors those who put Capernaum a little further up the lake, at Tell-Hûm, where there are the ruins of a place of importance. It is impossible to assign with certainty the sites of some of the places on the shores of this lake. Bethsaida may have been a fishing village where Khân Minyeh is. The Bethsaida which bore the name of the emperor's daughter, Bethsaida Julias, may have been on the opposite side of the river, or may have been a little removed from the shore. It is to be regretted that we cannot be sure regarding the site of Bethsaida, inasmuch as it was the home of Philip, Andrew, and Peter. It is suggested that Khân Minyeh may have been a government station, with a custom-house and other offices, and that Matthew may have been found there when he was called to be a disciple.

We watered our horses at the Fountain of Figs and rode on. We looked up to the Karn Hattîn, the hills whose cone-like shape have given them this name, the Horns of Hattîn. In the time of the Crusades the natives circulated a tradition that the Sermon on the Mount was delivered on this mountain. Indeed, the stone on which Jesus sat with the multitude around him has been pointed out. There is an older Greek story — that the feeding of the five thousand occurred in this mountain. This is simply the result of the common desire to assign places for important events. With the whole land open, places were readily selected, and the imagination of one generation became the belief of another. We saw Tabor far off. We rode through the village of Mejdel, — a forlorn collection of huts holding the ground where Magdala was, the birthplace of Mary Magdalene. Thus we came to Tiberias, where our tents were pitched in the yard of an old Crusader's castle. There, with the sea at our feet, and sacred memories and imaginations in our minds and hearts, we were very glad to settle down. It was a beautiful evening, and Mordecai engaged a boat for the next day, that we might have a ride on the lake and visit Tell-Hûm. It was more than romantic to have the night come to us on the shore of the Sea of Galilee, whose waters, dashing on the beach, gave the last sound we heard as we closed our eyes. Our night was to be less quiet than we thought. We were awakened by the fierce wind, which shook our canvas houses till it seemed almost impossible for them to stand. We waited patiently to see what the end would be. But above all the raging of the storm could be heard the loud voice of Keil, "Antoine! Antoine! our tent is coming down!" Then we heard the pounding which showed that the faithful Arab was driving in the stakes for that tent and the others. The wind kept blowing, and soon Keil's alarmed cry was heard again, "Antoine! Joseph! I think our tent is being blown down!" More pounding followed, and we waited for the light. In the morning our tents were still there. The sea had felt the wind, and the high waves and white caps witnessed to its severity. I have seldom seen a heavier sea than that which dashed upon the shore and broke against the wall, and threw the white spray over the towers. It was hard to believe that this was the quiet lake of the day before. Our excursion was given up, for a fisher's boat could hardly live in such a sea, and no boatman would venture out. Whatever we lost in this way was made up to us by the storm itself. We could realize how suddenly these strong winds arise, how hard it must be to row against them, how easily a boat would be filled and sunk. The thrice-told narrative of a company of men who launched forth upon these waters; of one who laid his head upon the boatman's cushion and in the quietness fell asleep; of the great storm of wind breaking upon them, and beating into the boat till it was full; of the cry of the frightened men as they woke Him who slept,— "Lord, save us; we perish!" of his rising and rebuking the winds and the sea so that there was a great calm,—all this was real and near as we thought upon the serene evening and the night of tempest and the troubled sea. This is one instance of the way in which the land of the Bible illustrates the book.

Tiberias is an imposing name. Its situation is very fine, with the sea in front and the hills behind it. It stands upon or near the site of a city which has perished. Columns of granite which are found indicate that the old city was a place of consequence. The new town was built by Herod Antipas, and in part upon the cemetery of its predecessor. This made the place unsuitable for the residence of Jews, if they were at all strict, and made it necessary to bring in strangers and slaves, and men of many classes, to make a people for the city to which the name of the emperor was given. Herod erected a palace and public buildings of magnificence, and adorned the city with gates and colonnades and statues, and built for the Jews a fine synagogue. The place soon acquired a large importance socially and politically, though as a commercial centre it may have been surpassed. The city was enclosed by walls, which were strengthened with round towers, and was thus protected from an assault by land or sea. The place is mentioned in the New Testament only by St. John, who calls the sea by the same name. It is supposed that our Lord never visited the place.

At the north of the city stands an old castle, deserted and partially destroyed. But it is strong and extensive as it is now seen, and could easily be made a defence against any force that would be likely to assail it. We wandered about its gloomy apartments, and, as in other places, tried to bring back the life which had once filled it. It was more satisfactory to ascend to the top of the broken wall and look down on the lake below us. I do not know why it has ever been questioned whether this sea of many names — Chinnereth, Gennesaret, Galilee, Tiberias — is beautiful or not. To us it seemed fair beyond description. There is not much which is attractive on the western shore, and it is unsafe to intrude into the country beyond its eastern banks. Tell-Hûm is ruins; Capernaum and the Bethsaidas have been lost; Magdala is a desolation, and Tiberias has lost its glory. But the waters are unchanged. The ships and boats have disappeared, for the Arabs have no use for them and no fondness for the sea. The lake has a lonesome look, if you compare the present with the days when many sails flitted from shore to shore, and many nets were drawn through the deep places, which still are tenanted with the fish, whom there are few to disturb. Yet the sea is there, and in itself is fair to look upon as it lies among the hills and mountains, which retain their places and their grandeur.

The shape of the lake or sea resembles a pear. It is about twelve miles long, and in its widest part some six miles broad. It is nearly seven hundred feet lower than the Mediterranean.

Tiberias has little to commend it. The streets are narrow and confused, and at least quite as dirty as in other Syrian towns. There are said to be three thousand people there, and more than half of them are Jews. Many of them have come from Poland, and the language of the people is therefore mixed. The Jewish men wear large felt hats, and keep the front lock of hair long and twist it into a curl. It gives them a queer appearance. The boys wear the hat, and arrive at the curl as early as they can. There are a few small shops, but the wares are not tempting. Girls came to the camp, wearing in the nose a small ornament which should have been of gold adorned with a precious stone. When we offered to buy one of these, a sale was quickly effected, and I presume we might have despoiled the maidens of Tiberias at a small expense. We bought some of these nose ornaments in the bazaars.

We were also visited by an aged Jew. He was poor, as his dress indicated. Indeed, it was his poverty which brought him to us, for he came begging. He was communicative regarding himself and his people. He told us that he had a daughter in the United States, — at St. Louis, I think, — and that he had spent a few years with her. He could not be content there. The Hebrew spirit was too strong for voluntary exile, and he had found his way back to Tiberias, where he was to end his days. He was still looking for the Messiah, with the old hope apparently unbroken. He knew his scriptures and traditions. He knew the rabbies and their tombs, and corrected some of the information which we had received. Beyond any one whom I ever met he was a Jew; a living piece of the old Jewry, with the national sorrow and desire. Despite his poverty and his sorrow, there was something sublime in this venerable personage, waiting in Tiberias, by the Sea of Galilee, for the fulfilment of the promise of his God, and knowing not the day of his visitation.

There are famous springs a little south of the town. The water is hot and sulphurous as it bursts from the ground, but it is believed to have medicinal virtues. There is a large bath-house, consisting for the most part of a huge circular tank, which is the common bathing-place. It is not an attractive place; — it is very unattractive. The steam which fills the room conceals some of the accumulated dirt, but enough is visible and enough more suggested to make a stranger willing to bear the ills he has rather than to plunge into the unsavory ones which invite him. Yet multitudes of persons to the manner born bring their maladies to this pool and seek to have them boiled away.

We visited a building near the baths which contains the tomb of a noted rabbi. The Portuguese and German Jews are in possession of this shrine, and visit it in numbers at Pentecost, when they make burnt offerings of clothes, jewelry, etc., placing them for this purpose on the top of pillars or pillar-like altars hollowed out at the top. The gold and silver are removed from the ashes and put to proper uses. Such is the tale which was told to us, and we saw the pillars. The Jews have a burial-ground west of the town, where many of their distinguished scholars have found a resting-place.

There is a small monastery in Tiberias,— belonging to the Greeks, I believe, — and also a school. There are many synagogues, of course, and one of them near the sea is very old. The interior of the town is in a dilapidated condition through time and earthquakes. Some of the houses have an arbor on the flat roof, which must be pleasanter than the spaces on the other side of the earthen floor in which the trees and vines are set.

Tiberias has its long and varied history, which I shall not attempt to relate or condense. I have spoken of it chiefly as I saw it, roaming through its rough streets, watching its uncouth people, and with delight looking on the sea, wandering on its shore, and dipping the hand into its waters to bathe the head. This is to-day. But there are thronging recollections of the events which have made the Sea of Galilee illustrious. The record of them is throughout the world. With this sea and the country around it the life of our Lord was intimately associated. Capernaum was here, and Bethsaida; and Nazareth was not far away. It was from the shores of this sea that He called his chief disciples, and through its waters he brought fishes to their nets. He trod these waves with the feet which for our advantage were nailed to the cross, and He stilled them with the voice which on one of these mountains taught the multitude, even as near by He fed the thousands with bread from these fields and fish from this sea. It was on this shore that He was seen by his disciples in the early morning, after the weary night, when He bade them "cast the net on the right side of the ship." Into these waters, on which once he had tried to walk, Peter cast himself that he might go to Jesus; and here, when Jesus had fed them with fish from the sea and fish from the coals, He questioned and commissioned the man who thrice confessed his love. It all comes back as you look upon the sea, the unchanged sea.

> "How pleasant to me thy deep blue wave,
>   O sea of Galilee!
> For the glorious One who came to save
>   Hath often stood by thee."

# CHAPTER XI.

FROM TIBERIAS TO JERUSALEM.

IT was in the early morning that we left Tiberias. We saw the sun rise over the Sea of Galilee. Long before it appeared we watched the clouds as they caught the light and were changed into masses of purple and gold. We lingered, enraptured by the glory, and then turned up the hill, often looking back upon the lake which we were leaving, and up into the sky which was fading "into the light of common day." At length sadly we looked for the last time upon the waters which had been so much to us, and moved on our upward way.

Above us, standing out against the sky, above the hill, we saw the outline of a camel descending towards us. Presently we saw that a woman was riding. She was dressed in white, and her appearance was very pleasing and picturesque. She might have been a king's daughter, in her morning ride, or a fair pilgrim communing with the rising sun. The light white folds, which revealed and concealed her, left us to imagine what we would of rank and beauty. Nor was the illusion dissolved till she came so near to us that we could see hanging beneath her moving drapery a pair of large, uncovered, uncomely black feet. Even then, might she not have been of Ethiop's royal line? It is possible.

Hermon we saw once more, with its gleaming snow and all its rugged grandeur, and the Horns of Hattîn rose up among the hills to remind us of the Beatitudes. Tabor's round summit was before us. High above us was Safed, famous for the honey which was gathered from the fertile fields around it; more famous as the "city set upon a hill." The description is accurate, and it may have been that our Lord pointed to Safed when he spoke of the city which cannot be hid, and told of men who ought not to be hid. Safed is still a city, with the remains of its castle and the recollections of Crusaders and Templars. It was one of the four holy cities, and had a rabbinical school and numerous synagogues. But its importance belongs in the past, though many Jews from many lands gather together there, sharing their superstitions and fanaticism. We looked into the Valley of Doves, but the birds which have furnished so much expressive imagery were not to be seen. David sang of "the wings of a dove covered with silver, and her pinions with yellow gold." The Song of Solomon praises the beauty of those who are loved with, "Behold, thou art fair; thine eyes are as doves' behind thy veil." "His eyes are like doves' beside the water-pools; washed with milk, and fitly set."

Then we reached Kefr-Kenna. It is a small, dreary-looking village, of some six hundred people, half Greek Christians and half Mohammedans. The only thing which gives the place any renown is the tradition that it is what is left of Cana of Galilee, the scene of our Lord's first miracle, and of the later one in which he healed the nobleman's son who was at Capernaum. It was there also that Nathaniel had his home. Kefr-Kenna needs something to commend it; but investigation, which spares so little, has wellnigh broken down the old tradition which is the life of the place. A church was built on the site of the house in which was held the wedding feast which was made forever memorable. We went into the building, which is very plain and unattractive. In a large barren room we saw two stone jars or pots, which were set in plaster. The settings differed, but that was not strange. There is as much mystery about the "six water-pots of stone" as could be expected. That they should survive somewhere would not be strange. When St. Willibald was at Kefr-Kenna, only one was to be seen. Centuries later, Lamartine appears to have seen the six. The Crusaders carried them to France, where one is now preserved. One is in St. Ursula's Church at Cologne, but that is much smaller than the two which are now seen in Galilee. The matter is not clear, therefore. Nor does the presence at Kefr-Kenna of the fountain from which the water was brought to fill the jars satisfy us either with regard to the genuineness of the two which are now exhibited, or the identity of the place with the Cana of the Gospel. It would be interesting to be sure of the place and of the water-jars. Yet this is not necessary. The truth and meaning of the narrative do not depend on such things. It is of greater profit to mark the gentleness and kindness which interposed in a time of real if not of extreme necessity, and made "the conscious water" blush that the bride might not blush to remember that the wine failed at her marriage.

There was one conspicuous house in Kefr-Kenna, a white building designed for a school to be connected with the monastery at Nazareth. Four or five miles north is the ruined town of Kâna-el-Jelîl, which is thought to be the place where Cana was. The name sounds more like Cana of Galilee. It is suggested that the guides have a preference for Kefr-Kenna because it is on the direct route from Tiberias to Nazareth. Can this have influenced the sober-minded Mordecai? Can this have helped to take from Kâna-el-Jelîl the honor which the earlier traditions ascribed to it?

We had our noon repast that day in an olive-grove at Er-Reineh, and then rode up a steep hill and had one of the finest views in Palestine, looking upon Nazareth, the plain of Esdraelon, with Hermon and Tabor and the range of Carmel reaching to the great sea. Nazareth is beautiful for situation and fine in itself far beyond any other place we had seen in the land. Its white houses, on the side of a' lofty hill surrounded by hills, make a fine appearance, which is greatly enhanced by the olive and fig trees and the cactus hedges which surround them. It seems like a city in a garden. As we look down upon it, it is the place which we should choose for the home of the Son of Man. In this beauty he grew up, in favor with God and man. Over these hills he wandered, looking far off to the mountains or towards the waters beyond. He plucked the flowers of these valleys, and heard the singing of birds in these trees. In the midst of this bountiful and beauteous nature he lived from his childhood till he was about thirty years old. The place was suited to the man. We can understand in some measure the strength and beauty of a character which was formed amid these scenes, and the love of nature which marked his life and entered so largely into his teachings. He liked the great outer world, which had retained so much of the nature given to it. We came thoughtfully down the hill and pitched our tents at the north side of the town, among the trees.

One thing far beyond all others gives to Nazareth its unchanging interest; yet it has had its history apart from the one life by which it has been consecrated. It finds no mention in the Old Testament, and has no commercial importance in the New. It was only a Jewish town till the time of Constantine. It is a tradition that the first church to commemorate the Annunciation was built by Helena. The vicissitudes of rough days robbed it of its increased honors, which were restored by the Crusaders who erected churches. Saladin wrested it from the Christians, and it was soon destroyed. The French became its patrons, and rebuilt the Church of the Annunciation, and added a cloister. The French and the Turks contended at Nazareth and in the plain below the town. After his victory Napoleon spent a few hours at Nazareth. The homage which he afterward paid to Him who was born there justifies the feeling that deep thoughts filled his mind as he stood with his conquering sword at the birthplace of the Prince of Peace. He must have seen his own littleness and the vanity of his pursuits as he lingered among the quiet memories of Nazareth. The present population of Nazareth I cannot give. The estimates run from five to ten thousand. Among these there are no Jews and a small proportion of Mohammedans. The place has a prosperous look as compared with others. There are steam-mills, which are a sign of modern life, and there is a considerable trade. It has connection by a road with Haifa on the sea and with the country at the east of its hills. In the time of Christ it was a stirring little place, as one of the caravan routes from the sea passed through it and brought into its market-place men of various nationalities. Its synagogue was important as one of the places where the priests met in preparation for their service at Jerusalem. It had, therefore, a close connection with the great city and its temple. Yet the inquiry of Nathaniel, who was of the neighboring town of Cana, "Can any good thing come out of Nazareth?" has suggested the comparative unimportance of the place and its isolation from the great interests of the nation, and perhaps the unpromising character of the people. But it is doubtful whether the guileless Israelite had in mind anything more than that the Messiah could not come from Nazareth. It was written that he should come from Bethlehem. It will be remembered that in the gospel Nazareth is spoken of as a city, which is an indication of its character at that time.

Hither the child Jesus was brought by Mary and

Joseph when Herod was dead and Archelaus was reigning over Judea. For the most part, his long thirty years were spent here. His father was poor. The humble offering which was made when the child was presented at the Temple shows this. Of the life of the child and youth at Nazareth little is told. He was brought up carefully, we may be sure, when we remember all which his mother knew of Him. At twelve He was taken up to the Temple, his Father's house, where He sat among the Doctors, amazing them with his understanding. Then we lose sight of Him till the time for his ministry has come. That He worked at the trade of Joseph is not unlikely. He must have had some trade by the common law. His education was scrupulously regulated. Till the Jewish child was ten, he was taught only the Bible. From ten to fifteen he studied the traditional law, and after that he was instructed in higher matters of theology. The home and the synagogue provided for the teaching which was deemed necessary. It is not difficult to think of this ingenuous boy growing to manhood under his mother's watch and ward. It is not so easy to imagine Him like one of these boys or one of these gay young men. Surely, He could never have dressed as they do, and never have had their bearing and demeanor. No; He was different from them. Yet He was a real boy and a true youth, for He was the Son of Man. If we shrink from placing Him on these rough streets and among these uncouth men, let us remember that it was the rough, rude world into which He came, that He might be in it the Truth and the Life.

Such thoughts come to one at Nazareth, and, while he muses on the past and strives to reproduce it, he is reluctant to go down into the city of to-day, so unlike the Nazareth of imagination and reverence. But we are here to see the place. Let us go down into its narrow streets.

Nazareth is divided between the Latins, the Greeks, and the Moslems. They have separate sections of the town, the Moslems having the smallest. When we had taken a general survey of the town, we naturally desired to see where the house of Mary stood. The house we could not see. Not even tradition could do much for us in this case. I do not know why the house was removed from its proper site. Probably some ecclesiastical exigency demanded it. Or it may have been thought that Nazareth could well afford from its abundance of sacred associations to surrender one for the benefit of distant neighbors. Or it may have been removed to save it from Moslem desecration. Whatever furnished the occasion, angels took up the house and carried it to the height of Dalmatia, near the head of the Adriatic. It was then taken across the sea to Recanati in Italy and finally to the hill of Loretto. There it remains, as multitudes of pilgrims can bear witness. They can testify also to the method of transportation, for only angels could have taken up a stone house, thirty-six feet by seventeen, and have carried it so far safely and speedily. The early history of the house is not known. It does not appear in the Italian records until the fifteenth century. The walls are encased in marble, though

the inner side of them can be seen. They seem to
be "of a dark red polished stone." In the west
wall is a square window through which the angels
of the Annunciation flew. It is "the most frequented
sanctuary of Christendom." It is "the
petrifaction, so to speak, of the 'Last sigh of the
Crusaders,'" and stands as a bit of Palestine in the
domain of the Church. The ages pay their devotions
at this shrine where a hundred priests are in
attendance, and kings and peasants wear the pavement
with their knees as they crawl around the
holy house. I have borrowed this description because
the house seems to deserve it in any account
of Nazareth. Indeed, there are two Nazareths, and
this house makes one of them in a strange land. It
is of course known to the monks who are in possession
of the Church of the Annunciation in Palestine
that the church has given its sanction to the house
beyond the sea. They make the best of their loss
by pointing out the place where it originally stood.
The church at Nazareth belongs to the Franciscans
and stands within the walls of their monastery. It
was very warm as we crossed the yard in front of
the church. We were soon admitted, and found
ourselves in a modern building, that is, one which
in its present form is a hundred and fifty years old.
It is not large, and its appointments are good. The
paintings are of the usual grade in such places.
Marble steps lead up to the high altar and the space
around it. But our interest was below. Fifteen
marble steps descend to what may be called the
crypt. We first entered the Chapel of the Angels,

where there are two altars, one for the angel
Gabriel, and the other for St. Joachim, the legendary father of the Virgin. By two more steps we
reached the Chapel of the Annunciation. The
chapel walls are of marble, and silver lamps shed
a mild light in the dimness. The altar is in a recess,
where a portion of the natural rock can be seen. In
front of the altar is a marble slab, with a cross in
the centre, and the inscription, *Hic Verbum caro factum est.* The stone is worn with the kisses of many
devout lips. It was here that the house of the Virgin
originally stood. It is readily seen that the house at
Loretto does not fit into the place. At the side of the
entrance to this chapel is a pillar marking the spot
where the angel stood when he greeted the Virgin,
" Hail, thou that art highly favored, the Lord is with
thee." Near this is the fragment of a granite column
hanging from the ceiling above the spot where Mary
sat as she listened to her celestial visitant. To prevent one from striking against this depending stone in
the attempt to pass beyond it, a column of marble,
or the part of one, stands directly under the other.
From this chapel there is an entrance to the Chapel
of Joseph, a small dark room with an altar, and the
inscription, *Hic erat subditus illis.* Beyond this are
steps cut in the rock which lead into the "kitchen
of the Virgin." It is simply a cave, small and dismal. It is hard to put the gentle Mary there. This
is not necessary, as the cave was doubtless only a
cistern, and the chimney was the mouth of it. We
made everything as impressive and suggestive as we
could. It needed all our imagination. It may be

granted that those who have built churches over the holy places had a reverent purpose, with their mistaken devotion. If places could have been left as they were, they would render a much better service and more easily. It is not helpful to go into the basement of a church to find a home. The place is gloomy, utterly unhomelike. The sanctity which has been superimposed is burdensome to the faith which would gladly connect sacred events with the places in which they occurred. But when all necessary divesting has been done, it remains that here, certainly very near this church and its dark chapels, the favored Virgin lived, and here was found by her great joy.

In the quarter of the Moslems is the house or workshop of Joseph. At least, that is the name of the small building which is also held by the Latins. It is not claimed that this was actually the building in which Joseph carried on his useful business, but that it stands on the spot where his shop was, and even rests on the same stones. A part of the original wall is also shown. The inevitable church now occupies the ground, with a painting in which the carpenter is seen at his work, and the child Jesus is working with him. We saw the synagogue, or the outside of it, into which Jesus entered when He came back to Nazareth after He had begun his wonderful life abroad; where He read from the roll of Esaias, and announced to his old friends and neighbors, who listened eagerly to hear what one would say whom they had known from his boyhood, that the prophecy of God was his biography, already fulfilled in their ears. The synagogue has gone, but the words remain. The angry hearers of that day "rose up and cast him forth out of the city and led him unto the brow of the hill whereon their city was built that they might throw him down headlong." The Mount of Precipitation is pointed out, but it is too far away to answer the description of St. Luke, if the city then was where the city is now. There are other places where the mad purpose of the Jews could more readily be carried out. It matters little what hill they sought, for his time was not yet come. In another small, bare chapel is to be seen the Mensa Christi, a part of the solid rock which was used by our Lord and his disciples as a table, before and after his resurrection. The table is some twelve feet long and ten wide. It would have answered very well for the purpose assigned to it. We had there the company of a German-speaking priest, a monk whose narrations flowed smoothly from his lips, but seemed to amuse him more than they convinced us, if we could judge from the laugh with which he accompanied his tales.

There is one thing in Nazareth which was probably there in the time of our Lord. This is the Spring of the Annunciation, or the Fountain of the Virgin. It is also called Jesus' Spring and Gabriel's Spring. It is found near the Church of Gabriel, or the Greek Church of the Annunciation. The water is taken into the church and led by the side of the altar, where it can be drawn and used by the Greek pilgrims who are refreshed as they bathe their eyes and heads. By a conduit the water is led to Mary's well, from which it is taken by the women of the city, who continually resort thither for water and gossip. It is a busy scene when they assemble there, of all ages and many conditions. We were amused at the trick of one girl. An old woman had put her stone jar down under one of the small spouts, and was waiting for the water to fill it while her mind was intent on pleasanter things. The girl cleverly put her finger at the end of the spout and diverted the stream into her own jar without disturbing that of her venerable neighbor, who was prompt in checking the diversion when she discovered it. The girls of Nazareth have a good repute for beauty, and they present a pleasant sight as they move from the well into the town, adorned with their strings of coins, and bearing on high their graceful earthen jars. Mary's well has long been used by the people of Nazareth. It may have been — it is more than probable — that Mary herself visited it with her neighbors. One tradition makes this the place where she received the salutation of the angel.

Nazareth maintains its religious character so far as institutions can do this. The Greeks have a church and a bishop; the Latins a monastery and nunnery, and the Protestants have a church and school and orphanage. We were much interested in a bright Christian school-boy who came to our camp. He spoke English well, and gave us a very cheerful impression of his school. We bought in the bazaar some flowers of Nazareth, which are the chief thing offered to strangers. We bought also at

the Bible rooms a copy of the New Testament in
Syriac. The flowers and the book were good souvenirs of our visit. Travellers are entertained at the
Franciscan convent, but we preferred our tents on
an old threshing-floor, where we could be closer to
the life of the old and new Nazareth.

It was in the early morning that we rode from the
town, and all was still. It was good to remind ourselves that we were in the streets of Nazareth. By
the side of the road in one place lay a huge iron
boiler for one of the mills. For the first time my
horse was afraid. He refused to go by till a native
took him by the bridle. He was true to his country.
With the true Syrian instinct he feared nothing but
civilization.

Our path now brought us into the plain of Esdraelon. It was a relief to get down from the hills
and to ride for hours on level ground. We could
ride side by side, or start out on separate raids
which proved the speed of our horses. It was a
famous place. "It is a wide reach of about twelve
miles in width between the mass of southern Palestine and the bolder mountains of northern Palestine." The plain is two hundred and fifty feet above
the level of the sea, and is marshy in some parts.
But the soil is fertile, and in the spring has the
appearance of "a vast waving corn-field." It has
been a renowned place in history. Here the low-
landers and highlanders met and contended for
supremacy. Here "the Lord delivered Sisera into
the hands of Barak." Here Gideon triumphed over
the Midianites and Saul was defeated by the Philis-

tines and "the beauty of Israel" was slain. Here Josiah met Pharaoh-Necho, King of Egypt, as he marched against Assyria; and here he fell, sore wounded by the archers. Among the battle-fields of later times Esdraelon has a place in keeping with its earlier fame.

We looked off upon the mountains of renown, and turned often to look at Nazareth. Its white houses were long to be seen. If at any time in the path we lost sight of them, it was only to regain the fair vision, which was a thing of beauty and delight through the greater part of the day. There were many places of interest on our route. We saw afar off "a city called Nain," once a place of importance, now ruins, with a few Moslems finding a home in the desolation among the graves. Only a few lines in the New Testament preserve its fame. We passed El-Fûleh. It is deserted now, but it has the remains of a castle of the Crusaders which was captured by Saladin. It was near El-Fûleh, in the invasion of Syria by the French in 1799, that Kleber was posted, and here he held in check the Syrian army, with fifteen hundred men against twenty-five thousand, fighting from sunrise till noon, when Napoleon came to his relief and frightened the Turks from the field. Mount Tabor, with its rounded height standing so quietly in the quiet plain, gave no sign that it had witnessed that conflict which bears its name. It is among the most difficult things which the imagination attempts to rebuild the cities which have fallen or restore the perished people to the places which they filled with life. It is perhaps even harder to bring contending armies into the silence and peace which rest on the fields where they fought with the fury of beasts and the brutality of men. We rode through Sûlem, the ancient Shunem. The old story comes up at the name. "And it fell on a day that Elisha passed to Shunem, where was a great woman; and she constrained him to eat bread. And so it was that as oft as he passed by, he turned in thither to eat bread." When she was persuaded of his holy character, she proposed to her husband to make a little chamber in the wall, and to furnish it with a bed, a table, a stool, and a candlestick. This was to be his room so often as he came that way, — the prophet's chamber, which has been repeated in many hospitable homes. It was on the prophet's bed that the good woman laid her son when he was dead, and it was in his room that he gave back to her the living boy. Familiar as it is, there is a pleasure in telling again the simple tale. There is an added pleasure in recalling the incident in its own place. But can this be Shunem? Can a great woman have lived here? In which of these houses would a weary prophet seek bread and rest and find his chamber? There are some two hundred families now there, it is said. But the town is little more than a collection of miserable hovels built of mud and stone combined. A few wretched survivors were sunning themselves, who had only energy enough to stare at the strangers. There must be times when they work, but this was not one of them.

Thus we came to Jezreel, which closely resembles

Shunem. Jezreel is conspicuous in the Old Testament, but there is nothing in the place to suggest this. It was here that Ahab and Jezebel lived, and there are stones now on the hill which belonged in their palace. So it is told, and I do not know why it may not be true. These stones are now the foundation of a much later building, and at the rear of this the inhabitants were sitting around an ox or some member of that family, who had recently been slaughtered and was then undergoing subdivision for the public good. It did not seem an enlivening occupation, but was sufficiently exciting for the participants. We passed a small stream in which, according to the local tradition, the chariot of Ahab was washed after he had been pierced by the Syrian arrow which was sent at a venture, and where the dogs licked up his blood, as Elijah had said. In the Book of Kings the washing is said to have occurred at the pool of Samaria. It was not easy to see how a chariot could be driven from the palace down to the plain. There must have been a road in that day which has been lost to sight. Thus we rode over the red fields of Esdraelon, with the mountains of Gilead in the distance and of Gilboa and Tabor close at hand. So we came to Ain Jâlûd, the spring of Goliath. It has this name from an unfounded tradition that in this valley the giant was overthrown by the young champion of Israel. The Fountain of Jezreel is a more appropriate name for the waters which spring up from the ground and form a pool, and in part issue from a cave in the cliff which rises above the plain. We had our noonday rest here. It was refreshingly cool as we lay on the rocks in the shade, and dreamed among the recollections awakened by everything which we saw. We were told, and the tale is not improbable, that this was the spring to which Gideon brought his army when he was to prove his men by the lapping of the water, and thus find the three hundred on whom he could rely.

Our afternoon's ride brought us to Jenîn, where we made our camp. Jenîn is the most important town between Nazareth and Nablus and is about equally distant from them. It was an old Levitical town under the name of Engannim, or the Garden-spring. That name could easily be corrupted into Jenin. The spring remains as one of the sources of the ancient River Kishon, and the town stands among gardens and orchards. The population is chiefly of the Moslem credulity, and numbers from twenty-five hundred to three thousand. There is a considerable business, especially with the Arabs, from a distance. There was nothing of beauty or interest to be seen. The houses were of the common shape and color, and the few streets had the Oriental characteristics. Our camp was in a grassy field among the huge cactus plants and beside a graveyard. The people of the town have so bad a reputation that the camp pistol was fired, the baggage chained to the tent-posts, and a watch kept through the night. Somebody constructed a scare-crow and put it against our tent. These precautions were successful, and the night passed without disturbance.

The next morning's ride had not very much

worthy of record. We rode by Kabâtîyeh, a large village of stone houses. Mordecai said that this was called "the village of robbers." Whatever the people had stolen they had used up, apparently, as there were no treasures in sight and no other signs of plunder. The place is reputed prosperous. Below us was the plain of Dothan. "And Joseph went after his brethren, and found them in Dothan." Very likely it was by the fountain which is still flowing that they were watering their flock when Joseph found them. It may have been into some one of these ancient cisterns hewn in the rock that they cast the dreamer. There was no water in it, but it would be a secure prison for the boy whom they hated. From Gilead came the Israelites with their loaded camels, carrying their spicery to Egypt, and to them the boy was sold. What story so full of tenderness and unchanging interest, from youth to age! Was it really here that they were, Reuben, and Joseph, and the rest, treading these fields, resting by this spring? Doubtless it was here, but we cannot quite bring it before our eyes. We passed Sânûr, a strong hill town. There was a Moslem fortress here, held by a rebellious people, who were besieged by Abdallah, Pasha of Acre, in 1830. The fortress was taken and burned. The town has been rebuilt, and the fortress again surmounts the hill. We rode across the beautiful plain which bears the name of the "drowned meadow," because in the winter it is covered with water. In the summer the lake dries up, and the rich soil is ready for the seed and the harvest.

We rode on among the hills till we came into a broad basin out of which rose another hill on whose summit was one of the renowned cities of the land. In the history of Omri, King of Israel, we read: "And he bought the hill Samaria of Shemer for two talents of silver, and called the name of the city which he built after the name of Shemer, the owner of the hill, Samaria." This city became the capital of the northern kingdom. There is another passage regarding the place, "I will make Samaria as an heap of the field and as the plantings of a vineyard; and I will pour down the stones thereof into the valley, and I will discover the foundations thereof." The sentence has been fulfilled. Ruins are on the top of the mountain, and on its side, and in the valley. The ruins stand where a great city was. The position was exceedingly strong. The hill was so high and so steep that it was easy to repel an assault. It was finally taken by Sargon, the Assyrian, after a siege of three years. The place had become the seat of idolatry, and there Baal had a temple which Ahab erected and Jehu destroyed. The town was rebuilt and again destroyed and again rebuilt. At length Augustus presented it to Herod the Great, who restored it and renewed the fortifications, and gave to it the name of Sebaste, in honor of the imperial benefactor. The glory long ago disappeared, but there are scattered remains of it. Columns are standing in their old places, and others have fallen which composed a colonnade of grand proportions which Herod probably erected as an ornament to the principal avenue of his city. These stone pillars have a strangely lonesome look as they rise above the desolation and stand as sentinels over a perished past. There are also the ruins of a church built by the Crusaders on the site of a basilica which was standing in the sixth century. The church bears the name of St. John, and there is a tradition that John the Baptist was buried here, while a later tradition has him beheaded here. On the broken walls are still to be traced the crosses of the Knights of St. John. In the court within the walls is the tomb of the saint, covered with a modern Moslem dome. The tomb itself is a grotto or chamber cut in the rock, and is reached by a flight of thirty-one steps. Besides the one who has given its chief fame to this sepulchre, Obadiah and Elisha are also reputed to have found their last resting-place within it. Near the church are the ruins of another building which may have been the residence of high officials when the church was standing. The modern village which has succeeded to the place of Samaria is called Sebastîyeh. There is nothing attractive in the town, unless it be the fallen columns and blocks of stone, some of which have been used for later building purposes.

Among the ruins, beside the standing pillars, we had our simple lunch. Men and children assembled around us and expressed a desire for bakshish. Thus far we understood the Syrian language. One girl rubbed her two forefingers together in a mysterious manner. Mordecai said that by this act she declared herself a Christian and of the same faith and fellowship with ourselves. We were more pleased with another girl who shared to the full the desire for a pecuniary offering, but could not claim it on the same ground. She was of a Mohammedan family, and therefore could not put her fingers together in the prescribed manner. She tried to compromise with her integrity, and brought the fingers as close to one another as a stubborn Syriac conscience would allow, but she could not give the sign. Her struggle and her victory were impressive. They were worthy of the place. We relied on Mr. Garry in such cases, and with his accustomed liberality he bestowed gifts on both the girls. Thus fellowship acquired the pledge it sought and fidelity received its reward.

A ride of two hours brought us to Nâbulus, Nâblus, Sychem, Sychar, Shechem. All these names the place has borne. It was Saturday afternoon, and we were glad to find our tents in readiness between Ebal and Gerizim. It was a good place for the Sabbath. Mr. El-Karey, the Arab missionary from whom we parted at Beirut, came to the camp and then conducted us into the city. We found ourselves in the usual narrow and crooked streets, with more darkness and dirt than in most places. Some of the lanes or passageways run under houses, or houses stand over them, and these tunnels have additional horrors, making them hazardous for the stranger. When a stream of water is rushing down the street the pedestrian finds new difficulties. The houses are of stone and have a substantial appearance. Trees and vines grow among the houses and add something of beauty where the addition is much needed. It is a busy town, having a trade in wool, cotton, grain, and cattle, with places on the sea-shore and in the interior. The olive-orchards enter largely into the domestic and commercial life of the people, who make a free use of the fruit and convert much of the oil into soap. Twenty-two soap-factories are reported, but, judging from the general look of things, nearly the whole product must be sent away. Of course we procured specimens, chiefly as a curiosity. Mr. Garry did the purchasing. The population of the town varies in different accounts. Conflicting statements were reconciled by the remark that one counted the women. There is material for reflection in this assertion, but we will not dwell upon it. There may be thirteen thousand people there, including a very small number of Samaritans and Jews, and a few hundred Christians, while the Moslems are the bulk of the inhabitants and are of a fanatical and rebellious sort. We were taken to the Samaritan synagogue, which is a small room whose walls are whitewashed. We were not invited to enter, but allowed to wait at the door, where the high-priest appeared, to whom we were formally presented by our guide. This ecclesiastic was a young man and had little of the bearing of one in his exalted position. The floor was covered with matting, and on this a few men in white were seated. Some were on a floor a little raised. They were reading their service, which did not seem to be impressive to them and which their manner did not make impressive to us. One of the readers lightened his labor by looking at us and then turning with unconcealed laughter to his neighbor. There is in the synagogue an ancient copy of the Pentateuch, which was written by the grandson or great-grandson of Aaron, — so the tradition informs the credulous. We wished to see it, and a roll of parchment was produced and opened. I presume that we were expected to believe that this was what we sought, but we knew that it was not the most ancient and most hallowed scroll. That El-Karey said we could not see. Much elaborate ceremonial and preparation was necessary before it could be taken from its silver case and satin robe and exposed to the eyes of a favored few of the sons of men. We paid three francs for the one which we saw, and that was three francs too much.

We looked into the great mosque, which the Crusaders erected as the Church of St. John. The gateway is in good condition, and certainly had claims to some beauty before the Mohammedans covered its stones with tawdry colors. The building has borne well the passing of the centuries.

There is not very much in Nâblus to detain travellers. The bazaars are like those in other places where the manufactures of the country are blended with those from the western world. The costumes are of interest, the people are a study, the camels are obtrusive, and the whole scene is Oriental, with a border from the newer world. It is the city of the elder days which engrosses the thoughts of the stranger, who is carried back by its history almost to the beginning of things. Shechem was here when Abram came into Canaan. "Abram passed through the land unto the place of Sichem. . . . And the Canaanite was then in the land." Jacob pitched his tent before the city and "bought a parcel of a field where he had spread his tent. And he erected there an altar, and called it El-elohe-Israel." I need not trace again the story of the city as it has been recorded. It was here that Rehoboam came to meet his people and be made their king, and here that the policy was inaugurated which divided the kingdom. The ten revolting tribes made this their capital, and here Jeroboam resided. After the captivity it became the seat of the Samaritan worship. The name of Samaria extended far beyond the city on the hill, and covered all of Palestine which was above Judea. The part on the east of the Jordan, and that which was afterward known as Galilee, Samaria lost, and thus became reduced to the middle one of the three districts of Palestine as we commonly see it. The Samaritans were separated from the temple and city which the nation had reverenced, and became idolatrous. The Assyrians finally swept them away and into their places were sent settlers from the east, who mingled with any who may have been left behind by the conquerors. Thus a mongrel people possessed the land, and their religion was like those who formed and used it. A new temple arose on Gerizim, and new rites rivalled those at Jerusalem. It is easy to see how there came to be the enmity which was so persistent and extreme between the two peoples and the two religions and which is expressed in the mild words of the Evangelist, "For Jews have no dealings with

Samaritans." Yet the Samaritans had a good place for their home; and a fine site for their chief city, between Ebal and Gerizim, in the plain over which passed the responsive blessings and curses of the old law. On Mount Gerizim are extensive ruins of a castle and a church. The site of the ancient altar is marked, so the Samaritans think, by a sloping rock, before which they take off their shoes. They point to the rock on which Abraham would have offered Isaac, though that was probably not on this mountain: and to the stones of the altar which Joshua built and on which he wrote the law, although in the book which bears his name that is said to have been on Ebal. But it seems probable that some of the stones that are now lying on the mountain belonged in the Samaritan temple. It would be expected that the building should leave such substantial traces of its presence, even if they gave no clear suggestion of the structure of which they formed a part.

Among these ruins the Samaritans continue to worship. The great festivals are still observed where they were kept in the days of prosperity, and the ceremonies are described as impressive, while they must be attended with a great sadness. There is a true pathos in the words of the Samaritan woman to our Lord, " Our fathers worshipped in this mountain; and you say that in Jerusalem is the place where men ought to worship." The temple of the Jews was then standing, thronged with worshippers. But there was a deeper meaning than she knew, deeper than the falling of the temple could disclose, in the words with which he replied to her: "Woman, believe me, the hour cometh when neither in this mountain nor in Jerusalem shall ye worship the Father." The years have brought their fulfilment. The mountain has been deserted and in the city the mosque casts its baleful shadow over all the altars. He meant more than this. He did not propose to exclude these places from the kingdom which was to come: but that worship should no longer be rendered especially at these conspicuous and contending shrines, but should be extended through all the earth. These are good thoughts wherewith to end the week.

It was pleasant to have Sunday morning come to us in Shechem. We had slept with a guard of four soldiers about our tents, and the day began with soldiery, for a procession of men went by the camp, followed by women who were wailing bitterly. El-Karey said that they were men who had avoided serving in the late war with Russia and were now being driven to the army to make up for their delinquency.

It had been arranged that we should have a service in Mr. Karey's chapel, and a man was sent to conduct us to the place. It was thought best to meet in his dwelling-house, and we were taken there, where we had an hour of worship. Including his man we numbered eleven. We sang from the Gospel Hymns, — the Lord's song in a strange land, — and worshipped "in spirit and in truth." The brief sermon could have but one theme. That Christ had been there, that he had rested at the well near by, was in our minds, and naturally formed the subject of the address. There was a rare delight in reading and repeating his words where they were first spoken. We lingered for some time with the Kareys and saw a little of their manner of life. Their house was quite large and very comfortable. But we fancied that the English ladies had not become entirely reconciled to their change of domicile. We invited them to dine with us, and in the afternoon they came to our camp. We enjoyed extending the stranger's hospitality to this missionary and his household. It was an event in our nomadic life. Mr. Mill and Mordecai and Joseph exerted themselves in honor of our guests, and a repast was provided which exceeded all our former experience. Everything was in the best of order. Fringes of paper adorned our candlesticks. All the elegancies which we had were brought forward. The luxuries of the time and the place abounded. Course followed course with precision and propriety. Best of all was it to have ladies at our table. I can never forget our feast under the shadow of the great mountains. When it was over, we ended the day in conversation, drawing from our missionary friend the information which he was glad to impart. Then as the evening drew on we said our last good-bys. Our friends went back to their home and their work. I wonder how it has fared with them since, — if the good wife has truly found a home in an Arab city, and if her sister still sings of " Sweet Beulah land, where mansions are prepared for me." There are many strange things to which the western dweller in the East must accustom himself or ever it can be made home to him. His house at least should be his own, and there his old life can preserve itself.

We saw on Saturday in Nâblus a funeral procession. Men were walking rapidly through the crowd, carrying a coffin on their shoulders, and singing a mournful chant. Mr. Karey said that when the coffin had rendered up its wrapped inmate at the grave it would be brought back for a like service in another's behalf. It seemed strange to us but not to them.

We thought of Abraham as the sun went down, and of those who had looked up to these hills in many generations, and then we slept with our soldiers watching before the tents.

It was well to rise early in the morning in which we were to leave Shechem that we might not be hurried as we wound out of the centuries which still remain in the mountains and the valleys. A short ride brought us to Joseph's tomb. "The bones of Joseph, which the children of Israel brought up out of Egypt, buried they in Shechem, in a parcel of ground which Jacob bought of the sons of Hamor the father of Shechem for an hundred pieces of silver: and it became the inheritance of the children of Joseph." This place answers the description, and there seems no reason to doubt that it was here that the coffin of Joseph was laid when his hundred and ten eventful years were ended. The Moslems say that the body was afterward carried to the cave of Machpelah at Hebron. But they join in paying reverence to this spot. H. B. M. consul at

Damascus in 1868 was so well assured of the identity of this grave that he put a wall around it and inserted in the wall a marble tablet commemorating his confidence and his conduct. The enclosure is perhaps twenty feet square, and is open at the top. It is divided into two parts. The grave is in the usual style and is about seven feet long by three or four feet high. At each end of the grave is a square pillar which was hollowed at the top so that the incense and possibly other things could be burned upon it. The superstructure of the tomb seemed to have been used for a similar purpose. Some of the cinders of past offerings remained. In the wall are niches in which lamps are placed on special occasions. There is nothing impressive about the place except as the visitor furnishes it out of his own thoughts. There is more than the usual difficulty in connecting the man and the tomb. For a life so romantic, so full of intense interest, with such a charm for youth and age, this is a dull and dreary resting-place. It seemed incredible that this could be its earthly consummation. We wanted more or less. Either less or more would have been fitting: more of nature or less of man.

Not far away is Jacob's well. This is disappointing, of course. Yet we were more familiar with it, and in itself it seems more a part of the time in which it belongs. The old is there, and changed but little except in growing older. It is agreed that the well and its name belong together, and that this is the well of which Jacob himself drank, and his sons and his cattle. Some have been surprised that he should have dug a well here, two miles from the city. It was its distance from the city which commended the spring to him, it is natural to believe. The people of the city would not wish to have him and his large flocks and herds depend upon their wells, while he would certainly prefer to be independent of them. He provided this well for his own house, and left it for those who should come after him. This personal character of the well has been preserved. At the opening of the fifth century a church stood around the well. It is reported that the church was in the form of a cross, having the well at the centre. Before the Crusades the church had fallen, and part of its ruins remain. At first you see only a mass of rubbish, in which is an opening into what is left of a vault which covered the well. You can go down into this vault and stand by the true mouth of the well. There is a stone over this some two feet square, and in this a round hole through which you may look into the neck of the well. This is perhaps four feet long. The well itself is about eight feet in diameter. Its depth it is not so easy to state. In 1697 it was given as one hundred and five feet, with fifteen feet of water. In 1841 it was seventy-five feet. The stones which have fallen and been thrown into it readily account for the difference in these measurements. A rough masonry lined the upper part of the well, and perhaps the entire interior. There is an unusual interest in Jacob's well from its association with him, and for the long years in which it rendered a rare and needful service to the travellers between Judea and Galilee. But beyond any other attraction is that which belongs to it because of its connection with our Lord. In no other place can one feel an equal confidence that we are on the very spot which his presence made sacred. The outer beauty and service have not remained. But the lessons which he taught, being here, have lost nothing of their meaning or inspiration.

He had no prejudice which kept him from passing through Samaria or restrained him from talking with a Samaritan and a woman. Perhaps she came at noon that she might meet no one. Why she was so far from Sychar, if that be Shechem, we cannot tell. Some work she had near the well, it may be, or her home even. She came to draw water, and found a stranger sitting on the curb, wearied with his journey. " Give me to drink," He said. It was a chance to triumph over him, this Jew, compelled to ask drink of a woman of Samaria. He was not vexed at her bantering words. " If thou knewest the gift of God, and who it is that saith to thee, Give me to drink, thou wouldst have asked of Him and He would have given thee living water." Again she saw her chance, yet was less trifling. "Sir, thou hast nothing to draw with, and the well is deep." Still, He would fain help her. " Whosoever shall drink of the water that I shall give him shall never thirst." " Sir, give me this water." She had grown to a suppliant in her manner, and half perceived there was a meaning in his sentences. " Go, call thy husband and come hither." She was startled at his knowledge of her, and made haste to shift the conversation from husbands to mountains. She drew out from Him that sublime declaration, "God is a spirit: and they that worship Him must worship Him in spirit and in truth." She was eager at last. Her slumbering hope was quickened. She forgot her shame in her awakened faith. "I know that Messiah cometh." "Jesus saith unto her, I that speak unto thee am He." All this was here. The woman here found what so few had discovered — that God was her Father, and that living water she could have for the asking. Here by this wellside she left the water-pot she had brought; left it, the sign of her old life; and, possessed of a new spirit and a new delight, she hastened into the city with her question, "Can this be the Christ?" It all comes back as we wait by Jacob's well, peer into the anxious faces, and hear the earnest questions and replies, and look off on the wide fields which even then were white with the harvest; the harvest which even yet has not been gathered in.

Patience, good Mordecai! When will you bring us to another place like this? "So when the Samaritans came unto Him, they besought Him to abide with them: and He abode there two days." But the sun is getting high, and the way is long before us. Let us move on.

This day we passed Lebonah, which gains the little interest which appertains to it from its mention in the Book of Judges in connection with the desperate attempt by the men of Benjamin to procure wives. They were told to go up to the feast in Shiloh, "in a place which is on the north side of Bethel, on the east side of the highway that goeth up from Bethel to Shechem, and on the south side of Lebonah." They were to lie in wait in the vineyard, and when the daughters of Shiloh came out to dance they were to come out and catch every man his wife, and carry her to his home. And they did so. "In those days there was no king in Israel: every man did that which was right in his own eyes." A few people remain in Lebonah, which is now Lubban, and there are tombs in the rocks which are memorials of better days.

Thus we came to Shiloh. The name promises a great deal, but the place does not furnish it. It was one of the early sanctuaries of the Hebrews, and in it the great Tabernacle was set up and the Ark of the Covenant rested. But from the time that the Philistines conquered Israel and captured the ark, which had been carried into battle, the place lost its importance. The sad story of Eli and the charming account of the boy Samuel invest it with interest, in addition to the other events which made it conspicuous. The traces of a vanished city are now to be found, and ruins are scattered over the hill. Cisterns and tombs remain in the desolation which has fallen upon the better past. We brooded over the changes which time and man had wrought, and realized as in few other places how much has perished out of the history of this land and its people, so prominent in the world's thought and life. Here at Shiloh, as we rested and mused at noon, we saw the remains of a church, with thick walls enclosing a room with an arched ceiling supported by columns.

Another building was near by where there was also a vaulted room. The sides of the building had a slanting appearance from a buttress which slopes up from the ground and sustains the wall. Surely this was very little for so great a name.

We came in the afternoon to Bethel. It received this name, the House of God, from Jacob, who there slept, with stones for his pillow, and saw in his dreams the ladder which reached from earth to heaven. In the early morning he changed his pillow into a pillar, and hallowed it with the oil which he poured upon it. "And he called the name of that place Bethel: but the name of that city was called Luz at the first." The city became prominent in the history of Israel. Indeed, it had an earlier importance. For it was near Bethel that Abram halted when he came into the land and set up his tent and altar. To Bethel he returned after his sojourn in Egypt, and from a neighboring hill he looked with his nephew over the surrounding country when he gave to Lot the choice of a dwelling-place for himself and his flocks and herds. There the young man showed the character which he held to the last. Perhaps the old man, who was as a father to him, had been over-indulgent towards his brother's son. Perhaps the experience of Lot in Egypt had brought him under the fascination of city life, so that Sodom was more attractive than the country towards the Great Sea. But it was here that God came to Abram when Lot had left him, and made to him the magnificent promise which has been so grandly fulfilled.

Here Samuel held his circuit court, and here Jeroboam established the worship of his golden calves. Beth-el became Beth-aven, the house of idols, or house of vanity. The situation of Bethel would prevent it from being a large place, but its renown did not depend on its dimensions, nor could it be preserved by them. It still existed after the captivity, but its glory had departed long before. The town now remains under the name Bêtîn, but is a collection of wretched houses where some four hundred people solicit bakshîsh and tobacco.

We made our camp in an old reservoir. This is about a hundred yards long and seventy wide. It was enclosed in substantial walls, large portions of which are now standing. We found an excellent place for our tents on the earth which now occupies the place of water. At the spring near us female Bêtînites were washing their jars and filling them. The process did not make us thirsty as we watched it. The girls seemed in excellent spirits, and would undoubtedly have been communicative but for certain linguistic difficulties. They looked more than they said, and the outstretched hand indicated hospitality less than bakshish. We walked into the village on the hill and examined the ruins of a church. These had signs of beauty and wealth beyond anything of the present time, and seemed strangely out of place. Part of an old tower stands in the village; but who built it, or when, nobody knows. A modern superstructure makes it of service to men who could not have erected it. There are some ruins in the fields, but none which are of any account.

Our next day's ride was of special interest. We passed through Dêr Diwân, a Christian village not far from where the city of Ai stood. Ruins once more. In the distance we saw Neby Samwîl, the mountain where Mizpeh, the watch-tower, is thought by some to have been. The name of the prophet belongs with the tradition that it was here Samuel was born and that here he was buried. We also saw Rimmon on its hill, where the survivors of the army of Benjamin took refuge after the battle of Gibeah when the enemy had chased the Benjaminites and trodden them down by the thousands, and gleaned of them in the highways. But six hundred men turned and fled to the wilderness, unto the rock Rimmon, and abode in the rock Rimmon four months.

We watered our horses at the robbers' spring, and had our nooning under a thorn-tree, whose thin branches were a poor protection from the hot sun. In the afternoon we had a good view of the Dead Sea, which we had before seen afar off, and the Jordan. We saw the mountains of Gilead, and the mountains of Moab, with Nebo, and the tomb in which Moslem tradition has laid the body of Moses. We passed the Mount of Temptation, with tombs on its side. Our way this day was harder than any we had seen. Much of the time there was no path, and the rocks were strewn and piled in such confusion that it was almost like descending a long flight of steps which had been shaken by an earthquake. We did more walking and leaping and climbing than usual, and the horses had enough to do to get themselves down in safety. We were coming near to Jericho. We rode past the old town, or what is left of it, on the hill-side. The ruins were more ruinous than is common. We came down to a narrow shallow stream, called the Sultan's Spring, which once furnished water for this city. We preferred to recognize it as Elisha's Spring and to receive the tradition that it was here Elisha cast in the salt and said, "Thus saith the Lord, I have healed these waters; there shall not be from thence any more death or barren land." We rode through the stream, letting our horses drink of the healed water from which our camp was also supplied. For we set up our tent near by and were not sorry that we were drawing near the end of our pilgrimage. Through the day we had two soldiers, in very unmilitary attire, as guides and guards. At night a man reputed to be the brother of the sheikh came in to take command of our forces and to be our security against assault. The principle seemed to be not that these armed men were in their valor strong against all comers, but that they were representatives of the ruling powers and would be content with what we chose to give them instead of helping themselves. The whole theory of Arab robbery, as it was explained to us, was that it is simply the act of the strong against the weak. If we were the stronger, we might fairly be expected to do the same thing. There is much in history to justify this view of the matter. It was also asserted, and probably with truth, that the Bedouins have no desire to harm the person and will only do so to secure a higher end or to protect themselves.

Probably a pistol is most dangerous to the traveller who carries it. He could hardly do a more hazardous thing than to use it against an Arab. To let it be seen or heard at a safe distance may be of some advantage. But it is best to trust to a good dragoman and purchase safety at a price which is not extortionate. It increased our sense of safety to see the doughty warriors at the head of our line. But to have the brother of the sheikh! There were no signs of royalty about him, though he was better armed than the other guardians of our peace. He was a pleasant fellow so far as we could have intercourse with him. On the other side of the bushes about our tents we heard the cries of jackals. Their sound was painfully human. In a great city we should have been certain that packs of the wildest street Arabs, crowds of hoodlums, were in their wildest games and most frantic warfare.

In the morning we set out for the Dead Sea. We soon came into the present village of Jericho. It seems absurd to give that name to the forlorn group of houses through which we passed. Low and dark, with rough walls of stone and a flat roof covered with brush on which earth has been laid, they are only less dismal than the people around them, who seem as unconscious as their houses that there is anything unattractive in their appearance. We saw the site of the house of Zacchæus, which is marked by a tower-like building and is certified to by a tradition which is not venerable. Near it is a Greek convent and hospice with the neatness and thrift which tell of a different class of residents. A camp of gypsies was also there, looking as such establishments always look, save that in the East their forlornness is unconcealed. Some work was going on, and some of the men, finding that we were willing to buy their weapons, offered them at prices which was a sign of their real poverty and our apparent wealth. Thorn-bushes abounded on our path. These serve a very good use as hedges, for they are impenetrable by man or beast, unless they are violently torn away. The belief that the crown placed upon our Saviour's head was made from thorns like these is rational. We saw the apple of Sodom, a fruit which resembles a small apple but has nothing else to commend it. Thus we came to the shore of the sea. The water was calm and clear, but the desolation was profound. Something may be ascribed to our preconception, but the whole scene is dreary. Death seems to be around the sea, as it is in its name. The silence was unbroken. The very sand and pebbles of the beach had a pale, forbidding look, and the scant bushes reaching out their white arms as if to repel an advance, while the brushwood and pieces of trees on the shore lifted up their weird, bleached forms as if they wondered at our intrusion. The old belief that these waters cover the cities of the plain, and that columns and arches can be seen in their old places under the surface, has long ago been dispelled. The sea, or a sea, was here while the cities were standing. Indeed, no one can tell where they were. They perished in fire, which could not have found it difficult to destroy places with a foundation of bitumen. No fish are found in these waters, no shell nor coral, and fish which are put into it are soon dead. But it is not true, as has often been said, that no bird can fly across the sea. The whole place is remarkable. It is thirteen hundred feet below the level of the Mediterranean, and thirty-seven hundred below Jerusalem. The scenery about it is pleasant. Ruins are found upon its banks, where hermits once found a place of residence suited to their peculiar purposes. Sometimes a storm breaks in upon the sea and raises its tranquillity into heavy waves, which soon become quiet when the wind has gone down. The heaviness of the water is its most obvious quality. Its specific gravity varies in different parts of the sea, but everywhere greatly exceeds that of common salt-water. It is easy to float on its surface and often difficult not to do so. If one loses his footing on the slippery bottom he finds it a hard matter to get on his feet again. Mordecai would not let the horses go in for fear that they would come to harm. Vespasian is reputed to have tied the hands of men behind their backs and then to have thrown them into this sea, where he could gaze at their helpless rolling and tumbling. When we came out of the water we felt as if we had been oiled. We were willing to leave the lake to the desolateness which is not likely to be broken unless the projected canal should take the Dead Sea into its course. We were told that French explorers used a steam yacht on the lake, and gave it to the neighboring sheikh when they were done with it. The Arabs came and broke it up, unwilling that the arts of the West should invade their barbarism.

We hurried up to the Jordan and dismounted at the pilgrim's fording and bathing place. The river is so very swift that there are usually few places where it can be forded or where bathing can be indulged in. The tradition that our Lord was baptized here has given to this place a sacred renown, and from early days it has been accounted a privilege to bathe here. At one time it is related that the banks were covered with marble and that a wooden cross stood in the stream. The priest blessed the water, the pilgrims entered it, and preserved the linen covering which they wore that they might be wrapped in it for burial. The water of the river is of a clay color. We went in with caution, but found it easy and agreeable to bathe as long as we pleased. We were glad to wash off the oily sensation we had brought from the Dead Sea, whose waters are much clearer in appearance, but much less pleasing in all other respects. Trees and bushes of different kinds were growing on the banks. We were kept busy during our intermission in thinking upon the events into which the Jordan runs, and gathering up the impressions which the place suggested. On our return we passed the ancient Gilgal on what many think to be the proper place for that name. A large tree is now in possession of the ground. If this is Gilgal, then here the Israelites encamped when they first entered Canaan after crossing the divided river. "And those twelve stones, which they took out of Jordan, did Joshua pitch in Gilgal." A church was built afterward upon this spot, and the twelve stones were enclosed within it.

We reached our camp at the close of an interesting day. The ride was an easy one. It gave me a good opportunity for a long talk with Mr. Garry, who told me many things out of his own life, and let me see how much of incident may come into the career of a quiet man. I cannot write the tales which he narrated. But, as I recall them now, it seems strange that we should have been riding to Jericho in conversation on things which happened long ago in the mountains of Pennsylvania. We had taken our home and our home-life with us, and under all the events and impressions of the Holy Land these held their place and were readily uncovered. As this was our last night together, our men gave us a characteristic exhibition. Some covered themselves with skins and represented bears or other wild animals, while their leaders set them to performing all manner of antics, yelling at them and beating them as if they were beasts in reality. It was a droll performance in the evening light beside Jericho, with these dancing, singing, howling men entertaining the western strangers. We appreciated their efforts, which were grotesque and exciting, but it is hard to give any impression of them in words. At length it was all over, and we stretched ourselves on our iron beds to rest till the dawning of the day in which we should see Jerusalem. Sing once more, Logan, before night fairly closes in upon us. Sing, "Are your windows open towards Jerusalem?"

The sunrise over the mountains of Moab was very fine as we prepared to move on. We took an early start. This was the day to which we had long been looking forward. We found the greater part of the road very hilly and rough. A part which had been recently built was very good. We passed the ruins of old aqueducts whose usefulness was over. We saw what is left of the Jericho of Herod. We came to the inn to which the Good Samaritan brought the man who had fallen among thieves. Three men were sent to help the poor fellow, but only one of them was good enough for the work which should immortalize him. There were no guests at the inn when we reached it. In fact, the inn itself was not there, but the floor of a ruined khân where travellers were once allowed to rest. We rode upon this floor and thought the story over. It was very near this place that the inn stood. Why not just here? The very spot where the Samaritan found the stranger was pointed out to us. The road was certainly one on which robbery could easily have been committed then, or in later times. Noon brought us to the Apostles' Spring or Fountain. As the name denotes, the apostles were accustomed to drink of its waters in their journeys between Jerusalem and Jericho. There was at one time a fine building over the spring, and part of it remains, holding an archway over the water. On the opposite side of the road was a ruined khân, where we had our simple repast and bade adieu to cold chicken. The water of the spring was good, and it is by no means unlikely that the apostles may have been refreshed by it in their time.

We rode up the Mount of Olives, saw Bethphage,

looking dull and dreary on its hill, and came into Bethany and rode among its dismal houses, so unlike any thought which we had had of the town of Mary and Martha. From the mount we had our first view of Jerusalem. It was the supreme moment of all our journey. This was "the joy of the whole earth," "the city of the great King," "beautiful for situation." We saw the hills and walls and gates; the great churches and the countless domes of the houses. We saw the city lying in peace where it had been for so many centuries; centuries holding the heart of the world's history. Far beyond all which we saw with the eye was that which we saw with the mind and the heart. For over all which was visible we looked upon the real Jerusalem.

We came down past Gethsemane and the Church of the Virgin. We crossed the dry brook of the Kedron, saw the swift, clear waters of Siloa's brook, and rode through the valley of Jehoshaphat and by its graves, past the tomb of Absalom and the pile of stones beside it, by the tomb of Jehoshaphat, the grotto of St. James, the tomb of Zechariah, the village of Siloam, the Mount of Offence, the Hill of Evil Counsel, the Potter's Field high up on a bluff, the cave in the hill, the pool of Siloam, and the Virgin's Fountain above the valley of Hinnom and its pool, past Job's well and Isaiah's tree, under which he mended his clothes, by Solomon's garden, which was very green; crossed Hosanna Street, and thus came to our resting-place.

Our entrance into the city was more exciting than we expected, and might have been disastrous. As we rode slowly up the hill, some boys with wheelbarrows were coming down. One saw his opportunity and started on a run. What horse of any spirit would endure such a descent upon him? Not Prince. He saw and started. I was not prepared for this, and for a few seconds it was doubtful what the result would be. I succeeded in keeping my seat till the good horse was quieted. But the episode was a startling one. My faithful attendant ran after the boy, but pursuit was useless, and we resumed our march. Soon we were at Teil's Hotel, near the Jaffa gate. We were in Jerusalem.

## CHAPTER XII.

### IN AND AROUND JERUSALEM.

I HESITATE to begin this chapter. The word "Jerusalem" suggests far more than can be written. The most sacred influences and associations cluster around this beautiful and despoiled city, this proud and humbled, this towering and buried capital. Who shall write of this? The guide-book which I carried opened its account of Jerusalem with Newton's familiar lines : —

> "Glorious things of thee are spoken,
> Zion! city of our God!"

Jerusalem is a mountain city. It is on a high table-land, more than two thousand feet above the Mediterranean. Standing on Mount Zion and Mount Moriah, the city well deserves to be called the "mountain throne" and "mountain sanctuary." "Beautiful in elevation, the joy of the whole earth, is Mount Zion, on the sides of the north, the city of the great King." The wall which now surrounds the city was built, or rebuilt, in 1542, by Suleiman the Magnificent, the successor of Selim I., the conqueror of Egypt. The population of the city is variously given, but is probably about twenty-four thousand. The Christians, Jews, and Mohammedans have their separate quarters, as elsewhere. The three nationalities have their separate claims to the renown of the place. To the two former it is pre-eminently the Holy City, while to the last it is one of the three sacred cities. Few places have so eventful a history as that of Jerusalem. That it was the Salem where Melchizedek reigned — that lonely, stately figure before which Abraham paid homage — is more than doubtful. But we read of Adonizedec, King of Jerusalem, in Joshua's time. When the Israelites came into the land, they took the city from the Jebusites who were settled in it; but the old proprietors retained Zion, which was their stronghold. David captured the fortress and established his capital where it stood. Solomon used his wealth and power in strengthening and adorning the city, and gave to it its chief glory when he erected the Temple which his father desired to build. When the kingdom was divided, this capital lost some of its importance, though it remained the centre of the real national life. I cannot trace its history through the rugged and broken years which followed until its final overthrow by Titus, when all the forces which cruelty, tyranny, and wealth could devise were leagued against the devoted, despairing, unyielding people, to whom the city and its Temple were more precious than life. It was a complete destruction. The Temple fell, yielding its splendor and renown to the unsparing fires, and the towers which the conqueror would have preserved as memorials of his costly triumph shared the common desolation. The ploughshare passed over the ground where the sacred house had been. A little town sprang up around the Roman garrison, and afterward Hadrian built another city with palaces and temples and the divinities of Rome. Wars upon wars, sieges on sieges, brought their violence against the city of peace. What names are clustered in its violent annals — Chosroes the Persian, the Caliph Omar, Godfrey of Bouillon, Saladin and Selim and Suleiman! It is no wonder that the city has gone, buried beneath its own ruins, and that its venerated places have been lost. The Jerusalem under the Crescent is not the proud city of David and Solomon. The stranger walks over the perished grandeur and treads upon the fallen sacredness. We are inclined to say that no higher purpose could be served by modern Jerusalem than the restoration of the old by the removal of the new. It would be a satisfaction here, as in other places, to stand where the past was in the days of its greatness. It is with profound satisfaction that the stranger sees that while the city has gone, the mountains which surrounded it still hold their place, and enable him in a remarkable degree to restore the Jerusalem which has perished.

I can write of but few things in Jerusalem, and I shall set them in no order. Perhaps in this way I can best take the reader along its streets. The air of antiquity is on almost everything which is Jewish or Mohammedan. What has the look of newness has been brought in from Christian lands. The streets are like all streets in this part of the world — narrow, rough, crowded. For that one cares little.

It belongs with the land. Mordecai felt a local shame as he walked with us through his own section, and he remarked, with a sigh or a sneer, "They make us pay taxes to keep the streets lighted, but they don't do anything. It takes all the money to support their wives." It is natural to seek the old Temple, or the place of it, that we may be in the city of ancient days. The hill on which stood the three temples of Solomon, Zerubbabel, and Herod is in the south-east quarter of the present city, Walls were constructed on the top of Mount Moriah, making a lofty platform for the sacred houses. The platform is irregular in its shape, and its dimensions are given differently by those who have measured it. For our purpose it is near enough to say that it is about sixteen hundred feet on the east and west sides, by a thousand on the other two. It is not clear on what portion of this large area the temples stood. Of the old buildings, of course, nothing remains unless it be in separate blocks of stone. But portions of the foundation walls, or the substructure on which they rested, have had firmness enough to hold their place.

It required the usual amount of diplomacy and expense to obtain the right to visit the hallowed enclosure and its buildings. This business was performed by others in our behalf, and we entered the Harâm esh-Sherîf. It is not long since Christians were prohibited from treading the holy ground. But western intrusion has opened the gates, and with our armed guard and a retinue of attendants we made our way in. We came to an elegant pulpit of marble, built in the fifteenth century. It rests on horse-shoe arches, and is surmounted by a canopy which is sustained by slender columns. The carving is abundant and graceful, and the whole structure is a pleasing specimen of the art which constructed it. There was no one to forbid us, and with the professional instinct and with the boy I ventured up the long marble stairs and stood where the duly authorized man preaches to the faithful in the fast of Ramadan. We felt that we could have discoursed to the edification of the faithful, or at least to their advantage; but they were not there to listen, even if our sentiment and pantomime could have passed for preaching. There were themes enough about us on every side and as far as the eye could reach over city and country. It needed more ceremony to visit the Dome of the Rock, the great mosque in which the interest of the place now centres. The mosque stands on a platform ten feet high, which is reached by flights of steps on three sides. At the top of the steps are elegant arches or arcades which bear the name of the Scales, because from them are to hang the balances in which the righteous and the wicked will be weighed in the Judgment. Protecting our feet and the pavement with appropriate slippers we entered the "noble sanctuary." This is octagonal in shape, and each side is sixty-six feet long. It was covered with marble, but porcelain tiles were placed on the upper part by Suleiman in 1561. Passages from the Koran form a frieze for the building. The Byzantine style and taste govern the design of the mosque. The dome, which gives its name to the house, is a fine piece of Oriental workmanship. It rests on four massive piers, and is itself nearly a hundred feet in height and sixty-five in diameter. It is made of wood, and is richly adorned on the inside. Under the dome is The Rock. Twelve columns stand around it among the piers of the dome, and an iron railing keeps off all intruders, while a crimson canopy hangs over it. It is a limestone rock, fifty-seven feet long and forty-three wide, and at its highest part is some five or six feet above the pavement. It appears to have been a part of the summit of Moriah, and to have been left when the top of the mountain was levelled to make a place for the Temple. What its history is cannot be told with certainty. That Abraham and Melchizedek offered sacrifice upon it, and that here Isaac was bound for a burnt offering, and that Jacob anointed it with oil, tradition claims. It is connected with Mohammed, which would be enough to make it renowned. It was the last place which his foot touched as he left the earth, and his footprint is still to be seen. The rock, naturally and unnaturally, proposed to accompany him, but was arrested in its flight by Gabriel, who left the mark of his hand upon the stone. The rock cried out when the prophet went up, and its tongue remains in sight. The rock now keeps its place without support, if we can believe it. This is difficult, because if one's eyes are to be trusted it has visible means of support. We went into the cavern under the rock, into the sanctuary of Abraham and David and Solomon and Elijah, where they were wont to pray. In the rock above us we saw the impression of Mohammed's head, which must have been immense. In the floor is a circular slab which covers a well or cavern of some sort, and gives a hollow sound when it is struck. It is worth adding that the Moslems regard this as the opening into Hades, and that within the gloom below the souls which have left the world above come twice a week for their prayers.

The place is rich in sacred associations with the past and the future. It has been called the centre of the earth. Here, some have thought, stood the holy of holies of the temple and the great altar of sacrifice. Here the throne will be set in the judgment when the last day shall come. But I have no room for more legends. The general appearance of the mosque is very pleasing, with its colored marbles and painted windows, its domes and arches, and it needs no fables to make it worthy of a longer time than the stranger in Jerusalem can give to it. There is another church, which bears the name of El-Aksa, a pile of buildings which with the Dome of the Rock really forms one temple. El-Aksa is said to stand on the site of the Mosque of Omar, although it is very much larger. But the building was originally a basilica founded by Justinian and dedicated to the Virgin. It has fallen with everything else. The Moslems hold it in high regard. It is ninety yards long and sixty-six wide, and has a nave with six aisles and many columns of many kinds. It is much more like a Christian church than any other mosque we saw. There is a handsome carved pulpit of wood with finely decorated stairs. Behind this is a stone which bears the mark of our Lord's foot. There are two columns so near together that it is not an easy matter to pass between them. Indeed one who has not been born in lawful wedlock could not force his way through. Some are more strict in another direction, and say that one cannot enter heaven unless he can pass through this narrow gate. An addition to the mosque proper covers the spot where the Mosque of Omar really was. In the nave of the church is a slab in the pavement which looks like the monument of a modern knight, but it is reported to be the tomb of the sons of Aaron. We descended to the vaults under the mosque, where we saw piers and arches, columns and walls, which are very old. Mordecai believed that they belonged to Solomon's Temple. Who shall say that it is not so? We went down into a small chapel or oratory, where we saw the "cradle of Christ," a niche which has long borne this name. There Simeon lived, and the Virgin mother passed a few days after the presentation of her child. So the story runs.

We went into vast subterranean vaults which are called "Solomon's Stables." Mordecai claimed that he and Dr. Wilson discovered them. Solomon's palace was not far from this place, and it may be that some of his numerous horses were quartered here. There are a hundred square piers of stone. Many of the columns have holes at the edges, in which a halter could be fastened, and there the horses of Franks and Templars have doubtless stood. The old and the new are strangely jumbled together in this ancient world. From the wall surrounding the temple area we gained a fine view of the valley and the hills around us. It was a good place from which to survey Jerusalem and mark all which belongs to it in its relations to the city towards which it looked. The moments were crowded with thoughts, and pictures rapidly succeeded one another as memory drew the lines. I must leave the reader, if I still have one, to think it out for himself.

The Golden Gate we saw in the wall of the Area. There is a projection from the wall six feet deep and fifty-five feet long, and in this is the double portal which has been called by many names, — the Golden Gate, the Eternal Gate, the Gate of Mercy, the Gate of Repentance. It is now walled up. A small door in the outer wall opens into the space between the two faces of the gate-way. In the time of the Crusades the procession on Palm Sunday passed through the Golden Gate, which was also opened at the festival of the Raising of the Cross. Strangers are sometimes admitted to the interior now as a special favor, and the Mohammedans use it as a place of prayer. But the gate itself cannot be opened. There is a tradition that on some Friday a Christian conqueror will enter by this gate and recover Jerusalem. It may be so. Yet the Christian conqueror will care little by what door he enters. The Moslems have another belief, that when He comes, Jesus will pass through this gate and take for His own the city which He could not save, and with it the whole world which lies about it.

We must not linger within the walls, hard as it is to go out. Let it be Friday afternoon when we betake ourselves to the base of the wall in the valley of the Tyropœon. It is a very old wall, and the stones in it and under it may have belonged to the house which Solomon builded. They have a lonesome look now. Thither for centuries the sad-hearted Jews have resorted, that they might weep over the desolation of their sacred city and cry for its deliverance. "In the palace that lies desolate we sit in solitude and mourn for the walls that are overthrown, for the great men who lie dead." We found some seventy or eighty Jews there. A few were rabbies, but the greater part were old women. The men could not be there, for they must be earning their bread in more promising pursuits, — that was Mordecai's explanation of their absence. The people who were there were chanting the Psalms in mournful voice, kissing the stones, and wetting them with their tears. The grief was obtrusive, but in many it seemed sincere. We did not understand their words, but we knew what they were sighing, "Be not wroth very sore, O Lord, neither remember iniquity forever; behold, see, we beseech thee, we are all thy people. Thy holy cities are a wilderness, Zion is a wilderness, Jerusalem a desolation. Our holy and our beautiful house, where our fathers praised thee, is burned up with fire: and all our pleasant things are laid waste." It was a solemn scene. We shared the pain and the lament. But we remembered that the city died by its own hand. Above the wailing and the weeping we could hear the voice of Him who came to save: "O Jerusalem, Jerusalem! how often I would, and ye would not!"

On the other side of the narrow space in which we were gathered were a few wooden boxes, on which some of the rabbies took their seat. We followed their example and rested as we watched. As the service grew monotonous, I had the curiosity to see what inscription was on the box which served me. Could it be anything appropriate to the place? Anything in harmony with the occasion? It needed but little knowledge of ancient languages to make out the words. There is one thing from the West which we found everywhere in the East. The inscription was of this, and not of temple or mosque, of ruined splendor or broken hearts. On my seat in the wailing-place in Jerusalem I read this, — " Bush and Denslow's Peerless Oil. Improved Patent Can. Guaranteed Safe, Pure, and Brilliant. New York."

When we would visit Bethlehem it was thought best, for the sake of variety, that we make use of the donkey of the country. He was produced in sufficient numbers, a larger beast than we see in America, and of a variety of colors. I have before alluded to the saddle which is put upon his back and which adds very much to the height of the rider, but lessens his comfort in the same proportion. The seat is insecure, which would be an annoyance were it not for the feeling that if one should roll off he could not fall very far. We had the usual retinue of boys to make the donkey's life a burden to him and to keep his rider in a state of physical and mental suspense, not unmingled with fear. Their spasmodic attacks upon the patient animals resulted in an irregular series of jumps and gallopings which made the ride exciting, if it was not perilous. A fine road between Jerusalem and Bethlehem was in process of construction. Men were working with considerable vigor, while women and girls were bringing dirt in baskets. The process was necessarily a slow one, but it answered its purpose. The distance between the two places is about four miles and a half. The ride is very pleasant on all accounts. On every side is seen something of immediate or of historic interest. The names of the places between which we were riding were enough to excite and engage our thoughts. Yet it is singular how readily a person becomes accustomed even to a country like this, so that the names are spoken with almost as little feeling as if they belonged to New England towns. It is so hard in the midst of the old world to realize that you are there. The discomforts which are felt are modern, — the weariness, the loneliness, the moods and methods of men; and these are intrusive and exacting, and in no small measure dull the senses to what is of far greater account, and cover from view the wonders of the land. One has to recall himself to himself, if he would make the most of that which he has come far to see. We rode by the Well of the Star, or the Well of the Magi, which marks the spot where the Wise Men from the East regained the sight of the star which was guiding them to the child whom they sought. We passed the monastery of Mar

Elyas, where a few Greek monks reside. Near this was the bed of Elias, a large rock which retains the mark of the reclining prophet. There is some doubt in regard to the genuineness of this couch, as it was not the prophet, but a Bishop Elias, who at some unknown time founded this house and gave his name to it. Elijah did indeed lie under a juniper-tree and sleep till he was touched by an angel. But there is no reason to suppose that he rested on this rock, in spite of the depression which it bears. The tomb of Rachel has more to commend it. "And Rachel died, and was buried in the way to Ephrath, which is Bethlehem. And Jacob set a pillar upon her grave: that is the pillar of Rachel's grave unto this day." The tradition which makes this the place of her burial is very old. For a long time there was a pyramid of stones here. Now a domed building of considerable proportions, similar to the tombs of many saints, stands over the grave. With all this there is room for doubt whether this is the place where the sorrowing Jacob erected his simple monument. In a little cemetery near the tomb there was a burial as we passed by. We could only look on the group of mourners whose grief was a part of the great human sorrow, which gains and loses nothing before legends and centuries.

We rode up the hill and under an arched house into the streets of Bethlehem. The town is very old, and, like other places, has its different quarters for different sorts of people. There are perhaps five thousand inhabitants, who for the most part live by farming. The fertile fields about the town justify the name Bethlehem, "the house of bread," and Ephrath, the old name of the place, which is thought to mean "the fruitful." It was here that David was born and was anointed to be king. We saw the "Wells of David," or the three cisterns in the rock which are called after him. Toward the wells of his boyhood the heart of the soldier turned when he was at war with the Philistines: "And David longed, and said, Oh that one would give me drink of the water of the well of Bethlehem, which is by the gate." Three mighty men broke through the Philistine ranks and drew the water which he longed for, and when they brought it to him he would not drink it because it was "the blood of the men that went in jeopardy of their lives." He "poured it out unto the Lord." Why should not these be the wells to which this romantic incident belongs? Here earlier were the fields of Boaz in which Ruth gleaned, when her devotion to the widowed Naomi had its reward, and the alien blood of Moab mingled with the blood of Judah, and the stranger became the mother of Obed, the father of Jesse, the father of David, and set her name into the proudest lineage the world has known.

Here were the fields where the shepherds watched their flocks by night, and "the glory of the Lord shone round about them," and the angel gave to them and to the waiting world the " good tidings of great joy." "And they said, Let us now go even unto Bethlehem, and see this thing which is come to pass." A part of the fields where the shepherds were when they heard the Gloria in Excelsis has been enclosed, to mark the place where the angel met them. A church and monastery were there, and there is still a subterranean chapel, which is called the Grotto of the Shepherds.

It was of this village the prophet Micah wrote, "Thou Bethlehem Ephrathah, which art little to be among the thousands of Judah, out of thee shall one come forth unto me that is to be ruler in Israel, whose goings forth are from of old, from everlasting." Seven hundred years after that there came a virgin from Galilee to be enrolled at Bethlehem, and there He was born of whom the prophets wrote and the angels sang.

Surely it was well that we were brought to the city of David. For the event of Bethlehem has become the centre of the world's life, and the Christmas joys are spreading through the earth. It is a prosperous place now. It was interesting to see that this town and Nazareth had lived and are now feeling the life of later days. Our entrance into the chief street was marked. The hospitality of the place was at once and profusely extended to us. We were not Galilean peasants but travellers from the far West. The merchants left their shops and clustered around our donkeys, and offered us as many inducements as their powers of illustrated speech permitted, to enter their warehouses and procure their goods. We were more than willing to comply, but there was difficulty in making our choice among the merchants. We chose liberally and examined the goods which were offered in abundance. Olive-wood and mother-of-pearl had been carved into numberless forms, of chains, necklaces, bracelets, paper-knives, pen-holders, crosses, charms, boxes; while the seeds of fruit were strung together into ornaments, and the black stone from the Dead Sea presented itself in inkstands and vases. There was variety, the goods were pleasing, and their associations with the place would always render them of value. When our purchases were completed, we left the dissatisfied merchants and proceeded to the more serious purpose of our visit.

The central point in Bethlehem is naturally the place of our Lord's nativity. On this stands, of course, a church, or two churches, which are used by three sects who are called after the Christian name, the Greek, Latin, and Armenian Christians, while each division has a monastery of its own, and the collection of buildings forms an imposing pile. The main part of the church belongs to the Greeks. The building is very old, and is by some traced to Constantine, and even to Helena. It has had its natural vicissitudes. In the front part of the church, which is nearly square, are the nave and double aisles, separated by columns of stone. The ceiling is of wood. The nave is cut off from the transept by a wall, in which are openings through which persons can pass to and fro. In the transept are the Greek altar, the throne of the Greek patriarch, and the pulpit. Abutting upon the transept is the church of the Latins, who were allowed to share in the sacred edifice through the kind offices of Napoleon III. Their portion is called after St. Catharine. It is quite long, but very narrow, and its decorations are more elaborate than among the Greeks. The Armenians have an altar in the Greek church. It is pleasant to see these three bodies of believers using the same church — that is, the theory of it is agreeable. There is less unity than would be expected; perhaps no more than would be found if they were not all of the same general faith. We marked that a Moslem guard was required to preserve the peace. We were told that there is so much jealousy that it is difficult to care for the house properly. When we were there some trifling repairs were necessary which either party would have been glad to make, but which neither would consent that another should make. Yet it was here that the Prince of Peace was born. That, however, was below. Two flights of steps lead from the Greek precincts and one from the Latin into the crypt. The Greek stairs lead at once into the most important part, the Chapel of the Nativity. It may have been here that our Lord was born. There seems to be no reason for questioning the tradition which hallows the spot.

There was no room in the inn, the khân, to which the strangers from the north came at the summons of the emperor, which had brought a crowd to the village. The rooms for travellers were occupied when they arrived, and they were glad to find a resting-place in some lower or adjoining room, which they must needs share with the quiet creatures of the fields. It is not uncommon in the East for a farmer to make this double use of a large room, placing in one part a raised platform for the family, while the lower portion is given up to his cattle. In the house which we occupied at Mejdel-esh-Shems, I found under our room a small household and a camel quartered happily in the same apartment.

A very early tradition places the Nativity in a cave. This is not history, but it is not improbable. The manger in which the Child was laid was probably like those now used — a box of stones and mortar, in which the Babe could be safely and pleasantly cradled.

The Chapel of the Nativity is about forty feet long and twelve feet wide and ten feet high. Its floor and walls are covered with marble. In a recess stands the altar, under which is a silver star with the inscription, "Hic de Virgine Maria Jesus Christus natus est." Around the altar fifteen lamps are burning, of which six belong to the Greeks, five to the Armenians, and four to the Latins. By three steps we descended to the place of the manger. The true manger was carried to Rome. Very near is the altar of the Adoration of the Virgin. The place from which water sprang out for the use of the holy family is further along in the Grotto. A little further on is the place at which Joseph received the command to take the young Child and his mother and go into Egypt. By five steps we went down to the Chapel of the Innocents, in which mothers took refuge with their children from the bloody edict of Herod, and where they were found and the children were slain. Near the end of the Grotto, hewn in the rock, are the Chapel and Tomb of St. Jerome and the Tomb of St. Eusebius. Jerome came to Bethlehem in the fourth century and retired to a cell, whither he was followed by some of his Roman converts, who used their wealth in founding monasteries. Over one of these Jerome presided, making it a hostlery for pilgrims. There he made his Latin translation of the Scriptures, the Vulgate, the version used by the Roman Church, and produced other works of interest. This chapel is reported to be the room in which he lived and wrote. Eusebius was a pupil of Jerome, or one of those who followed him to Bethlehem. Whether there is truth in the story which places Jerome here or not, his name and work do not seem out of place. A painting fittingly presents him with a Bible in his hand. This was a notable visit. Beyond all question, we were very near the place where the life began which is proving the Life of the world.

We saw but little of the monasteries. We were taken into a room where was a long table from which visitors may be fed. Entertainment for a few days is provided by the Latins. The monasteries serve a useful purpose in this way. There is in Bethlehem a Protestant school, under German direction, where a goodly number of boys and girls are taught.

I seem to have said very little of Bethlehem, where we saw and thought so much. But what can I do with words? The simple narrations of the Bible give to the place an unfailing charm. There one loves to linger and to recall the days which can never be lost in the past. Bethlehem will last while the world stands. There are not many places in Jerusalem which are associated with our Lord's life.

An immense reservoir, called Birket Israil, has been regarded as the Pool of Bethesda, on whose marble steps our Lord stood when waiting in the place where there was no man to put a cripple into the healing spring—the vacant place between divine mercy and human need. The pool is now nearly filled with rubbish, and there is no proof that it was ever the "House of Mercy." But it may have been. There is nothing interesting about it now except this possibility.

Of the Pool of Siloam we can be more confident. We read in the Book of Nehemiah that Shallum built "the wall of the Pool of Shiloah by the king's garden." It was to the Pool of Siloam that Jesus sent the man who was born blind, that he might receive his sight. That this is the same pool, and the same as that now known as Siloam, is generally admitted. At one time a church was built over it, after the custom of the country. Now broken walls surround it, and much rubbish has fallen into it. But it will always be held in special regard, whatever its condition may be. Now it is, like the land which holds it, a portion of the past.

When we come to the last days of our Lord's life, we can mark his way more clearly. Beyond the Zion gate is a group of buildings called by the name of David, and containing his reputed tomb. We were taken into a large upper room, in which, it is said, our Lord kept his last Passover with his disciples. The room is desolate, with nothing pleasing or suggestive in it. It is said that it was here the tongues of fire and the power of the Holy Spirit descended at Pentecost upon the apostles. A church once stood on the spot.

In the same building in which the Lord's Supper was instituted we were shown the tomb of David. In a recess behind an iron gate was a large structure, fifteen or twenty feet long, resembling a coffin. It was covered with a green cloth, on which is inscribed. "O David, whom God has made vicar, rule mankind in truth." Before this shrine is an arch, and within the recess a door and window. Over the door it is written in Arabic, "This is the gate of the garden of Paradise," words which commonly have reference to the tomb of a saint. It is claimed that by this door access can be had to the cavern in which David was laid. The sarcophagus which is seen is said to be a copy of the one below, which no one is allowed to look upon. The Mohammedans are jealous guardians of their sacred places. The neighboring Armenian convent is known as the House of Caiaphas. There in the altar of the small church is preserved the stone which closed the Lord's sepulchre, which the angels rolled from the door. There can be seen "the Prison of Christ," and the pillar on which the cock stood when his crowing warned or reproved Peter. This pillar is under the altar, and only small portions of it are seen through the plaster which has been put over it. The Latin, Greek, Armenian, American, and English cemeteries are here. We looked with respect on the tombs of the Armenian patriarchs of Jerusalem. On some of the stones in the Armenian cemetery

were what appeared to be the signs of the work of
the man who had been laid to rest, as a hammer and
anvil, an easel with brushes, and shears. There was
not very much to be credited in this visit to the
Moslem sanctuary of David. But there may be
truth under the traditions.

On our way back we passed the Potter's Field,
bought with the money of the betrayal. Far above
us as it was it had a dreary look. A lone tree but
added to the desolation by its legend that it was
from its branches that the traitor hung himself.
Some one suggested that it must have been very
small for that purpose eighteen hundred years ago.
I ventured one day to ask Mordecai his opinion of
Judas. "He was a bad man; hung himself." "Yes;
but what do you think of his conduct?" "He was
a bad man; he hung himself." "True; but he betrayed his Master and Friend. What do you say of
that?" "I don't want to talk about it. I have to
do with all kinds of people, and I must not express
opinions on such things." We changed the subject.

In the northeastern section of the city is the
Church of St. Anne, one of the churches of the
Crusades. It has kept its integrity very well, and
has received modern restoration. Napoleon III. was
presented with this church by the sultan, and it is
under French protection. The Arabs still attach
Saladin's name to it. Under the church is a crypt
cut in the rock. Formerly there were altars there,
and there is a story that there St. Anne lived and
the Virgin was born. The church is near St. Stephen's gate, by which one passes out towards the

Mount of Olives. The gate also bears the name of our Lady Mary. There seem to be reasons for both names; for not far away is a rock marking the place where Stephen is said to have fallen under the stones which were thrown upon him; and also very near is the Church or Tomb of the Virgin, where she was laid by the apostles and remained until her Assumption. The present building dates from the twelfth century, and is in good condition. We crossed the valley of the Kedron, passing by a bridge over the channel of the brook, and found ourselves close to the church. It is a curiously constructed building, being for the most part underground. A large porch with an arched portal, within which is a door, is the part which is seen on the outside. Steps lead down to the space in front of the church, and within a long and handsome flight of broad steps leads to the floor, which is thirty-five feet below the ground before the portal. On the right as you go down the stairs is a small chapel with two altars and the tomb of Joachim and Anne, who were brought from the Church of St. Anne that they might rest under the sanctity of their daughter. On the left is the tomb of Joseph, the husband of Mary. In the ground plan the church proper is cruciform, and the stairs enter at the west end of the transept. Two-thirds of the way down the nave is the sarcophagus of Mary, in a small chapel which is reached by a very narrow entrance. The Armenians honor and protect the deserted tomb by their devotions, as the Moslems were once allowed to do, while the Greeks and the Abyssinians have altars near the opposite end of the church. The Armenian service was going on at the time of our visit, and we had to wait until the dismal sounds had ceased before we could go behind their altar into the sanctuary where is the shrine of the Virgin to whom all hearts are drawn. A long side passage leads to the "Cavern of the Agony," a grotto fifty feet long, with three altars, and the remains of paintings on the ceiling. There used to be an altar to mark the spot where our Lord forgave Peter all his sins, and there was a well which was filled from the River of Paradise. On the whole, there is not much here which commends itself to faith. The most singular thing is the church. It has been conjectured that it is the filling of the valley which has left the house underground. Yet the ground about it seems to be no higher than it was centuries ago, and the oldest accounts of the church present it as a subterranean building. This must remain with many things which are not explained.

Crossing the road, we came to the Garden of Gethsemane. Here we could feel more confidence. For we know that Jesus, after his last Passover, went over the brook Kedron into the Mount of Olives, "where was a garden into which he entered, and his disciples." The Latins have enclosed with a high wall an irregular quadrangle whose circuit is given as about seventy paces. Entrance is easy, and the attendance is sufficient without being an annoyance. Very near the gate, outside the wall, is a rock marking the spot where the three disciples slept while Jesus was praying and suffering. The spot is also pointed out where Judas met his Master and gave the kiss of betrayal. The fragment of a pillar marks the place. Within the wall is a hedge enclosing seven olive-trees which are reputed to have been there in the Saviour's time. There is no reason to believe this, but the trees are certainly of great age, so that they need to be strengthened by having the trunk filled with stones, after the manner of the country. It is possible that they sprung from trees which were growing there when the garden became sacred. There are younger trees, which are of no special interest, and flower-beds, which are well cared for, and from which the visitor may carry away a memorial of the place. The oil of the olive-trees is naturally esteemed of rare value, and commands a large price. Between the garden proper and the wall is a passage containing oratories at which the devout can offer their prayers, with their hearts softened and quickened by the associations of the place. Was it just here that Jesus endured his agony and poured out his soul in supplication and submission? There is nothing to show this. But it was very near this place. It could not be expected that the Greeks would allow the Latins to hold the garden of Gethsemane. They have a rival garden further up the Mount. But, as Mordecai observed, "how can they get the olive-trees?" The very spot cannot be known, but here Jesus was met by the band which came out to arrest Him, and here He gave himself into their hands. The night comes slowly back as one waits reverently where Jesus was, and thinks upon the hours which sanctified the close of his life upon the earth, and brought Him under the shadow of the cross. No spot in Jerusalem is so dear, so sacred, as this. For we know that it was here He bowed under the olive-trees and felt the sorrows of death.

> "Mortal ! if life smiles on thee, and thou find
>     All to thy mind,
> Think Who did once from Heaven to Hell descend
>     Thee to befriend:
> So shalt thou dare forego, at His dear call,
>     Thy best, thine all.
>
> 'O Father! not My will, but Thine be done!'
>     So spake the Son.
> Be this our charm, mellowing Earth's ruder noise
>     Of griefs and joys:
> That we may cling forever to Thy breast
>     In perfect rest!"

It breaks the order of events, but while we are at the Mount of Olives let us pass to Bethany, which is on the road to Jericho. The Franks say Bethany. The Arabs call the place after Lazarus, El-Azarîyeh. We can reach the village by the same way over which our Lord walked, as we suppose, on which He was met by the triumphal procession which came out from Jerusalem to bring Him to the capital amid their hosannas. Bethany was a place dear to Him. There was the house of Mary and Martha, to which He was fond of resorting and where He was always made welcome. There the one sister wearied herself in her care for Him, and the other gave Him more delight as she sat at his feet and heard his words. He loved them both and accepted their ministering. The place where their house stood is shown. This is partly enclosed with walls. There is no house upon it now. A building occupies the site of the house of Simon the leper, where they made a supper for Jesus, and Lazarus sat at the table, and Martha served, and Mary broke her cruse of alabaster and poured the costly spikenard on the head of Jesus and filled the house with the fragrance of the ointment. In the insight of her heart she anointed Him for his burial, and gained in his Gospel remembrance for her devotion; and beyond this made the world sweeter ever since by her faith and hope and love.

The appearance of Bethany is forlorn in the extreme. Some forty hovels contain the Moslems who now dwell in the places out of which better people have gone. Those whom we saw were not attractive, though the begging of the younger portion was persistent. I suppose that we felt the dreariness the more that the place was associated in our minds with the pleasant village of the Gospels. It was hard to consent that this should be Bethany. The chief point of interest now remaining is the tomb of Lazarus. The Moslems hold him a saint and have put a mosque near his grave. There was a church over the tomb centuries ago. The tradition is therefore an old one which marks the sepulchre in which the brother of Mary and Martha was laid. Again it was difficult to attach the sublime narrative of the Gospel to the place now connected with it. We recalled the days which made Bethany illustrious, and the one day which gave it its greatest fame. The simple account of it, written by one who was present, can never fail to engage the attention and the affection of those who read it. Lazarus of Bethany was sick. His sisters, in their confidence, sent to Jesus the tidings which were so brief, which they knew would bring Him to them — "Lord, behold, he whom thou lovest is sick." He lingered, that the sickness might be "for the glory of God," and then went to them. The brother had been dead four days. He stood among those who bewailed him, with the sisters, whose hope was touched with fear. "Jesus wept," not because Lazarus was dead merely; for He knew what He would do, and that the sorrow would soon be changed to joy. But all men were dying and dead, and the burden of the world's grief and pain was upon Him. He spoke the words which have remained for the solace and the promise of countless hearts which have mourned their dead. In countless Bethanys, by numberless sepulchres, has He been heard, through the long and heavy centuries, still saying, "I am the resurrection and the life: he that believeth in me, though he were dead, yet shall he live. And whosoever liveth and believeth in me shall never die." At his bidding the stone was rolled from the door which it guarded. Jesus, when he had spoken to the Father, "cried, with a loud voice, Lazarus, come forth. He that was dead came forth, bound hand and foot with grave-clothes, and his face was bound about with a napkin. Jesus saith unto them, Loose him and let him go." It was here that Jesus stood. Let us believe it. Standing here, He spoke the words which proved him "the Resurrection." Here Lazarus came out of the gloom in which he had been lying, and opened his dazed eyes upon the world he had deserted.

"This is the tomb of Lazarus." So our guide said, as if it were a common place; and it meant so much to us. The door was opened for a price, and with candles we painfully groped our way down a long flight of worn and broken steps to a rude chapel where Moslems and Christians say their prayers. Then, bending low, we crept through a narrow passage and went up three steps into the small chamber where Lazarus had been, and out of which he was summoned. The dreariness and discomfort of the place made devout contemplation difficult. The dark, cold, rough walls repressed the feeling which we should have been glad to indulge. We retraced our way and came slowly back into the light, not to be greeted with the strong words of the Christ, or the glad cries of the women, but with the harsher sound which from many lips breaks the silence of Bethany, "Bakshîsh, Howadji, Bakshîsh!" We had returned into the world of to-day. It was memory alone which could invest the scene with interest. Perhaps we had expected too much. Can one enter Palestine and not expect what no other land has offered him? He should be thoughtful and moderate in his desires, but this is not the spirit with which he has sought the Holy Land. He must not expect to find the miracle there, or the record of it on the rock, or those who witnessed it, or any memorials which can add anything to the narrative of one who has written for us what he saw and heard. In this spirit he will find profit in standing where the Lord was, and those who were his friends. It is the New Testament, and not the tomb of Lazarus, which brings us the comfort of the Resurrection. In its living pages we find the times when the village of hovels was a village of homes. There too is lived before us the life of the Life. Palestine can well be visited while we remain in our own dwellings. If we do not see it there, we shall not find it in the desolateness of

"those holy fields,
Over whose acres walked those blessed feet
Which . . . were nailed
For our advantage on the bitter cross."

Leaving the Mount of Olives, we can enter the city by St. Stephen's gate, when we are in the Via Dolorosa, the street over which our Saviour is said to have carried his cross. The street is narrow and dark, and leads under arches and arched ways which add to its gloom. There are "stations" which mark special points. I need not say that no one knows that Jesus passed over this street in his sad walk to Calvary, or that imagination has set up the "stations." The tradition which makes this the "street of pain" does not appear to be very old. The first station is in the Turkish barracks, which are said to occupy the site of the Prætorium, the house of Pilate. The steps of the house, as everybody knows, are now in Rome, where the faithful ascend them upon their knees, and the less devout look on in a confusion of unbelief and wonder. But whatever may be the previous history of the stairs, they have a historic and abiding interest from their connection with Luther and that which he did for the world. The second station marks the place where Jesus received the cross. Beyond this an arch thrown across the street is called Ecce Homo, and the Arch of Pilate, because it was there that the troubled governor brought out his prisoner and said, "Behold the Man!" Adjoining this is a church, and opposite the church is a mosque. A broken column at the third station shows where Jesus sank under the cross. Passing the house of the poor Lazarus, we come to the fourth station, where Jesus met his mother. Passing the home of the rich man at whose gate Lazarus was laid, we reach the fifth station, where Simon of Cyrene received the cross. In a neighboring house is a stone bearing a mark made by Christ's hand as he fell upon it where it lay beside his path. The sixth station is near the tomb of St. Veronica, who gave her handkerchief to Jesus and received it back with the print of his face upon it. At the seventh station the Franciscans have a chapel and a school for girls. The eighth station, where Jesus spoke to the weeping women who followed him, is at the end of the Via Dolorosa. The ninth is in front of a monastery of the Copts. Here Jesus is said to have sunk under the cross. But the cross had already been laid upon the Cyrenian stranger.

We are thus brought to the Church of the Holy Sepulchre, within which are five more stations.

This is the central point, of course, in Jerusalem. The most profound interest would naturally belong to the spot where the Saviour was crucified and the sepulchre in which he was laid. It may be to guard us against an undue reverence for the places, and to fasten our minds constantly upon the events themselves, that it has been allowed to become impossible to tell where the cross stood and where was the new tomb wherein never before a man had been laid. It is not a very old tradition or belief by which the place has been selected on which this church now stands. It is said that Calvary was found in the reign of Constantine, while others have said it was the mother of Constantine who discovered both the cross and the sepulchre. We know that Golgotha was outside the walls, and this church is within. But it is possible that the walls may have been extended since the time when Golgotha was described by the Evangelists. But it may be added that scarcely any man of authority in such matters regards what is known as our Lord's sepulchre as that in which his friends placed him after he had been taken from the cross. Yet in the fourth century a church was erected here, and ever since the adoration of countless multitudes has been rendered at this sanctuary. Whatever other purpose this has served, it has kept in mind the facts of the crucifixion, the entombment, the resurrection, and has given them in literature and history a position which can never be lost. Here again we may say that we cannot be very far from the places where these events took place. Fragments of the old church remain. But the Persians destroyed the church, which was rebuilt, and partly burned, and desecrated by Mohammedans. Then came the church which the Crusaders found, and which they entered with bare feet and singing their psalms. In the twelfth century the Crusaders built a larger church, which has remained and has received many additions. The buildings of the Crusaders suffered at the hands of their enemies and the enemies of their faith and from fire; but a pious zeal continued to build and rebuild, till we have now what may be considered a modern church, though it retains part of the buildings which have preceded it.

I shall not add another to the numerous descriptions of this building or collection of buildings. There is a large central portion, with what may be termed three wings. The list of its apartments and their peculiar treasures is long. The mere reading suggests the wealth of sacredness which is here accumulated. The church is crowded in between other buildings, or rather other buildings have sprung up around it, so that there is nothing imposing in its appearance. In front there is a courtyard, which is below the street and is reached by a few steps. This is a fine situation for dealers in mosaics and relics, pictures and charms, and for the beggars, who are everywhere shrewd enough to look for their victims among the people who go to church. There are chapels at the sides of this court, but they are not of much account. Entering the open door, we soon came upon the Turkish guard, who preserve order among the Christians, and whose office at certain seasons is not a sinecure. Mordecai, being a Jew, would not be allowed in the church, and he intrusted us to the care of a guide whose knowledge of the church was less than his desire to make our visit profitable to himself. With an excellent guide-book and plan we had little need of an attendant. Very soon we came to the stone on which our Lord was wrapped in linen cloths with spices in preparation for his burial: we saw the marble slab which covers the true stone. The upper marble is held in great reverence, and pilgrims gather there, bowing before it and kissing it, and rubbing off its virtue with handkerchiefs. Many have brought their winding-sheets that these might be consecrated by contact with the holy stone, or with its representative. At the right of this stone are stairs which lead to Calvary. There is seen the hole in which the cross of Christ stood. The places of the other crosses are also marked, and in the rock is seen the cleft, a few inches deep, which was made when the rocks were rent. The sepulchre is on the floor which we left. In the centre of the large rotunda is a structure of white marble, twenty-six feet long and seventeen and a half feet wide. The interior is divided into two rooms. The first is the Chapel of the Angels, where may be seen a part of the stone which the angels rolled from the door. From this chapel we passed through a low door into the holy sepulchre itself. It is a small room about six feet square. Forty-three lamps hang from the low ceiling. A relief in white marble shows our Saviour in the act of rising.

Marble columns sustain the roof. The place is so covered with marble that the original form of the tomb, if such it was, cannot be seen. On one side of this small chamber is a marble shelf which represents the place where the sacred body was placed. There is very little to help the memory or the imagination in the effort to think of the events with which the place is associated. The words seem there more true than ever before, "He is not here."

In front of this sanctuary there is a raised place which serves as a porch, or an open ante-chamber. It is guarded by immense candlesticks and candles, and is furnished with parallel seats of stone. I went one day to the church in company with a clergyman of very high ecclesiastical principles, and we took our place for rest and meditation on one of these seats, and gave ourselves up to the impressions of the afternoon hour. Before long a young man whose dress and general appearance indicated that his position in the church was of a very low order, if of any order at all, stepped before us and began a system of pantomime which might indicate a disordered intellect. He stared at us very hard, and, putting one foot over the other, drew it back with vehemence. His behavior surprised us but did not produce whatever result he desired, for he immediately and with more emphasis repeated his strange conduct. It was still a failure. Then he took his seat opposite to us and threw one leg over the other and instantly jerked it back with his hands, pointing to my friend. His meaning was now clear. My clerical neighbor was sitting at the door of the holy sepulchre with one of his long limbs supporting the other. He saw the point and felt the reproof. It was very cutting, and he was unable to see the ludicrous side of it. He had been rebuked in church, and for an act of indecorum which had attracted the attention of the humblest servant of the house. Happily I had not offended. If I had I should have forgiven myself readily. It was not so with him. For he was put to shame in a matter where he was careful to be correct. I fancy that remains a sorrow in his mind as he recalls Jerusalem.

At the rear of the sepulchre, and touching it, is the Chapel of the Copts, and beyond that, out of the rotunda, the Chapel of the Syrians. The Greeks have the finest church in the Church. The Latins come next, with the Chapel of the Apparition, where Christ appeared to his mother after the resurrection. Almost every spot connected with those sacred days in his life is pointed out and permanently marked. The Chapel of St. Helena is below. There are found the altar of Helena, the altar of the Penitent Thief, and the chair of Helena, where she sat while search was made for the cross. Still lower down the natural rock is seen, and there is the Chapel of the Finding of the Cross. The name tells the meaning of the place and brings to mind the whole story in all its romance and interest. I have named but a portion of the things which are to be seen and believed within these sacred walls. But I ought not to omit the centre of the world, which is marked by the fragment of a pillar.

The Easter festival is naturally the time of exceeding interest in these sacred places. The ceremonies are elaborate and impressive for those who are in this way impressed. The miracle of the holy fire is still performed under Greek patronage, and still draws a crowd. The procession moves around the sepulchre, the lights are put out, the patriarch goes into the Chapel of the Sepulchre, priests and people pray, the fire descends from heaven and gleams through a hole in the wall of the sepulchre, the priests appear with lighted tapers, and the people crowd about them to light their own tapers, and soon the church is again illuminated. We did not see this. But we saw the place in the wall where the light appears.

Let us go into the open air. Again our steps bear us over the Kedron and up the Mount of Olives. We are following tradition in seeking at the summit the place of the Ascension. The Scripture does not tell it was there. — "He led them out as far as Bethany." Buildings were then on the top of the mountain. Still, for a very long time the Ascension of our Lord has been associated with this spot. Helena built a church there, but perhaps not because of the Ascension, for there was a sacred cave which needed preservation. There is a modern church now there. It is in form an octagon. The precise spot within it where Jesus last stood upon the earth is shown, and there is even a footprint which he left. All this goes for nothing. But the view from the top of Olivet is wonderfully fine. In the quiet of nature and its broad expanse there is a good place for thought. Near by is the place where our Lord taught the prayer which bears his name. In 1868 the Princess Latour d'Auvergne erected a church there, in the form of a Campo Santo. Around a quadrangle are covered passages, lined with slabs which contain the Lord's Prayer in many languages. A small convent is near at hand. A little further on is the chapel where the apostles did not form their creed. The church which was there is gone. The creed, which was written somewhere, and which is the record of the apostles, lives with an increasing life.

Not from the summit did the Lord ascend, — so we are told now. It seems fitting that it should have been from a height that he went up into his glory. Yet the mountain is not nearer heaven than the valley. Somewhere upon this sacred hill he stretched his hands over his disciples and blessed them, and was parted from them and carried up into heaven. — " It is good to be here."

There are a few more scattered notes upon Jerusalem which I must bring together. Among the pleasant hours which I remember are those which I spent with the American Consul, who added to his fitness for his official duties a rare interest in archæology, and a large knowledge of the land of which so few know anything. It was a great advantage to the traveller to have him for a counsellor and a guide. It was a credit to the country to have Selah Merrill for its Consul at Jerusalem. It is on all accounts to be regretted that the necessities of politics should have removed him from his place. One afternoon the Consul took me to a round hill not far from the Damascus gate, above the Grotto in which Jeremiah is said to have written his Lamentations, and to have been buried. The story is in great need of corroboration, but the prophet's name clings to the cave. The hill of which I have spoken is regarded by Dr. Merrill and others as the place of the crucifixion. It is shaped somewhat like a skull. An old Roman road leads towards it. Old Mohammedan graves are now upon it, and it is known that the Mohammedans do not put graves where a house has been, nor a house where graves have been. Putting together various points of circumstantial evidence, there seems to be reason to think that this was Golgotha. He took me to two churches near the hill, which had recently been unearthed and whose pavement has been uncovered, bringing to light the remains of paintings and mosaics. The owner of the ground wondered at the unproductiveness of this part of his estate, and, having enough energy to look for the cause, found two churches. An old Greek tomb had also been found, and we were allowed to go down into it. There were places for four bodies, and a Latin cross on the wall. I found that the Consul had no confidence in anything in Jerusalem which is above ground. But few know so much of what would be found if the new Jerusalem should suffer the old to come to light.

The Muristan was founded by Charlemagne as a monastery, to which a convent and church were added. After a time, the order of Hospitallers, or Knights of St. John, was formed, at first for the care of pilgrims, but afterward devoted to warfare on infidels and for the general promotion of the faith. In the changes of the times all this went down, and a great deal more. But there remains something of the old buildings, under the name of the Monastery of St. John. The ruins are meagre but interesting. The remains were given to the Crown Prince of Prussia, when he visited Jerusalem in 1869, and under his patronage excavations were begun, which have now ceased. We looked down into large and deep cisterns, and there must be other things concealed which it would be well to open to the light. We learned that a church and school and other buildings were to be put near the Muristan for the benefit of the German community. We went to the old and the later church of the Copts, and saw their place for the sacrifice of Isaac. We saw the stone on which the boy was to be offered. A black woman, who seemed to be at home there, said that the offering was not made at the stone but where a tree now stands, which she pointed out. Thus authorities differ. In the new church is a dove on the top and front of the pulpit, where the crucifix is more often seen. There was a prevailing lonesomeness about the whole place, which could not have been there in the ancient days.

The tombs about Jerusalem are a marked feature of the place. Among these, the chief are the Tombs of the Judges and the Tombs of the Kings, on the north side of the city. They are catacombs, with chambers and recesses, and were undoubtedly designed for the last resting-places of persons of distinction. The tombs of the prophets and the Grotto of St. James, on the east of the city, are much smaller. These rock tombs were stately burial-places; and besides these, which were carefully planned, are the many in the cliffs which stand above the plain. Some of the special tombs were prepared with great pains. The tomb of Absalom is cut from the solid rock, in the shape of a cube, twenty feet in each dimension, and with a round superstructure, terminating in a very low spire. The tomb of Zacharias resembles Absalom's, but is not so high, and the top is simpler, a pyramid resting on the cube which makes the body of the monument. The tomb of Jehosaphat has a broad entrance, and several chambers within.

Mordecai took us to what he called Solomon's quarries. He further declared that he and Barclay discovered them. They are an immense cavern from which stone has been quarried at some time. By Solomon? Who shall say? We groped our way in with candles, but it was rather difficult. Far within the cave we found a pool or well. It was a fearful place, and we were glad to emerge into the daylight.

The Russian buildings are conspicuous at the north-west of the city. There is a fine cathedral, with a hospital and hospice for men and women, and the Consulate. A thousand persons can be accommodated, and the poorest persons are taken in. In the yard we saw a huge column which had not been cut away from the solid rock to which it belonged. Portions of old columns were discovered when these buildings were erected. The Russians had more power in the land than any other nation, and their fine buildings made this evident. It was pitiful to see in what narrow and barren quarters our Consulate was housed.

Our hotel proved a pleasant home for us. It was modern, and well placed near the Jaffa gate. It was in the usual Oriental style, with the quadrangle and rooms around it. We had a good view to the north and west, and good air from the open country. Just within the Jaffa gate is the Citadel, or City of David, with its five square towers. The foundations, at least, are very old. This castle was the last place to yield to the armies of the Franks. Our attention was called to a hole resembling a mouth, in a wall near by. This was one of the stones which would cry out if men should hold their peace. I think the men were not silenced; but this may have been an impatient stone.

There are three Sabbaths in Jerusalem, — that is, there is none. Some shops may be closed on certain days, but the greater part are always open. The stores are small, but there are many fine things to be found in them. Excellent photographs were to be bought, while olive-wood presented itself in innumerable shapes. The dealers were anxious to sell, and the competition seemed to be eager. We could obtain all we wanted, at prices much below those which were asked and not expected. The wares were brought to the hotel, but we preferred the shops. Every one was good-natured, but there was, at times, more importunity than was agreeable. The beggars were numerous and more persistent than in most places. The Greek and Latin churches provide room and bread for their poor members, but still they beg. The Moslems do nothing for their poor. Why should they interfere with the will of God? A gentleman whom we met gave one of the regular beggars his stipend of so much a week, that he might not be assailed by him whenever he went abroad.

There was a small American colony in the city when we were there. They had come out by divine direction, and were waiting to be told what they should do next. Their means of living seemed uncertain, but they lived. Some of our company visited them, and brought back conflicting reports. Mr. Garry brought back one or two doughnuts, which were of the New England type, and were worthy of a place in the East. These people seemed harmless, but visionary. They belonged to a considerable class of whom a wise woman remarked to me that they came to Jerusalem to help the Lord fulfil his prophecies.

On Saturday night we went to the synagogues of the Jews. At the German synagogue I naturally removed my hat, when an old rabbi motioned to me to keep it on. Mordecai said that was the proper thing, and that it was expressive of the present homeless, wandering life of the people. Among the Spanish Jews we found four synagogues in one. The Sabbath service was just beginning, and seemed to us formal and hard, while it did not seem impressive to those for whom it was designed. In one synagogue we saw a harp hanging on the willows, which were breaking under the weight. We also saw a rude painting of a steamer. This seemed incongruous, but may have had its meaning to these strangers in a strange land.

We attended service on Sunday at Christ Church, which belongs to the English mission. It is a fine building. A goodly number of children from the English schools were in attendance, but the service seemed remote from them and their needs. Yet I have no doubt that they are well instructed in other places. Just beyond this church is the Armenian convent, with a fine garden.

I was glad to attend a meeting held by the English clergy on the afternoon of a week-day. It was in a room used as a vestry. The room was not very cheerful, but there was a gathering of the clergy and their workers and others. The rector presided. We sang, " Guide me, O Thou great Jehovah." A part of St. John's Gospel was read. The English gentlemen of the Society of Friends who were making a missionary journey took part in the service. One of them, Mr. Braithwaite, gave a warm Christian address. A German offered prayer in his own language. The service was simple, but sincere and helpful, and the more to be enjoyed because it was there. Is there a better place than this for me to close these desultory notes upon Jerusalem?

In view of all which has been said in these pages, it may be asked if it is well for one to visit Palestine. The answer is promptly given, and in the affirmative. Does it add anything to the sum of useful knowledge, or deepen religious impressions, or bring the heart and life into closer fellowship with Him whose presence made this the Holy Land? This it may do or may fail to do. It depends on the person.

It is of great interest to visit Palestine. It is an old land, which has filled an important place in the history of the world. From it have come forth influences which are felt at the ends of the earth and are steadily increasing. Men who have impressed themselves deeply on the human thought have there had a birth-place and a home. If we trace to its source what we are proud to call civilization, with our liberty and all which belongs to it; our homes, schools, governments; our art, science, business; we are carried past Italy and Greece to the narrow, neglected land which lies between the Jordan and the Great Sea. History, in any of its departments, is not thoroughly studied or clearly understood until the things which were wrought in Palestine are taken into the plan. It must always be with a peculiar and profound interest that an intelligent man journeys from the West to stand over the buried Jerusalem or to tread the narrow streets of Bethlehem and Nazareth. He should be able to see through what now is and to discern that which has been; to look past the men whom he meets to those of another generation, and to hold intercourse with them. A man must be independent of his immediate surroundings who would find in Palestine that which the land can give him, which he can find nowhere else. He will not look for the Christ there; but he can see where He was. If he has pictured to himself a paradise, an ideal land of broad meadows and still waters, of clear skies and fragrant airs, a land in keeping with the divine character which ennobled it, the illusion will pass away when his feet press the stony roads and he lies on the hard ground and the rains assail him from the clouds. But why should the man have made this mistake? Christ came into the world as it was. He came into its rough and stony places, with its sorrows and sins, among the actual men and women whose home was there. He saw the wilderness and the fruitful fields, the thorns and the flowers, the good men and the bad men. Men were poor, blind, maimed, bruised, sad and sick, sinful and dead. He came to them where they were and as they were. If such things are now seen in the land as He found in it, this should help us to comprehend the conditions under which his life of ministry and mercy fulfilled its purpose. If one knows the Christ, — knows his life, appreciates his design and his accomplishment, — it will be to him a rare privilege to stand where He stood, to walk where He walked, to feel what He felt. The best guide in Palestine is the Bible. The best preparation is sympathy with Him who came to Palestine for the world's advantage. For one who is thus furnished life will grow richer and stronger as he walks in the steps of the Son of Man, and lets the land and the people illustrate his life. Neither there nor anywhere is the letter enough. He needs the spirit. With this the days will be memorable, the land will be holy, and henceforth more than ever " Faith will have its Olivet and Love its Galilee."

# CHAPTER XIII.

### TO THE END.

Our last night in Jerusalem was marked by an exhibition which has a distant relationship to the East. Some wandering magician presented the usual attractions of men of his craft, and in the usual manner. Perhaps the masters of his art, who belong in the mystery of lands further east, and in the fascination of the Arabian Nights, would not have recognized his modest efforts at our hotel. But they were a diversion for an hour when we could not go abroad.

Our long journey seemed over. We went down to the stables where our horses were resting, and took an appropriate leave of those faithful companions of our journey, and of such of the men as could be found. We furnished Mr. Mordecai with an elaborate recommendation as an accomplished dragoman, and presented to him and to others the gratuities which were expected, and which seemed to give satisfaction.

It was on a Wednesday morning that a wagon came to the door, and we turned our faces homeward. Some of our company remained in Jerusalem. Mr. Garry, with his accustomed discretion, had left the day before. The other three of us distributed ourselves among the numerous seats, and set out for

Jaffa. The road was steep and rocky, and wound down the hill in many and short curves, around which our young Jehu drove his horses with an entirely unnatural celerity, which made us somewhat fearful touching our safety, even after all our experience of mountain roads. It must have been easier to go rapidly than slowly, or this juvenile native would not have broken the established rule of deliberation in everything. We soon lost sight of the domes and walls of the city, and felt ourselves fairly embarked on our Western journey. We passed the fine Russian buildings, the Austrian Consulate, the English Mission House, and other suburban and modern structures. We hurried by Lifta, the Nephtoah of whose fountain we read in the Book of Joshua. There is still a good spring there, and the remains of old buildings. On our right was the village of Kulôniyeh, which has sometimes been thought to be Emmaus, to which our Lord walked with two disciples, Cleopas and another, whose hearts burned within them as he talked with them, to whom he made himself known "in the breaking of the bread." But Emmaus was threescore furlongs from Jerusalem, so that this could not have been the place. But near by is the scene of David's conquest of Goliah, if we may confide in the tradition. Further on we saw where the young champion of Israel found the stones which he chose for his combat. He left a great many, and even then took "four more than he needed."

On our left was the village of Karyet el-Enab, which in late years has been known as Abu Gôsh or

Ghaush, from a mighty sheikh who with his brothers and attendants was the terror of the region. Pilgrims were his especial prey. The gang has been broken up, but it is said that the timorous native fears as he passes the castles, which may yet conceal some survivor. Dr. Robinson thinks that this was the Kirjath-Jearim, or city of woods, to which the ark was taken after its removal from Beth-Shemesh, where it was carried after it was sent away by the Philistines. He thinks also that it may have been the Emmaus of the Gospels. The village of Amwas, still further on, has a name which sounds like Emmaus, and some have thought that the honor of bearing the latter designation belongs here. It is possible that it may be so, though there are serious reasons against it. We can at least be certain that no one knows where the village was to which a single incident in the Saviour's life has given an interest so lasting.

For our noon rest we stopped at Latrûn. The name suggests robbers, and perhaps with good reason. It was a simple thing in finding places for events to fix upon this as the home of the penitent thief whose cross stood beside that of the Christ. His name is given as Disma. The place was a military station in the Crusades, and the remains of an old fortress and church can now be seen. In the third century Julius Africanus rebuilt the town and called it Nicopolis, in memory of Titus and his victories. The village itself has a most desolate and ruinous look. But it was interesting to us as the half-way place between Jaffa and Jerusalem. Howard has a very comfortable hotel there, for which the patronage is scant. We were told that it was necessary that he should keep a house on the road, or his rival, Cook, would do so. We greatly enjoyed our rest. The repose was perfect. Nothing broke the stillness. If we had not been beckoned away, we should have been glad to remain there and do nothing. After a generous pause, we climbed into our wagon and rattled on our way. We soon came to Ramleh, a large town of three thousand inhabitants, with a Latin monastery, and Greek and Russian hospices, with churches and soap-factories. The story of Ramleh is that it stands on the site of Arimathea, the town of Joseph, the wise and thoughtful Israelite who went to Pilate and asked the body of Jesus, and laid it in his own new tomb. It may have been here that he lived. Who shall say? The principal mosque was a Christian church, and stands as a sad witness to the profanation of a town which had churches before the coming of the Crusaders, and enjoyed a large prosperity. Its history is in the history of the land. The conspicuous object in Ramleh is its tower. It stands by itself, lifting its solitary grandeur and beauty above the surrounding desolation. It is twenty-five feet square at the base, and is divided into several stories, each of which has its own style and adornment. The top is reached by a flight of worn stairs in the interior. There are about a hundred and twenty-five steps. The history of the tower is uncertain. It belonged to a mosque, but whether that was its first use is not so clear. It has been known as the White Tower, and White

Mosque, and by other names. Portions of the building to which the tower belonged are now standing, but they are too small and scattered to tell much of its character. There are extensive vaults, and in them one tradition has buried forty companions of the Prophet, and another the same number of Christian martyrs. Some portions of the ruins look as if they were parts of a large khân. There are fine orchards at Ramleh, with olive and sycamore and other trees, but the place had a very dull appearance, and seemed very lonesome. We ordered our wagon, which we left at the entrance to the town, to go by the road and meet us near the tower. The directions were misunderstood, and to our dismay we saw the vehicle go past, pursuing its way to Jaffa. We shouted, but to no purpose. We ran, but the pursuit seemed hopeless. We found the rough ground very hard as we chased our chariot across the fields, A boy of the vicinage took in the situation, and volunteered in our cause. He was fresher and fleeter, and, putting his wings upon his unsandalled feet and exercising his lungs in the native vocabulary, he finally succeeded in stopping our impatient equipage. But for certain difficulties, growing out of a difference in language, we might have had an explanation from the driver, to which we could have added appropriate remarks. As it was, we contented ourselves with rewarding our Mercury, and then pushed on towards the sea.

It was dark as we entered Jaffa. We passed the house of Tabitha, who, under her other name of Dorcas, has been the patroness of so much ecclesiastical charity and has bestowed so many coats and garments which have gladdened the hearts of "saints and widows." We drew up at Howard's Hotel, where we found good quarters and a hearty welcome awaiting us. We had been told that it was important that we should reach Jaffa that night, as the steamer was appointed to sail for the North on the next day. We found that the steamer had not arrived. But it was not yet the next day. The morning came and we were still there. The steamer was not. Would she be in that day? Howard was non-committal. A less interested resident told us that she would not make her appearance. "When will she come?" "Nobody can tell. Last trip she was a week late. She is not often so late as that." There was nothing to do but to wait. It was tedious and annoying. My passage from England was engaged, and the day set for resuming work at home. Could I carry out my plans? It was hard to have the unsolved problem continually recurring, and in a place of no more attractions than Jaffa presented. The view from our hotel was interesting, although the interest was restricted. Across the road was a Muhammedan burial-ground, and beyond that the sea, over whose blue waters we were at liberty to gaze as far as we wished, and much longer. It would have been a pleasing sight if we could have been satisfied with a sight of the sea. Not a sail intruded itself on the far horizon or broke the tranquil surface of the boundless waters. It was indeed the unplanted sea. Thursday morning gave us a burial in the field below us, but that was not exciting. We explored our own premises. We found that Howard had a garden which was fine for this part of the world. He had, also, a barouche which he had imported from England for visitors of a higher rank than those to whom he did not proffer its luxury. He had, moreover, an apparatus for making ice by some chemical process. This would have afforded us a trifling solace on a hot day, but unfortunately it was not in working order. We walked out into the town. It was as others. The streets were narrow, rough, dirty, slippery. The bazaars were small, but had the usual variety of people and merchandise. Greeks, Latins, and Armenians were found to have their monasteries. The mosque was in its place, and its bare walls were uninviting. It was well that it was so, for it might have been hard to gain admission. We came upon a large well which is a place of popular resort. Standing in a court, covered with an eight-sided roof, or cupola, and showing something of the Saracenic character, it is a finer piece of work than anything else in the town, and it was a busy throng of men and beasts which was going and coming, through which with difficulty we made our way.

Friday was rainy, very. There seemed to be water enough before, as no steamer in these parts was in want of any. We had leisure to think upon the history of the place, but the amount of our historical knowledge was not large. It is said that the town was built before the Flood. It was the seat of an old Phœnician colony. When Solomon was about to build the temple, Hiram, King of Tyre, was appealed to for men and trees, and agreed to bring wood in floats by sea to Joppa, whence it could be carried to Jerusalem. The place came into the possession of the Jews, and Greeks, and Romans. Its name became changed from Yafa to Joppa. Christianity gained an early entrance, as we find from the Acts of the Apostles. The stirring centuries which followed left their mark, and the town was destroyed by Saladin. In the seventeenth and eighteenth centuries it came up again. The quay was constructed and walls were built. The present population is estimated by Baedeker at eight thousand, which seems large. There is quite an extensive trade with Egypt, Syria, and Turkey, in soap, grain, oranges, and other things. As the only port of southern Palestine, and therefore the gateway of Jerusalem and all which lies around it, Jaffa possesses a great advantage in its situation. The buildings come close to the sea and reach back from it to the base of a high cliff. A reef of rocks runs parallel with the shore, making a breakwater inside of which boats can find room. Large vessels must stop outside and in rough weather are often unable to effect a landing. Indeed, landing is very apt to be difficult, as it can hardly be said that there is a harbor. But all the conditions favored our remaining. We might have ventured out in boats, but it would have been to return in boats. Yet it was here that Jonah, when he was vainly fleeing from the presence of the Lord, found a ship which was going to Tarshish. "So he paid the fare thereof, and went down into it." That vessel seems to have been taken off the line.

Saturday brought more wind and rain, but brought no steamer in sight. We strained our eyes across the graveyard, and turned Howard's large glass towards the restless sea: but no wreath of smoke, no moving speck was to be discerned. At times we tried to fancy that we saw something unusual, but it was only to be disheartened once again. A few graves were dug in the morning, and later there was a burial. We went out when we were able to do so, and found that the rains had flooded the streets. They needed washing, and this was the only way in which they could get it.

We made a visit to the house of Simon the tanner, — to his two houses, in fact, his Latin and Greek residences. The Latin hospice covers the site of one of them, while a church has succeeded to the place of the other. Simon was a tanner of Joppa, whose house was by the seaside. Upon its flat roof, another Simon, surnamed Peter, received the vision which opened the Gentile world to him. We found a house by the seaside and went upon its roof. Not far away were tanneries. It could not have been far from the spot where we stood and thought upon Peter and his vision that the house of the tanner stood. For two hundred years tradition has dignified this site. The Moslems, as would be expected, have a mosque on the spot where they assert the house was. No one is very far out of the way, which is some satisfaction.

A little beyond the city was the settlement of a

German colony. Mr. Garry, with his usual enterprise, investigated the colonists and their buildings, and subsequently took us out to his new acquaintances. There was an American colony there, but that had disappeared. The present foundation dates from 1868. Some two hundred and fifty persons were reported in connection with it. The Jerusalem Hotel was in front, and back of this houses and shops. A variety of industries employed the people and furnished them with a good livelihood. The place was quiet, and everything had a peaceful and contented look. If the people deem it necessary to dwell in Palestine, in view of coming events, they seem to be doing it in quite a sensible way. The day wore on to night. There were no good omens in the air. It was here that Andromeda, daughter of Cepheus and Cassiopea, was taken from her boastful mother and chained to a rock where she would be devoured by a sea-monster. This is the rock. Sunday we kept at home. Showers were frequent, the streets were muddy, our spirits were low, the English service was on the other side of the town. In the afternoon we did go with Mr. Garry into a neighboring orange and lemon orchard. The Greek proprietor was very hospitable, and gave us all the information which his knowledge of the country and his ignorance of English would allow, and liberally endowed us with the immense products of his fragrant and beautiful trees. Still Perseus delayed to come for Andromeda. It was wearisome turning our anxious eyes towards the sea and the fair, far countries beyond.

Monday morning brought an unusual sound. It was the whistle of a steamer. No orchestra ever discoursed such music, no symphony was ever so delightful. We hastened to the balcony, and just off the town lay a small steamer—small but comely. Our preparations were quickly made, and we hurried to the quay. Mr. Mill went to the agent's office, while we repaired to the banker's to replenish our treasury. I asked for £20 and after an hour's waiting procured it. Meanwhile, Mr. Mill brought us the tidings that the *Selene* would not sail till the afternoon of the next day. He had found that the agent was in his bed-room at nine o'clock. Upon being aroused and brought into his office, he declared that no business could be done till he had refreshed himself with his hubble-bubble, or water-pipe. That was over at last, and the desired tickets were secured. I do not remember what we did, except that we waited and complained.

Howard did all he could for our comfort during our imprisonment. He fed us on the choicest which the market afforded. He ministered to our Yankee taste with what he called pumpkin-pie. If this had come a month earlier, before our imagination was jaded, we might have given it the same name. He did his best. He bore our detention better than we did. We were his only guests, and it was not for his advantage to send us off. I have a notion that he would have let us stay longer in Jerusalem if his hotel had not been in Jaffa. I believe that Mr. Garry was of that opinion.

I have mentioned the Moslem burials. They

were frequent and peculiar. We saw on the street a procession marching to what sounded like martial music. The music was made by a drum and two sets of cymbals. Men led the way, and were followed by women with black veils over their faces. A coffin covered with crimson cloth and trimmed with flowers was carried by men. At the grave the coffin and the women entered a tent. After a time the grave was filled up. I presume that the body had been taken from the coffin and laid in the ground. Then the company dispersed, hastened by the rain, though some of the women remained in the tent. There was what appeared to be a dispute about the grave or something connected with it. One woman talked in a loud voice and swung her arms violently, and the grave-digger, as I took him to be, responded in a befitting manner.

Women were in the cemetery early on this morning. Some were seated around a newly made grave. One elderly woman remained through the forenoon, when she was joined by another, who threw a handkerchief over and over, and laid it on the grave, repeating this many times with words that did not reach us.

In the afternoon there was another funeral. A procession came down the street and entered the ground, with a rude band and twelve flags. Men followed bearing an open coffin, in which lay the body, wrapped for its last slumber. Women in white, with black veils, followed. When the grave was reached, the women sat, while the men stood in a circle and sang a funeral hymn, throwing themselves backward and forward, swinging half-way round, bowing as they turned, finally reducing their movements to the shaking of the head. After this came the interment.

We walked on the shore of the Mediterranean, picking up pretty stones and shells, and wondering when we should go "sailing into the West." It is hard to make plans in this land of deliberation and delay. In Jaffa they draw water for irrigation by a system of buckets arranged on a rope. They had a similar method in Egypt in Pharaoh's time, judging from the pictures. The wheel is worked by a mule, whose eyes are covered with a cloth. If he could see he would not go, we were informed. It seemed probable. If he could see the men, his imitative instinct would prompt him to follow their customs, and the water would remain with the truth. He might use his energy in constructing a cigarette or raising the fumes of the nargîleh; but as a mule he would be a failure.

On Tuesday we were told to be on the steamer by half-past eleven in the forenoon. We were there. The sea within and without the breakwater was quiet, and we made the transit without difficulty. We sailed at half-past three. We waited, it was said, for the post. A general impatience prevailed after a time, and we whistled — that is, the steamer whistled — to hasten the operations on shore. The post finally arrived, and consisted of several letters. It is possible there may have been a paper besides, but we did not see any, nor did we know of any reason why there should be a paper, except that on such occasions papers are usually present. There was altogether about half a bushel of mail matter. At last we were off. Our destination was Beirût and Smyrna. We were to retrace our voyage along the coast. We regretted this. We had hoped for Egypt, but there had been a few cases of cholera some time before, and the quarantine laws were in force and likely to continue. We could have gone into the country, but when we could get out again it was impossible to say. Hence we left the pyramids and sphinx for another journey. We had hoped for a steamer which would take us directly to Italy; but the cholera had caused the quarantine, and the quarantine had deranged the shipping, so that we were forced to take anything which offered. In this frame of mind we drew a line over the water parallel to that which we had left on the land, and on Wednesday forenoon steamed again into the fine harbor of Beirût. There were the mountains of Lebanon, the finely curved shore, the imposing buildings, the schools, churches, hospitals, the printing-press and lemonade. But nothing was quite the same as before. Then we were moving into a strange and fascinating country. Now we were looking towards the home places and home friends.

The wind was strong through the night, and the *Selene* rolled more than seemed necessary. We stopped off Haifa, and could see the lights in the town, and, beyond and above, the mountains of Carmel, holding their long, dark line against the dark sky. The most interesting feature of the passage was the presence of an Arab, of whom, even now, it is a pain to write. When we were at the Mediterranean Hotel, in Jerusalem, as the guests of the American Consul, a fine-looking Arab was in charge of the dining-room, and he cared for us with dignity and intelligence. He was born in Egypt, and his parents were Moslems. They died when he was a child, and he was brought up in the Roman Catholic Church, and for twenty years had been a Christian. Being a Christian, he could not be forced into the Turkish army, and he had paid the tax which was accounted a substitute for personal service. But one morning, as he was on his way to market, he was seized, taken before the court, and made to draw from the drafting-box. Of course he drew a black paper, and was doomed to military service. He had a wife and four children, but he was not allowed to see them. He was at once started for Jaffa. His case was hopeless. Every one who knew with whom the man had to deal said that he would never come back. The interference of the Latin Church was hoped for, which might send the case to France. But if he was released, what would he gain? He would still be in the hands of the Turks. Or, as one man suggestively remarked to me, he would very soon die. Fatal maladies can be produced at an instant's notice. The plan was to have Mustapha walk to Jaffa. It was a cruel march, for it was a very long way, and the poor fellow was heavy and unused to exercise. Some of his friends found out what had been done, and sent a horse after him. But it was afterward learned that the men feared the soldiers and did not come up with them. He was forced to walk to Ramleh, where he succeeded in hiring two donkeys for himself and the officer in whose special charge he was, who needed, I believe, a further bribe to make him consent to this arrangement. So he reached Jaffa, where he was thrown into jail with some twenty ragamuffins, who had been seized on various pretexts and were destined for the army. There he was kept eight days in the greatest discomfort. He received some small kindness from friends, but his confinement was most painful to him. Whether he looked back to Jerusalem and his home, or forward to his unknown fate, his thoughts could only be burdened with anxiety and dread.

Mustapha was brought to our steamer, where we were able to talk with him. He thought that his seizure was due to the betrayal of his confidence by a Turkish effendi at the hotel. The charge against him was that he had abandoned the Moslem faith. Against this he had a good defence, if he had been in a country of law and justice. He was one of a sorry-looking company of Arabs, half-naked, ragged, infested with vermin. Falstaff would have spurned the lot. Mustapha made little complaint. He seemed submissive, and to cherish an indefinite confidence that things would turn out better than they promised. "I trust in the Lord," he said. We were glad of the trust, but we should have been glad to see more spirit on his own part. He had a hope that he might be released, through the efforts of his friends, when he would seek a home in America. At Beirût the men were taken on shore. The others were crowded into the bows of a boat, but Mustapha sat in the stern with the officers. He gave us a cheerful good-by as the boat pushed off.

We landed some brown monks, also, who were lowered into the boat by their arms. We enjoyed the process more than they did. We had rather a varied company, for a third of the upper deck was covered with canvas, making an apartment for a few Moslems.

We were at Beirût at nine in the morning. There was a high wind and sea, with rain, but the condition of things improved. At half-past one a boat came for freight. Some one, somewhere, seemed to have awakened to the fact that we were there to discharge a portion of our cargo. The men who came in the boats were fine-looking fellows, quick, strong, and willing. They were so much better than their betters. If only they could be made the rulers, and the palaces and offices emptied into the boats!

Thursday was a bright day, and the snow was glittering on Lebanon. The morning was well advanced before we received any freight. One important thing was accomplished. A barber came from the shore and shaved the captain. A French steamer came in, destined for Jaffa. There was in port an English steamer on her way to Port Said. But it was too late for the land of the Nile. We found that but one course was open to us, to return to Smyrna, and there at some time to catch a steamer bound somewhere. We went on shore, went to the hotel and read the latest papers, visited the Bible House and American school, and enjoyed a few hours of civilization. We remembered that at home this was Thanksgiving Day, and we gave thanks. When we returned to the ship we found that four or five hundred men had been taken on board and were to be forced into the Turkish army. There was a good deal of bustle, preparatory to our sailing. Mr. Mill planned to have Mustapha escape. He had been brought back to the ship. Mill had arranged with some one on shore to take care of him if he should get away. It seemed not very difficult, as no one was watching him, and boats were coming and going. He got a soft felt hat for him and a coat unlike that he had been wearing, and told him to watch his chance and slip into a boat which would carry him ashore. All went well. Mustapha made his way down the steps, and took his seat in a friendly boat. He was already quite a distance from the ship when some wretch, who should have been thrown overboard, screamed out, "One of your soldiers is running away." It was all over. Mustapha was brought back, his small store of money was taken from him, and an eye was kept upon him till we had left the harbor. He had no further punishment, so far as we knew. We saw him from day to day, and there seemed to be in him a mixture of Moslem fatalism and Christian faith. He was taken to Constantinople, I suppose, and sent somewhere into the interior, where he could not readily be found, and where he could expiate his crime of being a Christian.

The captain's clean clothes came off in the same boat with us, and there seemed to be nothing more to detain the *Selene*. At seven in the evening we sailed once more out of the beautiful harbor of Beirût. The next morning we were at Larnaka, on Cyprus, where we remained till one. Saturday was a pleasant day, but Sunday was dark and rainy. Patmos was covered with clouds. The day was in severe contrast to the Sabbath when we passed through the same waters, going in the opposite direction. But our voyage was made interesting by the soldiers whom we had on board. They were wretchedly clothed, but they seemed, for the most part, in good spirits. They had been seized in the fields and about their work, and hurried off as they were, under the charge that they had evaded the lawful military service, and must now pay their dues to the State, which deserved nothing. In themselves they were a good-looking set of men. They were well made, and their faces showed a fair degree of intelligence. I doubt if the same number of men swept in from any country would have made a better appearance. There was variety in their dress, or undress. They were like the men we had seen in our ride through the country. It was most interesting to watch them from time to time through the day. Some would be lying on the deck asleep. Here one would be telling his beads, and there one having his unkempt head gleaned by friendly hands. There was a kitten which did its part to relieve their monotony. Some would be found looking over their scanty clothes, and making any practicable improvement. The saddest sight of all was where one or two would be apart from their companions, sitting with mournful faces, thinking of the home and friends from which they had been torn, and of the dreadful life to which they were being carried. It seemed easy to interpret their thoughts. There one thought of his wife and children, left destitute, and wondering why he did not come in from the field. There a boy heard his mother's voice, and saw her anxious face peering into the gloom of evening, watching for his return. Here a young man, of fine bearing, with a face inexpressibly sad, submitted to his fate, while his heart was with the maiden whom he loved, who was to have joined her life to his when the harvest should be gathered in, who must wait while their sundered lives languished for the day which might never come.

We liked to watch the giving-out of rations. These consisted of olives and onions, with water. At first the men seemed to have bread in their bags. Some had brought oranges and grapes. After a time bread also was given to them. It was very hard. Even Arab teeth demanded that it be soaked. Once we found a dispute going on over the bread. Words grew loud, and scales were brought. Then the bread was weighed out in lots for six or eight men. It was in slices and pieces. The men were generally quiet while they were being fed. They had a natural courtesy. Once an officer who had been very rough in his manner towards them began to take off his coat that he might work more easily. They began to help him, and when the coat was off and he was holding it, a man offered to take it, and it was given into his keeping. A quarrel now and then enlivened the hours. Men from different parts of the country asserted themselves against one another, and blows followed. But blows come so readily among these men that there seems to be no ill-will in them, or only that which is of short duration. Once two men on board had a fight. One whipped the other. Whereupon the officer beat the victor, and equilibrium was restored.

We reached Smyrna at one o'clock Monday afternoon, and went to the Mille Hotel on the quay. Mr. Garry asserted that the terms offered by the runners of the house were not confirmed on shore, and he sought quarters of his own. But the rest were satisfied with the Mille. We found that on Wednesday a steamer would sail for Italy, *via* the Piræus. It seemed hard to lose another day. Yet it was expedient on our own account. The boy, who had been wonderfully well and happy through the entire journey, began to falter at Beirût, and on the voyage to Smyrna was dizzy and weak. The surgeon of the steamer, in intervals of comparative sobriety, looked at him, and expressed the professional opinion that the trouble was only of a temporary character. I think he expressed himself more seriously to others. It was a relief, therefore, that we could lie over at Smyrna. A German physician was called, who said there was a gastric trouble, for which he prescribed. Our time in Smyrna was therefore very quiet. Mr. Garry made an excursion to Ephesus. A guide who had volunteered to conduct him proved good for nothing, but to exact money, and the visit was not very profitable.

On Wednesday the doctor said we could go on, and his permission and warranty were most grateful. We thought that the boy would be as well off at sea, and we knew that he should be moving towards better care than he could have anywhere else. At two o'clock we went to the Italian steamer, the *Pachino*, and were hardly in our state-room before word was brought that the captain wished to see me. This was an unusual courtesy, but I responded to it. The captain was a man of substantial appearance, but of few words, and those chiefly in a language unfamiliar to me. But Mr. Mill was there. The captain remarked that I had brought a sick boy on board, and that he did not dare to take him. I remarked, through the interpreter, that the boy had been sea-sick, and was suffering from its effects. I cannot repeat the conversation. There had been cholera in Egypt, — more's the pity — but the cholera had made quarantine, and if the steamer reached Italy with sickness on board she might be detained for weeks. The agent for the steamer kindly expressed his belief that there was no danger, and that the boy should be allowed to go. The captain clung to his fears. "Would he regard the certificate of a physician?" He would. The agent and Mr. Mill jumped into a boat and went ashore, sought out the doctor, and came back with a written certificate that this was a case of *mal de mer*. Still the captain frowned. Not a ray of hope illumined his bronzed face. We had brought up from Beirût an Italian Consul, with his family. To him I appealed. I said, "You have seen this boy on the ship all the way from Beirût to Smyrna. You know the whole matter. Won't you please tell the captain that it is nothing but a case of sea-sickness?" "No; I won't interfere. I'm not a doctor." "But you know there's nothing the matter with the boy." "Are you a doctor?" "No; but here is the physician's certificate." I could make no impression on him. I became persuaded that it was he who had complained to the captain and awakened his fears. The little man was afraid that under the peculiar rules of his country there might come some inconvenience, and he preferred to have us suffer the inconvenience. Better that we should wait at Smyrna than that he should be detained at Brindisi. I was well nigh in despair. After so many delays, after so much anxiety and suffering, to be put off the last steamer which we needed did seem to be hard. But you can generally trust a sailor, if you can reach him. The captain was true to his calling. He consented that we should go to the Piræus. There, as he said, the agent of the ship would decide whether we could go further. I doubt if he meant to ask him. But the compromise answered a good purpose, and when the *Pachino* steamed from the harbor of Smyrna the boy was on board.

We were to have sailed at four o'clock in the afternoon. The sea was so rough that we did not leave until eight on Thursday morning. It was a very hard passage. I never saw the Mediterranean more angry and turbulent. The ship was lightly loaded and was tossed about in the most reckless fashion. I was the only one who was constant at meals, but I kept up the proprieties of the ship. The Italian consul came into a better feeling, and seemed to regret his churlishness. He told me that he spoke to the captain in my behalf. He exerted himself to make it plain to me how I could get from southern Italy to Switzerland, and at the Piræus he took his large household and went on shore to spend a week with friends, and to wait for a calmer sea. We reached the Piræus about seven on Friday morning. I found the captain on deck. "How is your son?" "Better." "Do you think you can get him through?" "Oh, yes." We heard nothing of an appeal to the agent.

We sailed again at noon. The distant glimpse of Athens was pleasing and attractive. But our thoughts were not with the past. Saturday was a hard day. The ship was jumping and rolling without pause or change. The boy was my anxious care. Yet he seemed to be doing well. Mr. Mill was attentive and he was something of a surgeon. The cook and steward did all they could in the way of tempting soups. Mr. Garry was most thoughtful and unselfish. He had always an encouraging word. "Ken will come through all right." He believed in dreams. I told him that in the night I saw a man standing over me as if he would strike me. "Well, he didn't strike you, did he?" "No." "Don't you know what that means? It is just as plain. You're anxious about your boy. The trouble is standing over you, but it won't strike you." Still, they were long hours and serious ones, day and night, night and day. Sunday was better. There was less sea. The boy was doing very well. I watched him and nursed him. I read through the Epistle to the Hebrews, and saw how much more it means when read as a whole. I cherished every hope which came to me. Late in the afternoon we reached Brindisi. A boat came off, and an officer was sent on shore. We were notified that we must be on deck early the next morning, when the quarantine officers would inspect us. On Monday morning the rain poured down. It was unlikely that the doctors would come to us, or at the time appointed. For some mysterious reason they were on hand promptly. They took their places at the side of the ship, and the crew marched by them and back again. The third-class passengers did the same. Our turn came. It was the critical moment. I told the boy that he must do his best. He was thin and pale, and uncertain as to his gait. The fortunate rain allowed me to conceal his face with an umbrella, while I let him rest on my arm. Mr. Garry considerately walked next, to cover any peculiarities of locomotion. We went past reasonably well, and, before we could make our way back, the doctors had pronounced us all right, and were on their way down to their boat. We were told that we could go on shore the next day. Why must we wait? Nobody knew. It had been said. We waited. It was a good place, if we must wait. But days were few and precious then.

The harbor was very pleasant. The stern castle frowned upon us with its round towers. We thought of the story of the old town which marked the end of the Appian Way and was thus bound to Rome. We were carefully watched lest we should escape to the shore. I do not know how they thought we might effect this. I doubt if they thought the matter out so far as that. Early on Tuesday morning we were called and counted, and ordered on deck. The government took every precaution against the few wanderers from the West. But when we reached the deck, the officers had completed their inspection and departed. We left the ship at half-past eight and with delight set our feet on the soil of Italy. We found a very comfortable hotel, the Oriental, where we established ourselves for a few hours. It was interesting to walk in the steep, narrow, winding streets, among the houses of stone which show their age, and to mark the signs of a new life which is coming in now that this is made the point of departure for steamers to the East. Brindisi has its history, but we were weary of the past. Still, we enjoyed this bit of the empire which has been preserved by its distance from the capital.

In the afternoon we took the train for the north. At Foggia Mr. Garry parted from us, as he was going to Naples. We regretted to have him leave, for he had been a very kind companion. We have not seen him since, but we heard of him while he was pursuing his exploration of Italian cities, where his tall form was conspicuous, crowned with his

Oriental fez, and asserting its nationality wherever it went.

At Foggia we changed to a *compartimento di letti*, a very convenient apartment, where the night's ride was as pleasant as it could be made. The road through much of its course ran close to the sea, and it was very restful to look out over the Adriatic as it lay quietly by our side, and to know that we were set free from its tossings and delays. We saw a little of Bologna from our windows, and there changed cars and came by a long day's ride to Torino. There we were put into a *coupelit*, a narrow compartment with a series of extension chairs on which we could stretch ourselves. Mr. Mill took leave of us, as his mission was ended, and we seemed qualified to finish the journey under our own guidance. We were to change cars at Culoz. If there is one thing that is more annoying than others in travelling in a strange country, it is to know that you have to leave one train and find another at some uncertain time in the night, and chiefly by your own wit. Sleep is too perilous to be indulged in. A moment's lapse may be the delay of hours. I kept awake as we entered and left one station after another, till at length I thought we must be near Culoz. No one spoke the magic word in my hearing. When my suspicions had become sufficiently strong, I inquired of the porter who opened our door if that was Culoz. Instantly he made it evident that it was not, and, further, that Culoz had been left behind. The unfortunate lapse had befallen me in spite of all my pains, and at the fatal time. With the hurried advice and vigorous assistance of the porter, the boy and I tumbled out of the car and stood on the lonesome, dreary, dismal platform of a large station and saw our train plunge on into the dark. Where were we?—At Amberieux. Nobody else seemed to be there. When we could leave no one could tell us. We made our way to a dimly lighted restaurant and sought information. To procure that we procured refreshments. The sleepy proprietor had more coffee than knowledge, or more which was available for our purposes, but there was a similarity in the quality of the two. Thrown upon our own resources, we scanned the walls of the room and discovered a railway poster. To our relief, we made out that a train would soon come along which would take us back to Culoz. It came. We were wide-awake when Culoz was called out. There we took a train for Geneva. Through our delay on the road we missed the train we meant to take for Geneva; but the station was large and comfortable, and the hour or two which we had to wait passed pleasantly enough. Then we went on to Lausanne, and thence to Vevey. Nobody at the station seemed to be expecting us. We made our way through the wet snow, carrying our luggage, and finally attracted the attention of the omnibus driver whom we sought. When he dropped us at the door of the Hotel Monnet this journey ended.

It was a good place for the end. The situation of Vevey is fine, as it looks out upon the lake and towards the snowy mountains beyond. It has been a favorite place of resort. The climate is milder than at Geneva, while the quiet of the little town is very restful. The name of Rousseau is associated with the place, and the traveller now finds a coffee-house where he found an inn. The streets which wind among the simple houses have a quaint and simple look, while the market-place has the attractions which belong to the assembling of busy people intent on the affairs of daily life. St. Martin's Church, nearly four hundred years old, stands high above the town, among the graves of the people. The view is very fine from the hill which it adorns. Within the church are the tombs of two English regicides, — Broughton, who read the sentence of death to Charles I., and Ludlow, his associate. There are other churches; among them a fine Russian chapel with a gilded dome, and a handsome English church. There is a boy's school, also, which has been well patronized by English and American families. The boys have excellent facilities for boating, and for other things which they delight in. Vevey has attractive shops for books and jewelry, while Mack's Bazaar is a museum crowded with things in general in an immense variety. There are delightful excursions in every direction. Montreux is not far away, with its figs and pomegranates, its laurels and its health, and the Castle of Chillon on its rocks in the lake. The prison is very gloomy, with heavy memories of Bonnivard worn into the pavement and lying on the stone where he sat in his weary years.

Vevey is indeed a charming place for resting and thinking. But for two persons who had come into its beauty and repose the chief pleasure was under the Three Crowns, where a united household sat around the blazing logs and talked of wanderings in the East and of the return to the fairer land across the sea. The hours were as a dream between two hurried days. I think of them as I write. Once again I look out upon the lake and over to the hills. At Vevey, with the gulls swooping to the windows, resting their broad wings on the still air, and plucking the bread from a child's hand, I lay down my pen.

# INDEX.

ABBOTTSFORD, 58
Acropolis, 208
Ægean, Sunday in, 273-275
Albana, River, 301
Athens, 200-231
  Acropolis, 208
  Agora, 218
  Areopagus, 215
  Eleusis, 224
  Herodes Atticus, 207
  Mars' Hill, 215
  Parthenon, 211
  Pentelic marble, 222
  Sanctuary of Æsculapius, 207
  Stadium, 204
  Temple of Zeus Olympius, 205
  Theseum, 220
  University of, 229
  Wine-making, 228

BAALBEC, 293
  Ruins of, 296
  Temples and walls of, 294
Baden-Baden, 132
  Castle of, 134
Bânias, 330
  Market-day in, 332
Bareno, 165
  Villa Clara, 166
Bedouins, Dwelling of, 334
  Customs and dress of, 335
Beirut, 276, 456
  Christian schools, 279
  Lemonade, 278
  Selection of horses, 281
Belfast, 17
Bergen, 64-68
Bethany, 392, 419
  Tomb of Lazarus, 420
Bethel, 382
Bethlehem, 406
  Chapel of the Innocents, 411
  Chapel of the Nativity, 410
  Chapel and Tomb of St. Jerome, 411
  Merchants of, 408
  Wells of David, 407
Blarney Castle, 12
Blarney Stone, 12
Borgund, Church of, 93
Brindisi, 464

CALEDONIAN CANAL, 45
Cana of Galilee, 350
Castle of Baden-Baden, 134
Castle, Blarney, 12
Castle of Chillon, 468
Castle of Dunluce, 21
Castle, Edinburgh, 48
Castle of Laufen, 150
Castle, Nuremberg, 145
Castle, Ross, 16
Cathedral of Cephalonia, 198
Cathedral, Cologne, 125
Cathedral, Dublin, 16
Cathedral, Glasgow, 29
Cathedral of Milan, 174-176
Cathedral of Strasbourg, 130
Cathedral of St. Mary, 40
Certosa di Pavia, 179
Chapel of the Angels, 356
Chapel of the Annunciation, 357
Chapel of the Innocents, 411
Chapel of Joseph, 357
Chapel of the Nativity, 410
Chapel of St. Jerome, 411
Chapel of St. Michael, 161
Chapel, Roslin, 50
Christiania, 100
  Frogner, 103
  Hospital, 104
  Kuriol, 106
  National Exhibition, 102
  Oscar's Hall, 106
  Viking's ships, 104
Church, Crimean Memorial, 264
Church of Borgund, 93
Church of Christ, 437
Church of the Copts, 433
Church of the Holy Sepulchre, 424
Church of Our Lady, 119
Church of St. Ambrogio, 177
Church of St. Justin, 184
Church of St. Lawrence, 138
Church of S. Maria degli Angioli, 168
Church of St. Martin, 468
Church of St. Peter, 128
Church of St. Sophia, 245
Church of St. Ursula, 127
Church, Trinity, 119
Cologne, 125
  Cathedral of, 125
  Church, St. Peter's, 128

# INDEX.

Cologne (continued)
  Church of St. Ursula, 127
Como, 170
Constantinople, 233
  Bazaars, 237
  Bible House, 262
  Bridge between Pera and Stamboul, 237
  Church, Crimean Memorial, 264
  Church of St. Sophia, 245
  Constantine, Grave of, 249
  Currency of, 239
  Dogs of, 252
  Hippodrome, 242
  Home or Girls' School, 259
  Public Baths, 251
  Robert College, 256
  to Damascus, 265
  Walls of, 244
Copenhagen, 119
  Church of Our Lady, 119
  Church of the Trinity, 119
  Thorwaldsen, 119, 121
  Tivoli, 120
  Rutchbauen, 120
Cork, 11
  Blarney Castle, 12
  Blarney Stone, 12
Culoz, 467
Cyprus, 276

DAMASCUS, 304-306
  Bazaar, 308
  Camels, 313
  Caravan, 313
  Citadel, 316
  Drama, 314
  Father of Antiquities, 309
  Great Mosque, 319
  History, 305
  Horse-market, 308
  Hotel Dimitri, 304
  House of Ambar, 317
  House of Ananias, 311
  House of Naaman, 311
  House of Shamai, 317
  Mosques, 318
  Plane-tree, 308
  Quarters and streets, 307
  Schools, 318
  St. Paul, 312
  Straight Street, 310
  Tomb of Bibaus, 320
  Tomb of St. George, 312
Dan, 334
Dead Sea, 387
Dome of the Rock, 398
Dothan, 366
Dryburgh, 59
Dublin, 16
  Cathedral of, 16
Dunluce Castle, 21
Dürer, Albert, 143

EDINBURGH, 48
  Castle of, 48

Edinburgh (continued)
  House of John Knox, 49
  Queen's Drive, 49
  St. Giles, 49
Eide, 84
Eleusis, 224
El-Fûleh, 362
Esdraelon, Plain of, 361

FAGERHUND, 98
Fall of Foyers, 46
Fingal's Cave, 42
Fjord, Hardanger, 68
Foggia, 465

GALILEE, SEA OF, 339, 343, 347
  Storm on, 341
Gap of Dunloe, 15
Gerizim, Mount, 373
Gethsemane, 417
Giant's Causeway, 18
Giant's Chair, 21
Giant's Well, 19
Gilgal, 389
Glasgow, 28
  Cathedral of, 29
  John Knox, Statue of, 29
  Norman Macleod, Statue of, 29
  Sunday in, 33-37
Golden Gate, 402
Good Samaritan, 301
Gudvangen, 89

HIPPODROME, 242
Holyrood Palace, 48

IONA, 39
  Cathedral of, 40
Ireland, 10
  Cork, 11
  Dublin, 16
  Giant's Causeway, 19
  Killarney, 13
  Muckross Abbey, 15
  People of, 22-26
Isola Bella, 166
Italian Lakes, 164-165

JACOB'S WELL, 377
Jaffa, 444
  Arrival of steamer, 450
  House of Simon, 448
  Moslem burials, 450
  Well in, 446
Jenin, 365
Jericho, 386
  House of Zaccheus, 386
Jerusalem, History of, 394-396
  American colony, 436
  Church of the Holy Sepulchre, 424
  Church of Christ, 437
  Church of the Copts, 433
  Church of St. Anne, 415
  Church of the Virgin, 416
  Dome of the Rock, 398
  El-aksa, 400

# INDEX.

Jerusalem (*continued*)
  Garden of Gethsemane, 417
  Golden Gate, 402
  Harâm esh Sheñf, 397
  Lord's Supper, Room of, 413
  Magician, 440
  Olivet, 430
  Pool of Siloam, 413
  Potter's Field, 415
  Sabbath in, 435
  Solomon's Stables, 401
  Tomb of Absalom, 434
  Tomb of David, 414
  Tomb of the Judges, 433
  Tomb of the Kings, 433
  Tomb of Rachel, 406
  Via Dolorosa, 423
  Wailing-place, 403
  Well of the Star, 405
Jezreel, 364
  Fountain of, 364
Jordan, River, 389

KÁSIÚM, 302
Kefr-Hawar, 323
Kefr-Kenna, 349
Khân Jubb Yûsef, 338
Killarney, 13
Knox, John, 29
  Desk in Hawthornden, 51
  House in Edinburgh, 49
  Statue in Glasgow, 29

LAST SUPPER, DA VINCI, 178
Laufen, Castle of, 150
Lebonah, 380
Locarno, Town of, 164
Loch Lomond, 31
Lucerne, 151
  Hofkirche, 152
  Lion of, 153
  Market-place, 152
Lugarno, 167
  Church of S. Maria degli Angioli, 168
Luino, 167
Lysicrates, Monument of, 206

MACLEOD, NORMAN, 30
Manessi, 201
Mars' Hill, 215
Mediterranean steamer, 197
Mejdel-esh Shems, 326
  Housekeeping in, 326
  Protestant chapel, 328
  Sunday in, 327
Melrose, 52
  Abbey, 52-55
  Sunday in, 55
Menaggio, 168-170
Merom, 337
Milan, 171
  Brera Gallery, 177
  Cathedral, 174-176
  Certosa di Pavia, 179
  Church of St. Ambrogio, 177

Milan (*continued*)
  Last Supper, by Da Vinci, 178
  Monastery of S. Maria delle Grazie, 178
  Sunday in, 176
  Mount of Olives, 391
  Muckross Abbey, 15
  Mustapha, 453-457

NÀBLUS, *see* SCHECHEM
Nazareth, 351
  Chapel of the Angels, 376
  Chapel of the Annunciation, 357
  Chapel of Joseph, 357
  Fountain of the Virgin, 359
  House of Mary, 355
  Life of Jesus in, 354
  Mary's Well, 360
  Synagogue, 358
Neuhausen, 150
  Castle of Laufen, 150
  Schweizerhof, 150
Newcastle-upon-Tyne, 61
Norway and Sweden, History of, 107-117
Nuremberg, 137
  Beautiful Fountain, 142
  Castle of, 145
  St. Lawrence's Church, 138
  Sunday in, 148
  Walls and towers of, 142

OBAN, 38
Odde, 71
Olivet, 430
Ördgaard, 97
Oscar's Hall, 106

PADUA, 181
  Chapel of St. George, 184
  Church of St. Justin, 184
  Church of St. Antonio, 184
  Scuola del Santo, 184
  Streets, 182
  University of, 183
  Palace of the Doges, 188
  Bridge of Sighs, 188
Parthenon, 211
Patmos, 273
Pentelic marble, 221
Piræus, The, 463
Polycarp, 269
Porlezza, 168
Portrush, 17
  Giant's Causeway, 18
  Premier Electric Railway, 18
  The Skerries, 17

RAMLEH, 443
Rigi, The, 155
Klosterli, 160
Sunday at, 162
Robert College, 256
Roslin Castle and Chapel, 50
Ross Castle, 16

SACHS, HANS, 143
Safed, 349
Samaria, 367
　Church of St. John, 371
　Woman of, 379
School at Athens, 203
Schweizerhof, 150
Scotch Lakes, 31
Shechem, 369
　Funeral procession, 376
　Samaritan synagogue, 370
　Streets, houses, and trade, 369, 370
　Sunday in, 374
Staffa, 42
St. John, 274
St. Paul, 217, 312
Sychar, *see* Shechem
Sychem, *see* Shechem
Syria, 282
　Tomb of Doris, 293
　Tomb of Noah, 291
　Travel in, 282, 291

TEMPLE OF BAALBEC, 294
Temple of Zeus Olympius, 205
Temple of Theseus, 220
Thorwaldsen, 121
Tiberias, 341
　Castle in, 343
　People, dress, and customs, 344
Tomb of Absalom, 434
Tomb of David, 414
Tomb of Doris, 293
Tomb of Joseph, 376
Tomb of the Judges, 433
Tomb of the Kings, 433

Tomb of Lazarus, 420
Tomb of Noah, 291
Tomb of St. Jerome, 411
Tomb of Walter Scott, 59
Trieste, 193-197

ULVIK, 81
University of Athens, 229
University of Padua, 183

VALLEY OF DOVES, 349
Venice, 184
　Academy, 189
　Armenian Convent of St. Lazarus, 190
　Bridge of Sighs, 188
　Palace of the Doges, 188
　The Frari, 189
Vevey, 467
　St. Martin's Church, 468
Via Dolorosa, 423
Vik, 73
　Church in, 79
Viking's ships, 104
Vitznau, 154
Vöringsfos, Excursion to, 74-79
Vossevangen, 85
　Church in, 86

WAILING-PLACE, 403
Well of David, 407
Well of Jacob, 379
Well of Mary, 360
Well of the Star, 415

ZANTE, 199

# THE SCHOOL OF HOME.

Let the school of home be a good one. Let reading be such as to quicken the mind for better reading still; for the school at home is progressive.

---

The baby is to be read to. What shall mother and sister and father and brother read to the baby?

BABYLAND. Babyland rhymes and jingles; great big letters and little thoughts and words out of BABYLAND. Pictures so easy to understand that baby quickly learns the meaning of light and shade, of distance, of tree, of cloud. The grass is green; the sky is blue; the flowers —are they red or yellow? That depends on mother's house-plants. Baby sees in the picture what she sees in the home and out of the window.

BABYLAND, mother's monthly picture-and-jingle primer for baby's diversion, and baby's mother-help; 50 cents a year.

---

What, when baby begins to read for herself? OUR LITTLE MEN AND WOMEN is made to go on with. BABYLAND forms the reading habit. Think of a baby with the reading habit! After a little she picks up the letters and wants to know what they mean. The jingles are jingles still; but the tales that lie under the jingles begin to ask questions.

What do Jack and Jill go up the hill after water for? Isn't water down hill? Baby is outgrowing BABYLAND.

No more nonsense. There is fun enough in sense. The world is full of interesting things; and, if they come to a growing child not in discouraging tangles but an easy one at a time, there is fun enough in getting hold of them. That is the way to grow. OUR LITTLE MEN AND WOMEN helps such growth as that. Beginnings of things made easy by words and pictures; not too easy. The reading habit has got to another stage.

A dollar for such a school as that for a year.

---

Then comes THE PANSY with stories of child-life, travel at home and abroad, adventure, history old and new, religion at home and over the seas, and roundabout tales on the International Sunday School Lesson.

Pansy the editor; THE PANSY the magazine. There are thousands and thousands of children and children of larger growth all over the country who know about Pansy the writer, and THE PANSY the magazine. There are thousands and thousands more who will be glad to know.

A dollar a year for THE PANSY.

---

The reading habit is now pretty well established; not only the reading habit, but liking for useful reading; and useful reading leads to learning.

Now comes WIDE AWAKE, vigorous, hearty, not to say heavy. No, it isn't heavy, though full as it can be of practical help along the road to sober manhood and womanhood. Full as it can be! There is need of play as well as of work; and WIDE AWAKE has its mixture of work and rest and play. The work is all toward self-improvement; so is the rest; and so is the play. $2.40 a year.

---

Specimen copies of all the Lothrop magazines for fifteen cents; any one for five — in postage stamps

Address D. Lothrop Company, Boston.

You little know what help there is in books for the average housewife.

Take *Domestic Problems*, for instance, beginning with this hard question: "How may a woman enjoy the delights of culture and at the same time fulfil her duties to family and household?" The second chapter quotes from somebody else: "It can't be done. I've tried it; but, as things now are, it can't be done."

Mrs. Diaz looks below the surface. Want o. preparation and culture, she says, is at the bottom of a woman's failure, just as it is of a man's.

The proper training of children, for instance, can't be done without some comprehension of children themselves, of what they ought to grow to, their stages, the means of their guidance, the laws of their health, and manners. But mothers get no hint of most of these things until they have to blunder through them. Why not? Isn't the training of children woman's mission? Yes, in print, but not in practice. What is her mission in practice? Cooking and sewing!

Woman's worst failure then is due to the stupid blunder of putting comparatively trivial things before the most important of all. The result is bad children and waste of a generation or two — all for putting cooking and sewing before the training of children.

Now will any one venture to say that any particular mother, you for instance, has got to put cooking and sewing before the training of children?

Any mother who really makes up her mind to put her children first can find out how to grow tolerable children at least.

And that is what Mrs. Diaz means by preparation — a little knowledge beforehand — the little that leads to more.

It *can* be done ; and *you* can do it ! Will you ? It's a matter of choice ; and you are the chooser.

Domestic Problems. By Mrs. A. M. Diaz. $1. D. Lothrop Company, Boston.

We have touched on only one subject. The author treats of many.

---

Dr. Buckley the brilliant and versatile editor of the *Christian Advocate* says in the preface of his book on northern Europe "I hope to impart to such as have never seen those countries as clear a view as can be obtained from reading" and "My chief reason for traveling in Russia was to study Nihilism and kindred subjects."

This affords the best clue to his book to those who know the writer's quickness, freshness, independence, force, and penetration.

The Midnight Sun, the Tsar and the Nihilist. Adventures and Observations in Norway, Sweden and Russia. By J. M. Buckley, LL. D. 72 illustrations, 370 pages. $3. D. Lothrop Company, Boston.

Just short of the luxurious in paper, pictures and print.

---

The writer best equipped for such a task has put into one illustrated book a brief account of every American voyage for polar exploration, including one to the south almost forgotten.

American Explorations in the Ice Zones. By Professor J. E. Nourse, U. S. N 10 maps, 120 illustrations, 624 pages. Cloth, $3, gilt edges $3.50, half-calf $6 D. Lothrop Company, Boston.

Not written especially for boys ; but they claim it.

The wife of a U. S. lighthouse inspector, Mary Bradford Crowninshield, writes the story of a tour of inspection along the coast of Maine with two boys on board — for other boys of course. A most instructive as well as delightful excursion.

The boys go up the towers and study the lamps and lanterns and all the devices by which a light in the night is made to tell the wary sailor the coast he is on; and so does the reader. Stories of wrecks and rescues beguile the waiting times. There are no waiting times in the story.

All Among the Lighthouses, or Cruise of the Goldenrod. By Mary Bradford Crowninshield. 32 illustrations, 392 pages. $2.50. D. Lothrop Company, Boston.

There's a vast amount of coast-lore besides.

Mr. Grant Allen, who knows almost as much as anybody, has been making a book of twenty-eight separate parts, and says of it : "These little essays are mostly endeavors to put some of the latest results of science in simple, clear and intelligible language."

Now that is exactly what nine hundred and ninety-nine in a thousand of us want, if it isn't dry. And it isn't dry. Few of those who have the wonderful knowledge of what is going on in the learned world have the gift of popular explanation — the gift of telling of it. Mr. Allen has that gift; the knowledge, the teaching grace, the popular faculty.

Common Sense Science. By Grant Allen. 318 pages. $1.50. D. Lothrop Company, Boston.

By no means a list of new-found facts; but the bearings of them on common subjects.

We don't go on talking as if the earth were the centre of things, as if Galileo never lived. Huxley and Spencer have got to be heard. Shall we wait two hundred and fifty years?

The book is simply an easy means of intelligence.

---

There is nothing more dreary than chemistry taught as it used to be taught to beginners. There is nothing brighter and fuller of keen delight than chemistry taught as it can be taught to little children even.

<small>Real Fairy Folks. By Lucy Rider Meyer, A. M. 389 pages. $1.25. D. Lothrop Company, Boston.</small>

"I'll be their teacher — give them private scientific lectures! Trust me to manage the school part!" The book is alive with the secrets of things.

---

It takes a learned man to write an easy book on almost any subject.

Arthur Gilman, of the College for Women, at Cambridge, known as the "Harvard Annex," has made a little book to help young people along in the use of the dictionary. One can devour it in an hour or two; but the reading multiplies knowledge and means of knowledge.

<small>Short Stories from the Dictionary. By Arthur Gilman, M. A. 129 pages. 60 cents. D. Lothrop Company, Boston.</small>

An unconscious beginning of what may grow to be philology, if one's faculty lies that way. Such bits of education are of vastly more importance than most of us know. They are the seeds of learning.

www.ingramcontent.com/pod-product-compliance
Lightning Source LLC
Chambersburg PA
CBHW051850300426
44117CB00006B/337